TWAYNE'S
RULERS AND STATESMEN OF THE WORLD
SERIES

Hans L. Trefousse, Brooklyn College
General Editor

JAMES MADISON

(TROW 13)

James Madison

By HAROLD S. SCHULTZ

University of Vermont

Twayne Publishers, Inc.   : :   New York

for Jacquelyn

Preface

THIS BIOGRAPHY IS A SHORT STORY OF A LONG LIFE. A GLANCE
at the bibliography beginning on page 229 will suggest how
much more can be said on the subject. One author who has
written much more than these two hundred pages is Irving Brant,
whose six-volume biography was invaluable in making this one.
His footnotes were my best guide to the primary sources; at
several points I have made use of information which he gained
from sources not seen by me; and in the main, his interpretations
have been confirmed by my own investigations. If there are
differences between the two biographies, other than of magnitude, I think they will be found in what the two authors say about
the nature of Madison's nationalism, the exact character of his
constitutional and political thought prior to 1786, the duration of
the political theory that distinguished his thinking in 1787, his
strategy in consequence of the Great Compromise, his successes
and failures as a delegate to the Philadelphia Convention and as
leader of the opposition to Washington's administration, his
policy toward alliances when he was president, and the criteria
for assessing his presidential leadership.

Edward Coles, Madison's secretary when he was president,
said: "If History do him justice, posterity will give him credit,
more for the goodness of his heart, than for the strength and
acquirements of his mind." This quotation explains the length
and method of the first chapter.

I would like to acknowledge my appreciation for the help
given by three women who had an intimate relationship to the
book at various stages. My wife Jacquelyn, combining the virtues
of Mary and Martha, received Mr. Madison into our home with
spiritual warmth and menial hospitality for what at one time
promised to be an interminable visit. Cheerfully and efficiently,
Pallas Braun and Carolyn Perry typed the manuscript.

Contents

Chronology

1751	Born at Port Conway, Virginia.
1762–1767	Attends Donald Robertson's school.
1767–1769	Tutored by Reverend Thomas Martin.
1769–1772	Student at Princeton.
1772–1776	At his father's home in Orange Country, Virginia.
1774	Elected to Committee of Public Safety, Orange County.
1776	Delegate to Virginia Convention and member of House of Delegates.
1778–1779	Member of the Virginia Council of State.
1780–1783	Delegate to the U.S. [Continental and Confederation] Congress
1784–1786	Serves in Virginia House of Delegates.
1785	Writes a *Memorial and Remonstrance against Religious Assessments*.
1786	Delegate to the Annapolis Convention.
1787	Delegate to the Philadelphia Convention.
1787–1788	Co-author of *The Federalists*; delegate to the Confederation Congress.
1788	Delegate to the Virginia ratifying convention.
1789–1797	Member of the U.S. House of Representatives; opposes Hamilton's financial policies and criticizes Washington's foreign policy.
1791–1792	Writes essays for the *National Gazette*.
1793	Writes "Helvidius Letters."
1794	Marries Dolly Payne Todd.
1795	Publishes *Political Observations*.
1798	Drafts the Virginia Resolutions of 1798 protesting against the Alien and Sedition laws.
1799	Member of the House of Delegates; writes report defending the Virginia Resolutions of 1798.
1801–1809	Secretary of State for President Jefferson.

1802–1803	Writes instructions for ministers who negotiated the Louisiana-Purchase Treaty of 1803.
1806	Publishes *A Memoir Containing an Examination of the British Doctrine, which subjects to capture a Neutral Trade not open in Time of Peace*.
1806	Writes instructions for negotiations carried out in London by Monroe and Pinkney.
1807	Instructs Monroe and Pinkney to continue negotiations after President Jefferson declined to submit to Senate the treaty which these emissaries had signed on December 31, 1806.
1807	Assists Jefferson in drafting message to Congress proposing an embargo on exports from the United States.
1809–1817	President of the United States.
1809	Opens trade with Great Britain but closes it again when agreement negotiated with David Erskine rejected by the British ministry in London.
1810	Proclaims the terms of Macon's Bill Number Two applicable against Great Britain because of an announced change of French policy.
1811	Supports ban on entry of British goods and ships into U.S. ports.
1812	Message to Congress justifies war against Great Britain.
1814	Public buildings in Washington burned by British army of invasion; President escapes to Virginia and Maryland for three days.
1815	Peace treaty negotiated at Ghent in December, 1814 submitted to Senate for ratification.
1815–1816	Supports national bank, protective tariff, federal aid for roads and canals, standing army, navy, national university.
1817	Retires to his home in Orange County.
1829	Delegate to the Virginia constitutional convention.
1836	Dies at Montpellier.

CHAPTER I

"A Good and Great Man"

ONE OF THE GREAT EPOCHS OF STATESMANSHIP WAS THE forty years of American history between the two wars with Great Britain. Madison's career was unique in spanning the entire epoch and notable for its continuity of officeholding.

His public life began in his twenty-third year, when he became a member of the Committee of Public Safety for Orange County, Virginia. During and after the Revolutionary War he served in the Virginia legislature and Congress of the United States. In 1786 he attended the convention at Annapolis which issued the call for a national convention to revise the Articles of Confederation. At the constitutional convention in Philadelphia in 1787 he was outstanding among about a dozen men who led the debates in that body. He was co-author of *The Federalist Papers* and a delegate to the Virginia ratifying convention.

He was a member of the House of Representatives throughout the presidency of Washington. In the first session of the first Congress he was a highly respected and influential debater and parliamentarian. He played a major role in adding a Bill of Rights to the Constitution and in passing legislation that provided the first taxes, executive departments, and courts for the new federal government. Although a trusted adviser to Washington during his first year in the presidency, he became thereafter a leading organizer of the Congressional opposition. During Washington's second term he was active in coordinating the Congressional opposition with propaganda and electioneering at the local level. He was pre-eminent among the men who founded the Republican party.

He declined to continue in Congress after 1797. In 1798 he prepared a set of resolutions protesting against the Alien and Sedition laws, which, in a slightly amended form, were adopted by the legislature of Virginia. In 1799 he was persuaded to serve in the legislature in order to defend the Virginia Resolutions of 1798 against criticisms contained in resolutions adopted by other state legislatures.

In 1801 Madison became Secretary of State in Jefferson's administration. In 1809 he succeeded Jefferson as President. His presidency was dominated by a prolonged diplomatic struggle and war with Great Britain. During the last Congress of his presidency, he gave approval to measures which he had contested when a leader of the opposition in the 1790's.

Madison died in 1836. As the last surviving signatory of the Constitution of 1787, he was the last surviving leader of the golden era of American politics.

During his nineteen years of retirement from public office the leading figures of the Congress and Supreme Court had known Madison as Secretary of State or President. What these practical political leaders who had personally observed his leadership said about him should be given serious consideration by all historians who attempt to assess his place in the early national history of the United States.

Three biographies of Madison were written in 1836 by politicians who had dealt with him as President.[1] Two were formal eulogies delivered to commemorate his death; one had been undertaken before his death as a contribution to an anthology entitled *The National Portrait Gallery*. Charles Jared Ingersoll, who had represented a Philadelphia district in the U. S. House of Representatives during the War of 1812, wrote the latter. One of the formal eulogies was delivered at the request of the Boston city council by John Quincy Adams, who had served as a negotiator for President Madison at Saint Petersburg, Ghent, and London. The other was delivered in Orange County, Virginia, by James Barbour, who had known Madison as long as he could remember and had been governor of Virginia and U. S. Senator during his presidency.

All three dealt with all stages and phases of Madison's life. Adams and Barbour told the story of Madison's public life within the framework of a narrative of national history. Ingersoll's was more strictly biographical. All three agreed on Madison's pre-eminence as a constructor of the Constitution and as an author of political treatises and state papers. All three described and praised his personal virtues, but only Ingersoll attempted to convey a distinct picture of his style and methods of leadership.

Adams and Ingersoll were fulsome in their praise of his various writings. They specifically cited his authorship of a Congressional report explaining instructions for negotiations with Spain (October, 1780), a Congressional Address to the States explaining proposed changes in the Articles of Confederation (April, 1783), a Memorial and Remonstrance against Religious Assessments (1785), *The Federalists* (1787–88), the Helvidius Letters (1793), the Virginia Resolutions of 1798 and their defense in his Report of 1799, and his *Examination ... of British* [Trade] *Doctrine* (1806).

Adams and Barbour were furtively apologetic about Madison's participation in the party strife of the 1790's; Adams shifted the narrative at this period to make Jefferson the chief antagonist of Hamilton and only incidentally referred to Madison. Adams' only praise for Madison in the 1790's was negative: his "temper and moderation" assuaged "the brain fever of party spirit." Barbour, who as a member of the legislature in 1798 had been a firm supporter of the Virginia Resolutions and had lodged in the same house with him in Richmond in 1799, insisted that Madison never uttered a word suggesting that the states use force to nullify the Alien and Sedition laws. Adams, who was in complete disagreement with the legal reasoning of the Virginia Resolutions, even to the point of accepting the constitutionality of the Alien and Sedition laws, managed to praise Madison by stressing his moderation in comparison with Jefferson. In his diary, July 29, 1836, Adams confided that the subject of the Virginia Resolutions was extremely difficult to handle in his oration, because Madison's party friends considered them perhaps the greatest of his services.[2]

Only Ingersoll appraised Madison's leadership in the U. S. House of Representatives as do present-day scholars. He wrote: "His participation during those eight years in all the acts and deliberations of Congress, was so prominent and pervading, that nothing of importance took place without his instrumentality, and in most of the leading measures his was the leading place; especially in all that concerned foreign affairs."

Ingersoll also thought his presidential leadership praiseworthy, a judgment at variance with the prevailing view of historians since Henry Adams published his history of Madison's presidency in 1891. His shortcomings as commander-in-chief, Ingersoll contended, were more than counterbalanced by his firmness in adhering strictly to constitutional processes. Madison proved, he said, that a republic could gain victory in war without suspending its constitution. He also pointed to the incontestable fact that the country was more united and more prosperous in 1817 than it had been when he was inaugurated eight years before.

An exhaustive study of the war in later years did not change Ingersoll's interpretation of his presidential leadership or his over-all assessment of his career. In his history of the War of 1812, published in 1845, he wrote: "There exists a remnant of inveterate, respectable federalists, who still deny Madison's merits. But the great body of his countrymen are unanimous in awarding him immortality. Much more than Jefferson, he enjoys undivided favor. He was no hero, not a man of genius, not remarkable for the talent of personal ascendancy. But his patriotic services are parcel of the most fundamental civil, and the most renowned military grandeur of this republic."[3]

Many years before Madison's death, two other men, who, like Ingersoll, had been in Congress during the War of 1812, had extolled his statesmanship, including his presidential leadership. Daniel Webster, a vociferous opponent of Madison's war policies, said in a private conversation in 1824 that he was "the wisest of our Presidents, except Washington."[4] Henry Clay, who had defended Madison's policies in Congress, said to a friend in 1829 that he was our "first political writer" and, after Washington, our "greatest statesman."[5]

In a discussion with Samuel Harrison Smith, Clay denied that Jefferson's administration was superior to Madison's.[6] Others who knew both men compared him favorably with Jefferson. John Quincy Adams publicly praised Madison's mind as the equal of Jefferson's and "tempered with a calmer sensibility and a cooler judgment" and in his diary wrote that he was "a greater and far more estimable man." Joseph Story of Massachusetts, whose thirty-four years of distinguished service as a justice of the U. S. Supreme Court began with his appointment by Madison in 1811, wrote to a man who had served with him in Congress when Jefferson was President: "I entirely concur with your estimate of Mr. Madison—his private virtues, his extraordinary talents, his comprehensive and statesmanlike views. To him and Hamilton I think we are mainly indebted for the Constitution of the United States, and in wisdom I have long been accustomed to place him before Jefferson."[7] James K. Paulding, President Van Buren's Secretary of the Navy, wrote: "I have always considered Mr. Madison, as emphatically the *Sage* of his time. He had not perhaps so much genius as Mr. Jefferson, but in my opinion his mind was more consummate and his faculties more nicely balanced than those of his predecessor."[8]

Webster, Clay, Adams, Ingersoll, Paulding—these were men

who had known Madison in the later years of his career. Only the man to whom he was most often compared was able to assess him on the basis of a personal knowledge covering the entire span of his career. Jefferson, writing in the 1820's, praised the "wisdom" of his presidency and declared that he had been "first" in every legislative body after he entered the U. S. Congress in 1780.[9]

Jefferson was most often mentioned when Madison's contemporaries compared him with other statesmen. In comparing the various stages of his career, they invariably accorded their highest praise for his work in framing and ratifying the Constitution, with which, as minister to France, Jefferson was not associated. Speaking in the U. S. House of Representatives in 1794, Richard Bland Lee said that all Americans knew "the share he had in forming the present Constitution, and promoting its adoption." The three men who eulogized Madison in Congress three days after his death—John Quincy Adams of Massachusetts and John W. Patton and William C. Rives of Virginia—stressed his role as "Father of the Constitution."[10] James Barbour, in August, 1836, said that the framing of the Constitution was a "culminating point" for Madison. "It is to him more than to any mortal, unless Washington be an exception, that we are indebted for our constitution, and, in consequence, for our union."[11] The next year, in the U. S. Senate, the two foremost expounders of opposing interpretations of the nature of the Federal Union, agreed when they came to assessing Madison's importance in making and interpreting the Constitution. John C. Calhoun, on February 18, 1837, said that "we were indebted to Mr. Madison at least as much as to any other man, for the form of Government under which we live. Indeed, he might be said to have done more for our institutions than any man now living, or that had gone before him."[12] Daniel Webster, on October 3, 1837, said: "He had as much to do as any man in framing the Constitution, and as much to do as any man in administering it."[13]

Madison was a prophet honored by his own countrymen in his own lifetime and honored most by those who personally observed him as a public and private man. Nor did recognition come only after he retired to private life. At the Philadelphia Convention of 1787 a delegate from Georgia wrote that "every Person seems to acknowledge his greatness." During the first session of the first Congress, Fisher Ames, at a time when he was displeased with Madison's advocacy of certain import duties which he thought harmful to the interests of Massachusetts, wrote: "He is our first man. ... He will continue to be a very influential man in our country." Congressman Swift of Connecticut, who disliked Madison's views on foreign policy, wrote during the third Congress: "The great Maddison, who has acquired so much undeserved celebrity ... has unquestionably the most personal influence of any man in the house of Representatives."[14]

Ames and Swift were New England Federalists who could criticize and recognize simultaneously. The eccentric Republican John Randolph of Roanoke only belatedly had a good word for his fellow Virginian. In 1806 he began a merciless attack upon Madison's foreign policy; he was one of only a few men who ever questioned the ethics of his diplomacy and politics. Madison's "insidious moderation" was an irritant to the caustic nature of Randolph, who, according to James Parton, used to say that Mr. Madison "was as mean a man for a Virginian as John Quincy Adams was for a Yankee." Not until the very end of Madison's presidency did Randolph relent. In the House of Representatives, January 31, 1817, he praised Madison's services in the Virginia legislature and remarked that "even he would not be deterred from saying of him that he was a great man—for such he unquestionably was in some respects."[15]

Foreign observers in the United States were among the first to assess Madison's standing as a political leader. The French minister at Philadelphia wrote in 1784 that his sound judgment was highly regarded in the Confederation Congress. J. P. Barissot de Warville, who dined with him in New York in August, 1788, wrote in his *New Travels in the United States*: "The name of Maddison, celebrated in America, is well known in Europe, by the merited eulogium made of him by his countryman and friend, Mr. Jefferson. Though still young he has rendered the greatest services to Virginia, to the American confederation, and to liberty and humanity in general. ... He distinguished himself particularly, for the acceptation of the new federal system." In 1789, two British diplomats who were critical of his views on U. S. commercial policy alluded to his "good sense" and his reputation for being "a gentleman of the first abilities in America."[16]

Madison's greatness in statesmanship was the result of a rare combination of mental qualities and character traits dedicated without stint to public service. For forty years, his every emotion, feeling, sentiment, and interest were subordinated to politics. His thought and energy were much more absorbed in the political than his good friend Jefferson, whose versatile interests and varied emotions required more attention to the arts and sciences and more occasions for introspective musings and extrovertive amusements. He shared most of Jefferson's interests to a degree, but they were kept in abeyance during his forty years in public office. "His breeding was altogether that of a statesman," said Charles Ingersoll.[17] His wife, in a brief matter-of-fact description written three years after his death, said that he had a scientific interest in agriculture, "but from his public occupations it necessarily became more of a theory than practice as was the case in all business pursuits other than the political."[18]

Observers less friendly than Mrs. Madison commented not only upon his preoccupation with public affairs but also upon the disciplined mind that ruled his whole being as a politician. "He is well versed in public life, was bred to it, and has no other profession," Fisher Ames wrote when they were in the first Congress together in 1789. "Yet, may I say it, it is rather a science, than a business, with him." Zephaniah Swift, who observed him in the third Congress, said that he was "the most artificial, studied character on earth ... he calculates upon everything with the greatest nicety and precision ... I never knew a man that better understood to husband a character and make the most of his talents."[19]

If there was a taint of censoriousness in the characterizations of Ames and Swift, there was only a shading of difference between what they said and what was said by his closest friends and enthusiastic admirers. "His life, from first to last," according to Ingersoll, "was passionless and thoughtful; though his affections were kind and his attachments constant. ... Taking nothing for granted, by intuition, or sympathy, he worked out every result like a problem to be proved." Jefferson strongly implied in his autobiography that Madison succeeded in transforming shyness into self-possession through the power of a commanding mind.[20]

Even Washington, famed for his self-restraint, lost his temper a few times. Madison never did. His constancy in the suppression of his emotions impressed his friends as one of his salient virtues. They saw him as patient, forbearing, and imperturbable. His quality of imperturbabilty was especially emphasized by those who observed him as a negotiator with European diplomats, as a presidential candidate subjected to the abuse of partisan attacks, as commander-in-chief of an army that suffered one defeat after another, and as the head of state whose executive mansion and capital buildings were burned by enemy invaders. The wartime governor of Virginia said that he had never seen his serenity disturbed under any circumstances. John Quincy Adams referred to his coolness, forbearance, and "imperturbable patience."[21]

Mrs. Margaret Bayard Smith described his calm reaction to partisan abuse and military disaster. During the presidential campaign of 1808, she said, he accepted slanderous and insidious attacks with "imperturbable serenity." With "unaltered equanimity" he "continued his social intercourse with persons of all opinions; the chiefs of different parties met at his house with perfect good humor." When Madison returned to Washington a few days after the British had burned his residence and public buildings housing the executive departments, she found him "tranquil as usual, and tho' much distressed by the dreadful event, which had taken place not dispirited."[22]

Ingersoll, who was a U. S. Representative when the British burned the halls of Congress, wrote in his biographical sketch of 1836: "Victory never elated, disasters never depressed him beyond measure; always calm, consistent, and conscientious, there was confidence that he would do right, come what might. Exposed to that deluge of abuse which the leading men of free countries, with a licentious press, cannot avoid, he was perfectly serene and unmoved by any vindictive emotion; true to friends, patient with adversaries, resolute but forbearing even with public enemies."[23]

In a letter of December 23, 1854, Edward Coles recalled: "During the six years I lived with him as his Secretary, I had opportunities of witnessing his conduct under very trying circumstances, and in justice to him, I will say, amidst all the troubles and excitement attendant on a foreign war, and provoking feuds at home, I never saw Mr. Madison in a pet or heard him utter one petulant expression, or give way for one moment to passion or despondency. No, he was always cool, collected, and self-possessed, conscious of doing his best, and feeling confidence in his fellow citizens and in the Government which he had been most instrumental in establishing."[24]

Friend and foe alike assumed that Madison had feelings and thoughts which neither his face nor his words revealed completely. All saw him as cool, calm, moderate, temperate, dispassionate, cautious, and reserved. For his admirers, his reserve was reticence, his caution the equivalent of circumspection. For his detractors, his reserve was a manifestation of indecisiveness, his so-called caution a disguise for timidity or cowardice. For his admirers his reserve derived from strength of character; for his detractors, his reserve derived from weakness: this was the only disagreement among his contemporaries as to his character. The exact meaning that should be attached to his reserve is to this day at the bottom of the varying interpretations of his presidential leadership.

Those who observed timidity and indecisiveness in Madison sometimes associate these attributes with his bookishness, and, in the period when the Constitution was being made and first administered, with his obvious interest in political theory. Fisher Ames in May, 1789, thought him "too much attached to his theories ... too much of a book politician, and too timid in his politics." Alexander Hamilton told a British diplomat in October, 1789: "The truth is, that although this gentleman is a clever man, he is very little acquainted with the world." Samuel Taggart, in January, 1808, said that he was unqualified for the presidency because he was "a theoretic, closet politician." Senator Adair of Kentucky, although convinced that Madison by 1806 had acquired a complete ascendancy over President Jefferson, agreed with Senator Plumer of New Hampshire that he was too "timid" to be President. John Beckley, who had collaborated closely with Madison when he was in the House of Representatives, wrote to Monroe in 1806 that he was "deemed by many, too timid and indecisive as a statesman." Congressman Calhoun wrote privately, April 18, 1812: "Our President tho a man of amiable manners and great talents, has not I fear those commanding talents which are necessary to control those about him."[25]

Mistakingly informed that Madison was to be governor of Virginia, Eliza House Trist, whose mother kept the lodging house in Philadelphia where Madison lived when he was in the Confederation Congress, wrote to Jefferson on April 13, 1784: "He deserves every thing that can be done for him. But I am afraid he will not increase his happiness by an acceptance [of the governorship of Virginia]. ... I am convinc'd he will have enemies the moment he accepts it and I feel unhappy at the thought. He has a Soul replete with gentleness humanity and every social virtue and yet I am certain that some wretch or other will write against him. You I am sure woul'd not advise him to it. I have no Idea that men are to live only for the

Publick. They owe something to them[selves]. Mr. Madison is too amiable in his disposition to bear up against a torrent of abuse. It will hurt his feeling and injure his health, take my word."[26]

Eliza Trist was not alone in failing to perceive the inimitable and subtle talent which for thirty years enabled Madison to commit himself in public controversies without eliciting personal attacks from rivals and opponents—or in failing to judge his capacity to withstand criticism when it finally came. Throughout his career he was misjudged by those who failed to see that his modesty and reticence concealed a strong will and rare talents.

Madison's character and intellect were conspicuous in his public speaking and writing. The French minister in Philadelphia in 1784 said that "almost always he speaks justly and obtains the approbation of his colleagues." William Pierce at the Philadelphia convention said that he always came forward "the best informed man of any point in debate" and blended together "the profound politician with the Scholar." Fisher Ames in 1789 said: "He states a principle and deduces consequences, with clearness and simplicity." Jefferson said that he always soothed the feelings of his adversaries by civilities and softness of expression and gained a prominent place in Congress by the rich resources of his mind and his extensive information. John Quincy Adams contrasted "the dazzling but beclouded genius and eloquence of Patrick Henry" with Madison's mild-mannered, steady, informed, and cogent argumentation. Madison's "conciliatory gentleness of temper," Adams said, disarmed "the adversary by the very seeming to decline contention with him." John Marshall said that if eloquence included "persuasion by convincing, Mr. Madison was the most eloquent man I ever heard."[27]

Charles J. Ingersoll said that all of his state papers were "calm, respectful and forbearing, while earnest, candid, and forcible, the diction chaste and elegant, seldom impassioned." His diplomatic writings as Secretary of State, Ingersoll said, showed a "depth of research, power of argument, and force unsurpassed by any state papers." In the judgment of John Quincy Adams, Madison's Helvidius Letters scrutinized the President's diplomatic powers with an "acuteness of intellect" which had perhaps never been surpassed.[28]

Madison's speeches commanded attention from their content alone. They received no enhancement of appeal from the appearance of the speaker, the language he used, or his manner of delivery. James Barbour said that he "used little or no gesture; his style of speaking was pure and simple, and without ornament." Fisher Ames said he spoke "decently, as to manner, and no more." Zephaniah Swift said he had "a correct stile without energy or copiousness."[29]

Ames and Swift reported that his speaking voice was "low"; and Barbour, who described his speaking voice as "inconveniently feeble," said that "the members, lest they should lose a word, were accustomed to gather around him." The stenographer at the Richmond ratifying convention of 1788 noted that he could not hear some of Madison's remarks. Mrs. William Seaton said that his voice in delivering his second inaugural address was so low "that scarcely a word could be distinguished."[30]

Some of course found Madison's style of speaking and writing dull or tedious. Fisher Ames, reputed one of the great orators of his day, said of him: "In speaking, he never relaxes into pleasantry, and discovers little of that warmth of heart, which gives efficacy to George Cabot's reasoning, and to Lowell's." Zephaniah Swift thought he was "awkward" and "uninteresting" in comparison with Ames: "he is wholly destitute of vigour of genius, ardour of mind, and brilliancy of imagination. He has no fire, no enthusiasm, no animation."[31]

Senator Plumer of New Hampshire found Madison's *Examination* of British trade doctrine (considered by John Quincy Adams one of the best diplomatic papers produced by an American statesman) "obscure and sometimes unintelligible." Although admitting that it contained many useful facts and exposed the fallacies and inconsistencies of the British courts of admiralty, he confessed in his diary that he had never read a book that "fatigued" him more than this two-hundred-page book. Of the same treatise, John Randolph said in the House of Representatives: "Sir, I have tried, but I could not get through this work. I found it so wire-drawn; the thread so fine, that I could neither see or feel it; such a tangled cobweb of contradictions, that I was obliged to give it up."[32]

Those who described Madison's writings and speeches made few comments upon his use of language. Ames said his language was "very pure, perspicuous, and to the point," and Jefferson said it was "pure, classical and copious," but neither took note of certain characteristics which distinguished his language from their own and which impress the modern reader as the most obvious feature of his style. They said nothing of its lacking imagery, idioms, figures of speech, analogies, epigrams, anecdotes, and a vocabulary conveying a sense of visible things.[33]

Madison's style, involved and ponderous at times, could easily be adapted to dignified equivocation or obfuscation. When he was President it undoubtedly served him well in dealing with a party that was sharply divided on issues of foreign policy. In private, Congressmen often professed to be in the dark as to the meaning of his pronouncements on policy. On one occasion in early 1810, a member of his own party, Crawford of Georgia, expressed his bewilderment to the U. S. Senate:

The President's Message of the 3d instant has been introduced ... in support of this bill. Feeble must be the aid which this measure can derive from that source. This Message, in point of obscurity, comes nearer my ideas of a Delphic oracle than any State paper which has come under my inspection. It is so cautiously expressed that every man puts what construction upon it he pleases. Is he for war? The Message breathes nothing but destruction and bloodshed. Is he for peace? The Message is mere milk-and-water, and wholly pacific. Is he for the bill before you? The Message calls for its passage. Is he a friend to a large standing army? Why then the Message means 20,000 regular troops. Is he friendly to the militia? The Message does not call for regular troops—it means militia. Thus, sir, this Message means anything or nothing, at the will of the commentator.[34]

Madison's use of language reflected his rational practicality. In the thirty-seventh *Federalist* he wrote:

The use of words is to express ideas. Perspicuity, therefore, requires not only that the ideas should be distinctly formed, but that they should be expressed by words distinctly and exclusively appropriate to them. But no language is so copious as to supply words and phrases for every complex idea, or so correct as not to include many equivocally denoting different ideas.

A weakness of the intellectual in practical politics may be his tendency to be bewitched by the magical power of words, just as the naïvely "practical" intuitionist may tend to underestimate their potency. Madison avoided the pitfalls of both tendencies. Words for him were instruments for forming his own thoughts and communicating them to the exact extent that he desired they should be revealed. He was no coiner of happy phrases, no contriver of catchy slogans, no composer of the felicitous expression. Compared with Jefferson, Franklin, or

Wilson, his language was gawky and unadorned, and compared with Patrick Henry or Fisher Ames, cold and dry. The result, however, was that his own thinking process was never impeded in its substance by the temptation to cling to ideas because of the attractive costume in which they had been first enveloped; and those who read his writings or heard his speeches were necessarily influenced only by the information and ideas contained in them and not by their verbal trappings.

Madison used words to excite the mind—not the glands. If, as a practical leader, he neglected the great potentialities to sway large numbers by appealing to the primitive, irrational, even neurotic passions and feelings of mankind, he at least did not, like so many demagogic leaders who have successfully exploited such appeals, permit his own sober mind to become intoxicated with his own words. He never became a victim of his own propaganda.

In conversation, Madison revealed the same intellect and manners that came forth in his public speeches and his writings. For those who talked to him on formal or official occasions, he appeared much the same as when observed in making speeches. But with a small number of friends or amiable visitors, he often displayed a sprightliness not observed in his public speaking or writing, or indeed, in his private correspondence. The Baron de Montlezun, who visited him in September, 1816, said: When "he can disengage himself for a moment from the cares attached to ... being the head of a republican government, his brow unwrinkles, his countenance becomes animated: it shines then with a fiery spirit and sweet gaiety; and one is surprised to find in the conversation of the great politician and wise administrator as much playfulness as gravity."

The British diplomat Augustus Foster said that he was "a social, jovial and good-humored companion full of anecdote and sometimes matter of loose description relating to old times, but oftener of a political and historical interest." In his "parlour," Richard Rush reported in a letter to his father, he was "not to be surpassed in whatever is kind-hearted, hospitable, and amiable." George Tichnor, who saw the President at a dinner party during one of the gloomiest periods of the war, found him "more free and open" than he had expected, "starting subjects of conversation and making remarks that sometimes savored of humor and levity." After dinner, "at which he usually took a liberal portion of wine," William C. Preston recalled in his memoirs, "he became free and even facetious, telling with great archness many anecdotes," some of a sort that were no longer thought proper in "good society." Edward Coles, his secretary for six years, said that "few men possessed so rich a flow of language or so great a fund of amusing anecdotes, which were made the more interesting from their being well timed and well told." In his history of the War of 1812, Ingersoll wrote: "He was fond of table-talk; and, though temperate in all things, enjoyed not only fine wine, but the lively, and even the sometimes more than lively freedom it produces. Jefferson, with uncommon colloquial powers, was constitutionally modest, and would blush at any indelicate allusion. Madison, more diffident of opinion, was fond of free chat, and rather enjoyed what his instructor would have shrunk from."[35]

In language, manner, and content, Madison's private correspondence resembled his public writings and speeches more than his private conversation. Even letters to his intimate friend Jefferson had none of the gaiety and playfulness ascribed to conversations. Like his public writings, his letters were serious discussions of public issues and factual reporting of public events, with little attention to the personalities or setting of the political drama. References to matters of personal concern were brief and barrenly factual. He sometimes mentioned, usually in a few concluding sentences, the weather, his health, conditions of crops, money transactions, or acquisitions of books and furnishings.

The epistolary Madison was neither an introvert nor an extrovert. Only the faintest traces of his ego can be seen in his letters; thoughts of the kind we called "innermost" were omitted. His letters were not about himself; they were about the world outside himself; but they were about the world in its intangible and invisible form; it was a world of ideas, institutions, policies, conditions, and circumstances. What his eyes saw in his physical environment was as meagerly reported as what he felt inside himself; portrayals of people, buildings, and landscapes were as scarce as expressions of his own emotions, feelings, and sentiments.

A singular occasion when Madison revealed his perturbation to a visitor enables us to see how little of his emotions were expressed in his letters, even to his trusted friend Jefferson. William Wirt visited Madison about three weeks after the burning of Washington; the first harsh terms presented by the British negotiators at Ghent were then known and secession was rumored to be the secret purpose of the forthcoming Hartford Convention. Wirt described the President in a letter to his wife: "He looks miserably shattered and wo-begone. In short, he looked heart-broken. His mind is full of the New England sedition. He introduced the subject, and continued to press it,—painful as it obviously was to him. ... I diverted the conversation to another topic; but he took the first opportunity to return to it, and convinced me that his heart and mind were painfully full of the subject."[36]

Nothing of what Wirt reported, however, is discernible in letters written by Madison. Judging by two he wrote to Jefferson, on October 10 and October 23, 1814, the President was apprehensive only about the "very critical" situation at Sackett's Harbor. The severe demands of the British were summarized, but nothing suggesting a gloomy reaction was uttered. Neither of the letters mentioned the situation in New England.[37]

The reader of Madison's letters sees Stoicism personified. There are no complaints, excuses, or solicitations of sympathy.

On the subject of religion, the adult Madison was reserved almost to the point of silence. In his letters he said nothing of his religious beliefs and practices, and only a few of his contemporaries commented upon the religious side of his life. Ingersoll said simply that he was "inscrutably reserved in his religious opinions."[38] The many comments upon his probity and integrity neglected to associate his ethical behavior with his religious beliefs. And most remarkable of all, his political opponents made no attempt to exploit his silence on religion; they never subjected him to the abuse that Jefferson received in the campaign of 1800.

George Tichnor's conversing with Madison about religion was unprecedented. In a letter addressed to his father in Boston, January 31, 1815, Tichnor wrote: "He talked of religious sects and parties, and was curious to know how the cause of liberal Christianity stood with us, and if the Athanasian creed was well received by our Episcopalians. He pretty distinctly intimated to me his own regard for the Unitarian doctrines."[39]

Bishop William Meade, in his *Old Churches, Ministers and Families of Virginia*, written in the 1850's, said of his religion: "Whatever may have been the private sentiments of Mr. Madison on the subject of religion, he was never known to declare any hostility to it. He always treated it with respect, attended public worship in his neighbourhood, invited ministers of reli-

gion to his house, had family prayers on such occasions,—
though he did not kneel himself at prayers. Episcopal ministers
often went there to see his aged and pious mother and adminis-
ter the Holy Communion to her. I was never at Mr. Madison's
but once, and then our conversation took such a turn—though
not designed on my part—as to call forth some expressions and
arguments which left the impression on my mind that his creed
was not strictly regulated by the Bible."[40]

Madison was thought to be a man of frail health, but his
letters tell us little more than the timing of some of his illnesses.
He never described his symptoms or complained. Often in-
capacitated for short periods by illness, he failed to be stricken
by the disease that killed a brother and sister in 1775, and he
escaped the epidemics of yellow fever in Philadelphia.

A few of his illnesses came at difficult times for him, inter-
rupting or delaying his participation in important public controversies. He was twice sick when involved in proceedings at
Richmond: at the ratifying convention of 1788 and in the legislature of 1799 while he was preparing the report defending the
Virginia Resolutions of 1798. He was delayed in returning to
the second session of the first Congress in January, 1790, by a
rather prolonged illness. He was ill during the period when the
tie vote between Burr and Jefferson was unresolved. His departure for Washington in 1801 was delayed by illness, and he was
still not feeling well when he took up his duties as Secretary of
State in May. The most important negotiation he conducted in
Washington, that with the British envoy George Rose, was carried out in part from a sickbed.[41]

By far the most severe illness he suffered during his adult
years came during the War of 1812. He was in poor health
throughout the summer of 1813. On July 29, 1813, Mrs. Madison wrote to Mrs. Gallatin: "You have heard no doubt of the
illness of my husband, but can have no idea of its extent and
the despair in which I attended his bed for nearly five weeks.
Even now I watch over him as I would an infant, so precarious
is his convalescence. Added to this are the disappointments and
vexations heaped upon him by party spirit."[42] On August 28,
1813, Madison himself reported from Montpellier, his home in
Orange County to which he had gone for recuperation: "My
own health has greatly improved since my arrival here, but I
have not been without several slight returns of fever, which are
chargeable rather on the remnant of influenza than the cause
which I suffered in Washington."[43]

Madison's attitude toward travel may have been influenced by considerations of health. He turned down several invitations to serve the United States at posts abroad during his lifetime, for reasons which he never announced. We do know, however, that one of the reasons he gave to Jefferson for not visiting France in 1785 was that "crossing the sea would be unfriendly to a singular disease of my constitution."[44] On the other hand, his recreational travels in the United States were sometimes intended to benefit his health. He occasionally visited the warm springs of western Virginia for his health, and he was always eager to get away from Philadelphia and Washington during the heat of the summer, which he thought not only uncomfortable but harmful to his physical condition. He gave health as one of the reasons for accepting Jefferson's invitation in May, 1791, to travel northward to Lake George and Lake Champlain. After their tour that summer, Jefferson reported that "his journey with me to the lakes placed him in better health than I have seen him, but the late heats have brought on some bilious dispositions."[45]

Madison's correspondence tells us little of his daily habits, except, implicitly, that he was an inveterate letter writer. Mrs. Madison said that he "passed a part of every night in writing, reading and study." He required only a few hours of sleep, she said, and kept a candle burning all night so that he could read or write whenever he awoke. In a letter written a few years after his death, she testified: "Mr. Madison was most temperate, but reasonably fond of generous diet and good wines, tea and coffee. He never used tobacco."[46]

His dress was plain, dignified, and, when he was in his fifties and sixties, considered old-fashioned. Edward Coles, his secretary from 1809 to 1815, recalled that he "always appeared neat and genteel, and in the costume of a well-bred and tasty old school gentleman. . . . I never knew him to wear any other color than black. His coat being cut in what is termed dress fashion; his breeches short with buckles at the knees, black silk stockings, and shoes with strings, or long fair top boots when out in cold weather, or when he rode on horseback of which he was fond. His hat was of the shape and fashion usually worn by gentlemen of his age. He wore powder on his hair, which was dressed full over his ears, tied behind, and brought to a point above the forehead, to cover in some degree his baldness, as may be noticed in all the likenesses taken of him."[47]

Madison's demeanor, as well as his dress, sometimes gave an

impression of stiffness, gloom, or coldness. When he was thirty, Mrs. Theodorick Bland described him as a "gloomy, stiff creature." Eight years later, Fisher Ames wrote: "Madison is cool, and has an air of reflection, which is not very distant from gravity and self-sufficiency."[48] William C. Preston, who as a youth lived a few months with the Madison's in the White House, remembered him as having an abstract air and a pale countenance. Francis Jeffrey, of the *Edinburgh Review*, who visited Washington in November, 1813, said that President Madison reminded him of a schoolmaster dressed up for a funeral. Mrs. William Seaton wrote in January, 1814, that the President was "very formal, reserved and precise, yet not wanting in a certain dignity." "His grave and sober character and retired life" seemed to Joseph Story "very little fitted" for the levees held by Mrs. Madison every Wednesday evening. The Baron de Montlezun said he was cool, reserved, and affable. Ingersoll, who described his lighter side in private conversation, said that his public manners were shy, cold, circumspect, and reserved without being taciturn. "His ordinary manner," Edward Coles remembered, "was simple, modest, bland and unostentatious, retiring from the throng and cautiously refraining from doing or saying anything to make himself conspicuous. This made him appear a little reserved and formal, and had the effect, like similar traits in the character of General Washington, to keep applicants and other obtrusive persons from approaching too near and being too familiar with him, particularly when he filled high offices and possessed patronage."[49]

Although reserved in his public manners, he was neither discourteous nor ceremonious. Augustus Foster, a British diplomat who observed him as Secretary of State and as President, said that "he was allowed on all sides to be a gentleman in his manners." Francis James Jackson, British minister to Washington in 1809, described him as a man "of great simplicity of manners, and an inveterate enemy to form and ceremony." Jackson was first received by the President in an afternoon frock suitable for ordinary occasions and was introduced as one gentleman to another.[50]

Those who described Madison's appearance mentioned his stature more than any other feature. He impressed those who saw him for the first time as "a little man." Tichnor in 1815 was astonished to find how "short" the President was. Edward Coles, his secretary, is authority for his exact height: five feet, six inches.[51]

His other physical features were less remarkable. Coles said he had a "tawny complexion" and that his hair had been "dark brown."[52] A few who left accounts of seeing him in retirement at Montpellier referred to his blue eyes, which for Mrs. Margaret Bayard Smith "sparkled like stars from under his bushy grey eye-brows" and for James K. Paulding twinkled "most wickedly, when lighted up by some whimsical conception or exposition." By his sixties his face was wrinkled, or as Augustus Foster remembered, "rather wizened." Contrasting the President with Mrs. Madison and her sisters, Washington Irving exclaimed: " . . . but as to Jemmy Madison—ah! poor Jemmy!—he is but a withered little apple-John."[53]

Dolly Payne Todd, whom James married when he was forty-three years old, was an asset to his later career. When he was Secretary of State and President, she arranged and presided over the social life of the capital.[54] She was universally acknowledged to be a charming and delightful hostess. Her most prominent trait was a pleasure in pleasing others. The worst ever said of her, except for the warped innuendoes of John Randolph, was that she took snuff and used rouge.

Dolly was a help to James when he was a presidential candidate. She brought to his dining and drawing room a variety of political leaders. According to Senator Samuel Mitchell of New York she was an "aid to his pretensions" while George Clinton, the Vice President, had "nothing of female succor on his side."[55] She was the perfect helpmate for a man of Madison's disposition. She was much more sociable, less burdened by conventional ceremonies, much more attentive to the mundane things of everyday living. Unlike her husband, she had an extrovertive interest in the external appearances of places and people. She was clearly interested in helping with the social life of the politician, but she never tried to influence his decisions. She solicited information on politics from him, but what her husband told her was kept in the strictest confidence. His opinions were her opinions, and she was even more reticent than her husband in the realm of politics. At her dinner parties and levees, she was noted for her impartiality. Men of all factions and of both parties were received with equal grace and cordiality.

Dolly complemented James without in any way disturbing the ways and habits he had established in the first forty-three years of his life. She added to his life without dislocating it. This perfect adjustment seems to have rested upon certain basic qualities they shared in common. Despite Dolly's greater sociability, she resembled him in certain important ways. She too was lacking in introspection. She too accepted hardships, failures, frustrations, and sickness without complaint. Like him she was tactful, gentle, even-tempered, and discreet. Like him she was incapable of uttering a vicious word about anyone. Like him, she could remain silent on many subjects.

Dolly was born in North Carolina, but spent her childhood in Hanover County, Virginia. Her father, John Payne, a conscientious Quaker, after manumitting his slaves, followed an unprosperous business career in Philadelphia until his death in 1792. She was a twenty-six-year-old widow with a two-year-old son when she married Congressman Madison. Her first husband, John Todd, Jr., had died during the yellow fever epidemic in Philadelphia in October, 1793, and her infant son had died shortly thereafter. She was introduced to Madison, at his request, by Senator Aaron Burr. She was then living with her mother, Mary Coles Payne, who was keeping a boarding house. Her marriage to Madison took place on September 15, 1794, at the home of her sister Lucy, Mrs. George Steptoe Washington, at "Harewood," in Jefferson County, Virginia (now West Virginia).

Before she married Madison, she consulted a lawyer friend in Philadelphia. He replied: "Mr. M—n is a man whom I admire. I know his attachment to you and did not therefore content myself with taking his Character from the Breath of popular applause—but consulted those who knew him intimately in private life. His private Character therefore I have every reason to believe is good and amiable. He unites to the great Talents which have secured his public Approbation those engaging Qualities that contribute so highly to domestic Felicity. To such a man therefore I do most freely consent that my beloved sister be united and happy."[56]

Others who knew Madison also lauded his integrity. Jefferson praised his "pure and spotless virtue." From "three and thirty years trial," he wrote in 1812, "I can say conscientiously that I do not know in the world a man of purer integrity." As early as 1783, Jefferson had written to his young nephew: "His judgment is so sound and his heart so good that I would wish you to respect every advice he would be so kind as to give you, equally as if it came from me."[57]

Edward Coles thought that the greatness of "his mind and the fascination of his conversation" were but decorations to set off to advantage his pure and incorruptible virtue and integrity. If history do him justice, posterity will give him credit, more for the goodness of his heart, than for the strength and acquirements of his mind. It will show him to have been the most virtuous, calm, and amiable, of men; possessed of one of the purest hearts and best tempers, with which man was ever blessed. Nothing could excite or ruffle him. Under all circumstances he was collected and ever mindful of what was due from him to others, and cautious not to wound the feelings of any one. Never letting prosperity or adversity, underserved praise or wrongful abuse affect him; as cautious in making engagements and promises as he was punctiliously particular in fulfilling them; ever bearing in mind what was due to himself, as well as personally or officially, and acting on his maxim that public functionaries should never display, much less act, under the influence of passion. He acted not from the fear of punishment, or from the apprehension of censure, but from an innate love of virtue, and the pleasure it gave him to do what was right.[58]

"No man had a higher reputation among his acquaintances for probity," was the testimonial of the man who represented Great Britain in Washington just before the War of 1812. Fisher Ames in 1789 said that he was "a good man," and Alexander Hamilton in the same year told a British diplomat that he was uncorrupted and incorruptible. His private life was "without stain or reproach," said Charles Ingersoll; and among the "torrents of abuse which enemies and opponents showered upon him, not one accused him of selfish ambition or arbitrary power." Senator William C. Rives of Albemarle County, Virginia, characterized him as "a model of public and private virtue." And James Barbour, addressing his neighbors, friends, and fellow citizens of Orange County, said: "Our Madison, uniting extraordinary capacity with great virtues, furnished to the world that rare combination of the good and great man."[59]

CHAPTER II

Toward Manhood and Nationhood

MADISON'S GREATNESS WAS NOT FORECAST BY HIS CHILDHOOD and youth. In college he seemed least likely to succeed in public life. For no announced reason, he was the only member of his class who failed to have the honor of speaking at his commencement exercises. That his ultimate fame would exceed any one of his eleven classmates, among whom were Philip Freneau and Hugh Henry Brackenridge, seemed most unlikely.[1]

Not even his posthumous memorialists saw in his early years signs of his future distinction. His goodness, however, they did recall. Adams said that Dr. John Witherspoon, President of the College of New Jersey, "always delighted in bearing testimony to the excellence of his character." Baverour, as "proof of his extraordinary and persevering assiduity," cited his practice at Princeton of limiting his hours of sleep "to the least number consistent with his health." Ingersoll said that "his health was impaired by over-ardent study" while at college, where he "laid the deep foundations of those attainments, habits and principles, which gradually, but without fail, raised him to after eminence."[2]

Despite his lack of formal honors at Princeton, his intellectual capacity and interests were demonstrated many years before he entered public life. After learning to read and write at home, he began, when he was about eleven years old, to attend a school in King and Queen County kept by Donald Robertson, a graduate of Edinburgh. During the next five years, under the tutelage of Robertson, he studied mathematics, geography, Latin, Greek, French, and literature, including some works of recent times, of which Addison's essays in *The Spectator* left the strongest imprint on his memory. Two more years of study at home with the Reverend Thomas Martin, rector for the local parish, provided him with ample preparation to attend the College in Princeton, New Jersey, then called Nassau Hall or the College of New Jersey. By passing an examination that exempted him from the first-year courses and by taking more courses than the usual student, he was able to obtain his baccalaureate degree after only two years of residence. Graduating in September, 1771, he continued to study at Princeton under Dr. Witherspoon for another six months.[3]

Madison engaged in no public speaking during these years, despite the fact that the two college clubs competed with each other in forensic activities. Perhaps he was too shy to speak before an audience. Perhaps for the same reason that he did not take part in public debates he did not speak at his commencement exercises. For his Princeton years, there is no explicit testimony of his shyness or his speaking, but a few years later his diffidence and his reluctance to speak in a legislative body were noticeable to Edmund Randolph and Thomas Jefferson.

As a member of the recently organized American Whig Society, Madison did produce some writings in the form of satirical doggerel lampooning the rival Cliosophic Society. Preserved fragments of these verses indicate that his enjoyment of the kind of stories that would have made Jefferson blush was not entirely dependent upon imbibing wine at the dinner table.[4] Presumably these extracurricular literary efforts, of dubious literary and educational merit, escaped the notice of Dr. Witherspoon, who told Jefferson that "in the whole career of Mr. Madison at Princeton, he had never known him to say or do an indiscreet thing."[5]

The records of James's childhood and youth tell only of his schooling; they tell us nothing of diversions from his books. Nothing is known of his daily life on his father's estate. We cannot know whether he had playmates or pets, glided in swings, climbed in trees, built rock fortresses, made castles in the sand, explored in the woods, threw snowballs in the winter, roamed in the meadows, tossed horseshoes, swam, hunted, fished, or rode horseback for fun; fraternized with slaves or chatted with neighbors; whether he ever did a naughty or impish thing—chased the chickens or poked the cows, squirmed in church, quarreled with his brothers or teased his sisters, sassed his mother or argued with his father; whether he played cards, danced, or flirted with the girls.

For four years after he left Princeton, James lived at his home in Orange County. Except for his studies and reading, he did little beyond tutor his younger brothers and sisters, write letters to a few friends, receive several visitors whom he had known at Princeton, and make a trip to Philadelphia and Albany. Despite his studies, these were not happy years for him. He looked back upon his days at Princeton with nostalgia; Virginia seemed less desirable to him than Pennsylvania, where his friend Bradford lived, and he suffered from a disquieting debility of mind or body.[6]

References to his illness at twenty-one were even more cryptic than at fifty-one. Madison reported to his friend William Bradford in a letter of November 9, 1772, that he felt "dull and infirm" and did not expect, because of "sensations" which he had experienced "for many months past," to have a "long or healthy life." On April 28, 1773, he wrote that his health was a "little better" because of more "activity and less study" recommended by the physicians. On September 5, 1773, he told Bradford that he hoped to visit him in Philadelphia in the spring "if I should be alive and should have health sufficient."[7]

In his letters of 1774 and 1775 he made no reference to his health. Nor did Bradford inquire of his health. Only in his reply to Madison's of November 9, 1772, did Bradford write of the illness; he expressed alarm but added: "I believe you hurt your constitution while here [at Princeton], by too close an application to study; but I hope 'tis not so bad with you as you seem to imagine. Persons of the weakest Constitutions *by taking a proper care of themselves* often out live those of the strongest."[8]

Bradford did not live long enough to know how prophetic he had been when he wrote those words of reassurance; he died forty-one years before Madison died.

The extent to which James was still suffering from the illness in 1774 and 1775 is uncertain. In an autobiographical statement made when he was eighty or more, he said that he "continued for several years in very feeble" health after his return home from Princeton.[9] Edward Coles, in a memorandum checked for accuracy by Madison himself, stated: "He remained in bad health for many years, having an affection of the breast and nerves; but for which circumstance he would have joined the army."[10]

Even if he had not recovered sufficiently to serve in the army, there are good reasons to think he had continued to improve after April, 1773. His silence on the subject of health in his letters to Bradford, a more optimistic outlook expressed in those letters, his trip to Philadelphia and Albany in May and June, 1774, his reporting on his marksmanship in June, 1775, and his being commissioned a colonel in the Orange County militia in October, 1775—all these add up to a firm impression that his mental and physical state was not what it had been during the first year after his return from Princeton.[11] After 1773 he did not write like one who was expecting to exchange "Time for Eternity."[12]

At Princeton and for several years after his return home, Madison had a strong interest in theology and moral philosophy. When he was twenty-two he wrote that divinity was "the most sublime of all Sciences."[13] His readings were mostly from learned divines who defended orthodox and traditional Christianity; he was distrustful of reviews of books published in English monthlies because they were enemies to "serious religion" in their encouragement of inquiry that "destroys the most essential Truths" and their biased selection of citations to justify their censures and condemnations. Nevertheless, he shared some of the anticlerical attitudes of the Deists. He was quite ready to ridicule evangelistic enthusiasm, enforced conformity, hypocrisy, or stupidity in the pulpit.[14]

His letters to William Bradford indicate that his determination to be silent about his religious beliefs had not yet been made when he was twenty-two. To Bradford he expressed his religious opinions freely, and in a letter of September 25, 1773, declared that there could be no "stronger testimony in favor of Religion or against temporal Enjoyment" than for men of rising "reputation and wealth" to declare publicly "their unsatisfactoriness by becoming fervent Advocates in the cause of Christ."[15]

Except for this lack of reticence in expressing his religious opinions, the young Madison, as revealed in his letters, had a striking resemblance to the later statesman. Even during the first two years after leaving Princeton, when living a life of solitude and study at home, he offered only a few introspective observations about himself, he never described his surroundings, and his references to personal matters largely pertained to the acquisition of books, news of mutual friends, and his health. His language was matter-of-fact and prosaic, employing perhaps only a few more metaphors than in his later years.

The few introspective observations contained in his letters to Bradford indicate that James placed great value upon the control of feelings and avoidance of worldly pleasures. He considered himself "very sedate and philosophic" and rejoiced that his friend had the same characteristics. He was pleased that his friend had "so early seen through the romantic paintings with which the World is sometimes set off by the sprightly imaginations of the Ingenious" and urged him to keep at "a becoming distance" from "those impertinent fops that abound in every City to divert you from your business and philosophical amusements."[16]

Ascetic in his values, he could never quite make cultivation of the intellect an end in itself. He was a stoic, not a quietist or a dilettante. The mind for him was above all an instrument for governing conduct, a power for subduing and avoiding evil. At the same time, he assumed that learning and study would be of vocational benefit. A few months before he was twenty-three he confessed that he was losing interest in "amusing Studies." In the past, he wrote to Bradford on January 24, 1774, he had had "too great a hankering after" poetry, wit, criticism, plays, and romances—now he was beginning to discover that they deserved "but a moderate portion of a mortal's time," and that something more substantial, durable, and more profitable were befitting "a riper Age."[17]

When Madison wrote this letter to Bradford, his "affections" for the "belles-lettres" were being "loosened" by a growing interest in public affairs.[18] His first recorded statement about politics was apologetic. On September 25, 1773, he had written: "We have a very great scarcity of circulating cash in this colony. . . . I do not meddle with Politicks but this Calamity lies so near the heart of every friend of the Country that I could not but mention it."[19] How exquisitely fitting that the future expositor of economic determinism should have had his interests in politics thus aroused!

The subjects which became of absorbing interest to him in 1774 and 1775 were religious freedom in Virginia and British imperial policies in all the colonies. His letters show a young man who had no trouble making up his mind about which side to take in the controversy with Great Britain. There was no conflict in his mind between British and American patriotism. Completely missing were any expressions of sentimental attachment to the mother country or the monarchy. There is no indication that he had any doubts or misgivings about the justness and wisdom of the American cause. He became a revolutionary and American nationalist without any discernible mental anguish.

His opinions of British imperial policies were popular in Virginia and well defended by the most prominent leaders in the colony. His views on the Anglican Church, however, were less acceptable to a large segment of Virginia society.

His own family was of course Anglican. His father was a

vestryman. These ties did not, however, render him indifferent to the disabilities placed upon the dissenters by law and public opinion. He resented the jailing of Baptist ministers in adjoining counties, despite his distaste for their emotional fervor. Apparently he argued the subject with his neighbors in Orange County, for on January 24, 1774, he told Bradford that he had squabbled, scolded, abused, and ridiculed so long about the harassment of the Baptists that he was not "without common patience."[20] The nearest Madison ever came to expressing passionate indignation was when he denounced persecution of men because of their religious beliefs.

Sympathies for the Baptists led him to think about the fundamentals of state-church relations. His other political opinions, however, rested on foundations which he did not debate. In his letters to Bradford, philosophical and ethical justification for resistance to Britain were taken for granted as he discussed questions of strategy, tactics, and morale. How to resist, not why, was the subject of his discourse.

Madison was not yet advocating independence in 1775. For himself at least, and probably for the Virginians he knew, Madison remembered correctly when he wrote to Jared Sparks, January 5, 1828:

You wish me to say whether I believe "that at the beginning of the Revolution, or at the assembling of the first Congress, the leaders of that day were resolved on Independence?" I readily express my entire belief that they were not, tho' I must admit that my means of information were more limited than may have been the case with others still living to answer the enquiry. My first entrance on public life was in May, 1776, when I became a member of the Convention in Virginia, which instructed her delegates in Congress to propose the Declaration of Independence. Previous to that date, I was not in sufficient communication with any under the denomination of leaders, to learn their sentiments or views on the cardinal subject. I can only say therefore, that so far as ever came to my knowledge, no one of them ever avowed, or was understood to entertain a pursuit of independence at the assembling of the first Congress, or for a very considerable period thereafter. It has always been my impression that a re-establishment of the Colonial relations to the parent country previous to the Controversy, was the real object of every class of people, till despair of obtaining it, and the exasperating effects of the war, and the manner of conducting it, prepared the minds of all for the event declared on the 4th of July, 1776, as preferable with all its difficulties and perils, to the alternative of submission to a claim of power, at once external, unlimited, irresponsible, and under every temptation to abuse, from interest, ambition, & revenge. If there were individuals who originally aimed at Independence, their views must have been confined to their own bosoms or to a very confidential circle.[21]

At age twenty-three James could not see that advocacy of resistance to British policies would culminate in support for national independence. Likewise, he could not see that his shedding theology and literature was to be an essential step toward a choice of career. For four years after finishing his studies at Princeton he had, perhaps excused in his own mind by his poor health, avoided a choice. In a letter to William Bradford, December 1, 1773, he said that he had decided "to read Law occasionally," but he said nothing about his future career, and, more than a half century later, he recalled that he had "never formed any absolute determination" to practice law. He paid high tribute to the ministry as a profession and divinity as a subject for study, but neither in his letters to Bradford nor his octogenarian memoir did he give any inkling of a desire to become a clergyman.[22]

In his letters to Bradford, James gave not even a hint of hidden aspirations for political leadership or public office. When he announced his intention to read law, however, he showed that he was attracted by public, not civil or criminal law. "The principles & Modes of Government," he wrote, "are too important to be disregarded by an Inquisitive mind and I think are well worthy [of] critical examination by all students that have health & Leisure." These words were written in December, 1773, just before stirring events in the colonies became the main topics of his correspondence.[23]

The translation of Madison's political interest into a career required moving from observation to participation. This step was taken in association with his father when he became a member of the Committee of Public Safety for Orange County in December, 1774.

His father, then fifty-one years old, was chairman of the committee. James Madison, Sr., was the son of one of the first settlers in Orange County. During the life of his son James, he had added greatly to the land and slaves he had inherited from his father. For the upper Piedmont, his holdings were large-scale; he was one of the wealthiest men in his county. In his county also he held a position of social and civic prominence commensurate with his wealth.[24]

When he was in his twenty-sixth year he had married Nellie

Conway, then aged nineteen. Their first child had been James, born March 16, 1751; their tenth and last child was born October 4, 1774. There were then living five boys and four girls, one boy having died in infancy.[25]

The senior Madison's bookish interests, judging by the titles in his library, associated learning with practicality.[26] His positions as vestryman, justice of the peace, and county lieutenant associated the life of a planter with public service. There was nothing in his life that associated learning with genteel leisure and nothing that associated moneymaking with either unlettered ignorance or avoidance of public service. Why he financed his son's schooling or tolerated his excessive concentration on book learning is not known. Like other Virginia fathers who provided a comparable education for their sons, he probably expected such learning to have an ultimate vocational and public utility.

The elder Madison, it seems, had inculcated an ethic, and, for reasons not known, permitted a contraction of interests and activities that left his son James at twenty-one a choice between the life of an invalid and the life of a man of affairs. He had permitted book learning to become his sole proficiency; indeed, to pre-empt his whole being. By example surely and by precept presumably, he had taught his son that book learning was not for idle purposes. For James at twenty-one to have repudiated book learning would have been to give up his one recognized accomplishment, indeed, would have created a total void in his life. To cling to his book learning as a recluse would have been to repudiate ingrained ethical assumptions. To hold to his book learning, probably a psychological necessity by age twenty-one, his own ethic demanded illness or a career. A healthy life of genteel exemption from vocational employment or public usefulness, even if financially permissible, was a psychological impossibility.

But why did not James combine scholarship with agriculture? Why did he become a literary politician rather than a literary planter? Perhaps his father's age and continued presence as head of the Orange County estates precluded any but an uncomfortable subordination. Perhaps, as he was to later admit, he disliked dependence upon the labor of slaves. Certainly he had shown no interest in agriculture. He at no time intimated to William Bradford that he might be considering the life of a planter, although his friend, whose father was a printer and bookseller, had written that he was considering a mercantile career.

Madison's interests and his knowledge at twenty-one were most suitable for the ministry or the law. But something about these professions or something about himself caused him to avoid a choice for four years. Then, caught up in the swirl of a great political storm, he was brought to his life work without knowing exactly when the choice was made.

Election to the Committee of Public Safety, of course, was not in itself a choice for a civil career in government, any more than his practice with Orange County riflemen was a choice for a military service. He might have retreated from this first step in politics just as he retreated from military service after June, 1775. But something latent in his personality enabled him, perhaps compelled him, for the sake of a public career and a great cause, to overcome his poor health and shyness.

If Madison's poor health was physiological, his own explanation for not continuing in the military service is adequate. If his illness was psychological, then one must ask why he was too ill for one but not too ill for another occupation. Perhaps his size alone would not permit his thinking of himself as a commanding person among military men, although a short stature had no such effect on Alexander Hamilton or Napoleon Bonaparte. Perhaps his obvious lack of self-assertiveness ruled out a military career, although the same characteristic hardly recommended him for a career in politics. Between the military and civil career, his choice, if not determined by physical disability, was probably made on the basis of capacities and interests developed during his first twenty-three years: his verbal aptitude and erudition would be of greater use in a civil than in a military career.

Vestiges of the withdrawn lad of twenty-one were observable throughout Madison's public career. Some seeing only his outward diffidence and bookishness, failed to take into account the invisible will that kept such a person in public life. They thereby failed to perceive whatever it was that constituted the fundamental strength of his personality.

CHAPTER III

For a National Community of Interests

IN APRIL, 1776, MADISON WAS ELECTED ONE OF TWO DELE-
gates from Orange County to attend the convention that made
the colony of Virginia into a state. This convention, held in Williamsburg between May 6 and July 5, first instructed the Virginia
delegation in the Continental Congress to propose a declaration
of independence, formation of a union of the revolting colonies,
and negotiation of foreign alliances. Then, while also acting as a
provisional government, it adopted a constitution, issued a Declaration of Rights, and elected Patrick Henry governor.

At Williamsburg, Madison found himself surrounded by men
who had led resistance to English policies for a decade. He was
also probably the smallest man in a body that included many tall
men. Young, inexperienced, and shy, he did not enter into the
debates from the floor, and it is improbable that he spoke very
much in committee.[1] He was a good listener, however, and his
whispered comments were delightful to those who sat near him.
Edmund Randolph, two years younger than Madison and the
youngest delegate, later wrote:

Madison, even then, attracted great notice. Until the meeting of the
convention he was unknown at the metropolis. He was educated at
Princeton College in New Jersey, and had been laborious in his studies,
which ranged beyond strict academick limits, but were of that elemen-
tary cast, subservient in their general principle to any science, which he
might choose to cultivate in detail. As a classical scholar, he was mature;
as a student of belles lettres, his fancy animated his judgment; and his
judgment without damping his fancy, excluded by the soundness of
criticism, every propensity to tinsel and glitter. It still glowed, but it
glowed without glare. His diffidence went hand in hand with his morals,
which repelled vice, howsoever fashionable. In convention debate his
lips were never unsealed, except to some member, who happened to sit
near him; and he who had once partaken of the rich banquet of his
remarks, did not fail to wish daily to sit within the reach of his conversation. It could not be otherwise; for although his age and the deference,
which in private circles had been paid to him, were apt to tincture him

with pedantry, he delivered himself without affection upon Grecian, Roman and English history, from a well digested fund, a sure presage of eminence. A very sensible foreigner observed of him, that he never uttered anything, which was not appropriate, and not connected with some general principle of importance. Even when he commented upon the dignity, with which Pendleton filled the chair, it was in that philosophic spirit, which looks for personal dignity in officers of a republic as well as of a monarchy. While he thrilled with the ecstasies of Henry's eloquence, he detected what might be faulty in his reasoning. Madison was enviable in being among the few young men, who were not inflated by early flattery, and could content themselves with throwing out in social discourse jewels, which the artifice of a barren mind, would have treasured up for gaudy occasions.[2]

If Madison did any more than register the consent of Orange County to the proceedings of the convention, it was done behind the scenes. Late in life, Madison remembered that he had taken no part in debates but had occasionally "suggested" amendments, "the most material of which was a change of the terms in which the freedom of Conscience was expressed in the proposed Declaration of Rights."[3]

As reported to the convention by committee, a version of the Declaration of Rights drafted by George Mason asserted that "all Men sh'd enjoy the fullest Toleration in the Exercise of Religion, according to the Dictates of Conscience." Madison, desiring to declare religious freedom an absolute and natural right, drafted a substitute resolution which deleted the word toleration. Agreeable to a motion introduced into the Committee of the Whole by Edmund Pendleton, the convention eliminated the word toleration and approved Madison's phraseology declaring that "all men are equally entitled to the free exercise of religion."[4]

Madison left among his papers the draft of a resolution on the free exercise of religion which was not accepted by the convention. If broadly interpreted, this resolution could have been used to sanction separation of church and state. It declared "that no man or class of men ought on account of religion to be invested with peculiar emoluments or privileges; nor subjected to any penalties or disabilities."[5]

As a member of the Convention, Madison became automatically a member of the House of Delegates under the new constitution. In its first session at Williamsburg between October 7 and December 21, 1776, he served on two committees that dealt with the subject of state-church relations. The first was

discharged without making a report. The second drafted legislation in accord with a set of principles adopted by the Committee of the Whole.[6]

Nothing is known of Madison's activities in these committees,
but the legislation drafted by the second committee embodied
principles to which he subscribed. The committee proposed to
remove certain legal disabilities of the dissenters and to terminate tax support for the Anglican Church. As amended by the
House, suspension of tax payments was limited until the next
session of the legislature.[7]

In 1777, Madison lost his seat in the legislature. In April, he
was defeated by Charles Porter. "Sundry freeholders" of
Orange County, in a petition requesting disallowance of the
election, charged that Porter won by means of bribery and
corruption.[8] Madison blamed his defeat on his refusal to
"recommend" himself to the voters "by the corrupting influence of spiritous liquors, and other treats, having a like tendency. ... The voters were not pleased with this departure
from an old custom, and fancied they saw in it a higher spirit
of independence than they were disposed to encourage in a
young candidate for their favor."[9]

In April, 1778, the candidate who believed that treating voters to drinks was "inconsistent with the purity of moral and
republican principles" was elected by the constituency which
rejected him the year before.[10] Whether his opponent or the
voters underwent a reformation during that year, he never explained.

On May 27, 1778, the House of Delegates ruled that Madison
was ineligible for membership in the General Assembly because
of another office which he then held. On November 15, 1777,
he had been elected by the General Assembly to the Council
of State. William C. Rives said that he was nominated to this
post "without his knowledge or his wish."[11]

Election to this body of eight men whose collective power
equalled that of the governor indicates that the quiet young
legislator of twenty-five had made a favorable impression upon
his elders. On the first ballot he received 30 of 108 votes divided among seven candidates. On the second ballot, he defeated Meriwether Smith by 61 to 42.[12]

Madison was sworn in as a member of the "Privy Council" on
January 14, 1778. He served for two years. Until June, 1779, he
was working with Governor Henry; for the rest of the year,
with Governor Jefferson. Although the council had eight mem-

bers officially, rarely were all present at one time. Madison seems to have spent little time in Williamsburg between July and November, but when not at his home in Orange County or visiting at Berkeley Springs during these months, his attendance at the council meetings was good. In May, 1778, he was absent for about a week because of illness.[13]

A few years later he recalled that he had "long regarded the Council as a grave of useful talents, as well as objectionable in point of expence."[14] Despite this harsh judgment, his two years of service in the council provided valuable experiences for the young man. In a group that usually varied between four and six men, his voice could be heard and his shyness could be overcome much more easily than in a large legislative body. Furthermore, the deliberations of the council were about the same practical problems that had interested him when he had written his letters to William Bradford in 1774 and 1775: furnishing supplies and men to fight the war, checking disaffection, directing frontier defenses against the Indians, guarding the coast against enemy vessels and landing parties, levying taxes and seeking loans, maintaining discipline in the militia, setting up prison camps, and exchanging information with the Continental Congress and General Washington.[15] While Jefferson, during Governor Henry's term, was dedicating his labors to constitutional and legal reforms of long-term significance, Madison, to be known ten years later as a speculative and bookish philosopher, was grappling with the daily business of a wartime executive.

Madison's friendship with Jefferson began when he was a member of the council. In a letter of September, 1830, he recalled: "During part of the time whilst he was Governour of the State, a service to which he was called not long after, I had a seat in the Council associated with him. Our acquaintance there became intimate; and a friendship was formed, which was for life, and which was never interrupted in the slightest degree for a single moment."[16]

In December, 1779, the General Assembly of Virginia selected Madison as a delegate to the Continental Congress. At twenty-eight, he was the youngest of the four selected at this time; the others were thirty-five, forty-eight, and fifty-two. When he took his seat in March, 1780, he was the youngest man in the Congress.[17]

In the Continental Congress, he served in a body which was much smaller than the Virginia House of Delegates and which, through small committees, conducted executive business similar to that conducted by the Virginia Council of State. He was therefore not entirely unfamiliar with what came before the Congress and its methods of operation. There were, however, differences in his legislative role and the scope of his activities. He was no longer in a subordinate relationship to the leading men with whom he was associated. In the committees, despite his youth, the responsibility of chairmanships and authorship of formal reports was often assigned to him. He not only shared in making decisions as he had in Williamsburg but also was called upon to justify or to explain them in the form of instructions to diplomats abroad and addresses to the state governments. The production of major public documents became for the first time an important feature of his career. For the first time, too, he assumed a position of leadership in a legislative body. He became an active participant in debates and undertook to manage the formation of legislative majorities.

Diplomacy, for which his intricate but orderly mind was eminently suited, was of course necessarily a much more important phase of his activities than when he had served in the Virginia capital. He served on numerous committees dealing with diplomatic problems and shared in the preparation of instructions for American negotiators. He had not yet been in the Congress a year when he was being talked about as a possible candidate for the new position of Secretary of Foreign Affairs.[18]

In his attempts to shape diplomatic instructions, Madison sought to safeguard Virginia interests by linking them with the maintenance of other interests. The great danger, as he saw it, was that each distinct interest in the nation would seek to gain diplomatic concessions from Great Britain or Spain by granting concessions which abandoned what others were seeking. From the standpoint of Virginia, the threat was that several states, in seeking a Spanish alliance or bargaining for the access of their fishermen and shippers to British and Spanish colonies, would be willing to place the western boundary along the Appalachian range, abandon navigation on the Mississippi, or exclude certain American exports from areas controlled by Britain and Spain.[19]

Madison was convinced that all the distinct interests represented in Congress would gain their objectives if, in addition to giving mutual support in negotiations, French help was obtained for policies opposed by the British and Spanish governments. He was a staunch supporter of the French alliance. He trusted French intentions. Unlike his fellow delegates Arthur Lee and Theodorick Bland, he saw nothing sinister in the time taken to get French troops and fleets to America or in the dipolomatic consideration given by France to her ally Spain. He supported the instructions which required the American commissioners to consult with the French in negotiating a peace treaty with the British.[20]

When the reports of a preliminary peace came to Philadelphia in March, 1783, he was placed in a painful dilemma. The terms were highly favorable, but they had been obtained from the British in violation of their instructions to consult with the French, and the treaty contained a secret article on the boundary of West Florida. Although he did not call for censure of the American commissioners, he thought that "candor, rectitude, and plain dealing," required some explanation to the French government.[21]

Madison's notes and letters while serving in the Congress during these years are filled with references to the special interests of the several states and the shifting alignments formed in their behalf. Virginia was especially interested in navigation on the Mississippi, land titles in the West, national reimbursement for state financing of military operations in the Northwest, and reservation of land in the West for Virginia veterans who had been promised land bounties. All the Southern states were interested in the method of assessing land and slave values, in legislation affecting exports, and in the future western boundary of the United States. Importing states stood to gain more than Connecticut, New Jersey, and North Carolina from levying their own duties. Pennsylvania and Massachusetts, where creditors of the United States were more numerous than in the other states, had compelling reasons for supporting measures for funding the national debt. States such as South Carolina, Georgia, New York, and Rhode Island had suffered damages from invading armies while Virginia had incurred unusual expenses to fight the British in North and South Carolina. New York and New Hampshire, claimants to land between Lake Champlain and the Connecticut River, opposed the admission of Vermont into the Union, while states with no western land sought to admit a delegation that seemed likely to vote against Virginia's terms for ceding her lands to Congress. Massachusetts was eager that her fishermen continue to have access to the coastal waters of Newfoundland after independence. All the states disputed whether the national capital should be located on the Potomac, Delaware, Hudson, or Chesapeake Bay, with the Southern states generally favoring the most southerly and the New England states the more northerly sites.[22]

No one issue, Madison found, could be discussed solely from the standpoint of a presumed generalized national interest. Special and local interests were always present, whether considering contributions that each state should make in money, men, and material; deciding upon the location of continental troops and vessels; preparing instructions to govern negotiations with France, Spain, and Great Britain; or arranging terms with the states for the cesandn of their western lands to the Confederation. Despite repeated frustrations and defeats, he adhered to the belief that conflicting and rival interests among the states could be compromised through reciprocal concessions. Always implicit in his Confederation politics was the proposition that the short-term losses that some states might incur in making the compromises necessary to form a united front would be less in the long run than the territorial and commercial gains which a powerful Union would be able to obtain from Great Britain, Spain, and France.

Madison's interpretation of Virginia interests usually coincided with the majority in the state legislature. The greatest difference between him and a large segment in the legislature occurred on the issue of taxation. Although he had himself voted against the impost proposed by Congress in February, 1781, he subsequently supported its ratification and was distressed when Virginia in December, 1782, repealed its earlier ratification. When he proposed in March, 1783, that Congress be empowered to levy import duties and to requisition sums from the states in proportion to population rather than land values, he was acting contrary to positions approved by the Virginia legislature. He acted out of his conviction that the legislature failed to understand the crisis then facing the Union.[23]

When devising the legislation of March, 1783, he had hoped that his proposal to have Congress assume some of the state war debts would make the tax and requisition amendments more palatable in Virginia. To his chagrin, Congress submitted to the states only those measures which were most objectionable in Virginia. Notwithstanding his disappointment in the failure to provide "bait" for Virginia, he consented to write the Address to the States which Congress accepted as the official explanation of the measures submitted for ratification.[24]

Delegate Madison did not propose structural revisions in the Confederation or drastic changes in the powers of Congress. In his speeches and letters one does not find proposals of the kind that the young Alexander Hamilton was making as early as 1780. During the war years he seems to have believed that use of force against states that carried on trade helpful to the enemy or against states that failed to provide money requisitioned by Congress would enable the Union to accomplish its military and diplomatic objectives. After Yorktown, he seems to have assumed that granting Congress the power to tax imports and to requisition sums from the states in proportion to population would enable the United States to pay its debts and current expenses. At no time during these years in Congress did he propose to add new Congressional powers in order to accomplish new objectives.[25]

Like Hamilton and Jefferson, Madison did not believe that the doctrine of implied powers depended upon an "elastic" clause giving to Congress the power to enact legislation "necessary and proper" for implementing the specified powers. With no such clause in the Articles, Madison argued that the power to regulate or prohibit trade helpful to the enemy could be implied from the war-making power and that the power to use land and sea forces against delinquent states could be implied from the statement in the Articles which obligated the states to abide by the determinations of Congress.[26]

His willingness to exercise powers not expressly granted by the Articles did not mean that he would accept without question any power that a controlling majority in Congress would approve. When, on May 26, 1781, twenty members of Congress, including three from Virginia, approved plans for a national bank, Madison was one of four who voted in the negative.[27] In a letter to Edmund Pendleton, January 8, 1782, in which he hinted that he had recently acquiesced in chartering the Bank of North America because of its financial benefits and "a recommendation to the States to give it the necessary validity within their respective jurisdictions," he expressed an aversion to "the poisonous tendency of precedents by usurpation."[28]

Madison wrote many letters to Virginia while in Congress. He usually sent several a month to Edmund Pendleton. He often wrote to Joseph Jones and Edmund Randolph when they were not serving as delegates in Philadelphia. Only occasionally, before 1782, did he write to Jefferson. His letters to these men were reports and commentaries on public business. They reveal a man absorbed in the day-to-day affairs of a government at war. They reflect the mind of an intellectual only in that they were orderly, analytical, calculating, and unemotional. Madison the bookish and speculative philosopher is not to be seen in them. Ideas as discussed by the philosophical-minded are totally missing. Long-term objectives and underlying assumptions are implied, not debated. If Madison during these years was the theoretical and philosophical statesman which he was generally thought to be after the year 1786, he apparently preferred either to remain silent about his theories and his speculations or to confine his expression of them to private conversation.

Letters received from his friends in Virginia were similar in content to his own. Judging from what Madison said about the diplomatic correspondence of John Adams and John Jay, one can surmise that he was quite satisfied to confine his correspondence strictly to business. Adams' letters were less interesting than Jay's, he told Jared Sparks, because they were too long and "contained much extraneous matter, discussions and speculation on government, and narratives of events abroad."[29]

Except for many complaints about the failure of the state treasury to remit enough money to pay his living expenses, he said little in his letters about his personal affairs.[30] He said nothing about his health. Only in several letters to Jefferson did he tell, in veiled language, of his first courtship.

In January, 1783, when Jefferson was staying at the same house where Madison lived in Philadelphia, he became acquainted with the daughter of William Floyd, member of Congress from New York and a co-signer of the Declaration of Independence. Her name was Kitty and she was sixteen years old. Jefferson noticed that Madison, showing some interest in Kitty, was subjected to "raillery" among his friends in the household. From his own observations, too, Jefferson began to believe that there was "some foundation" for a courtship. "I wished it would be so [he wrote to Madison on April 14] as it would give me a neighbor whose worth I rate high, and as I know it will render me happier than you can possibly be in a single state. I often made it the subject of conversation, more exhortation, with her and was able to convince myself that she possessed every sentiment in your favor which you could wish."[31]

On April 22, Madison wrote to Jefferson: "Your inference on that subject was not groundless. Before you left us I had sufficiently ascertained her sentiments. Since your departing the affair has been pursued. Most preliminary arrangements, although definitive, will be postponed until the end of the year in Congress. At some period of the interval I shall probably make a visit to Virginia. The interest which your friendship takes on this occasion in my happiness is a pleasing proof that the dispositions which I feel are reciprocal."[32]

But, alas, the plans of the benign match-maker from Monticello and the delicate negotiator in Philadelphia came to naught. During the summer a young medical student won the affections of Kitty; or, as Madison reported to Jefferson, August 11, "one of those incidents to which such affairs are liable" had brought "the object" he had been "pursuing" to an "uncertain state."[33]

When Jefferson received the disappointing news of August 11, the quoted words were not yet scratched over, as they were to be many years later when the letter once more came into the possession of its author.[34] Even without the later marks of censorship, the anonymity and ambiguity of Madison's allusions would have rendered their meaning obscure to anyone who knew nothing of the affair. Jefferson of course understood exactly what he was being told, and on August 31 he wrote a consoling reply: "I sincerely lament the misadventure which has happened from whatever cause it may have happened. Should it be final however, the world still presents the same and many other resources of happiness, and you possess many within yourself. Firmness of mind and unintermitting occupations will not long leave you in pain. No event has been more contrary to my expectations, and these were founded on what I thought a good knowledge of the ground. But of all machines ours is the most complicated and inexplicable."[35]

At the end of August, 1783, Madison went to Princeton, Congress having fled to that village in June when about three hundred soldiers surrounded the State House in Philadelphia demanding back pay. He was not eager, despite his recent matrimonial disappointment, to be away from Philadelphia. For the first and last time in his life, he complained in his letters about the discomfort of his living conditions. In a letter to Edmund Randolph, he wrote on August 30: "We are crowded too much either to be comfortable ourselves or to be able to carry on the business with advantage. Mr. Jones & myself on our arrival were extremely put to it to get any quarters at all, and are at length put into one bed in a room not more than 10 feet square." The same complaint was made in letters to his father and to Jefferson. Not a word was said about seeing people and places he had known at Princeton eleven years before.[36]

If Madison disliked this stay in Princeton, he had no desire to return to Virginia, at least not without a wife. The other delegates returned periodically for visits, but throughout his period of service in the Congress, he never returned. Early in 1783, after he had already been absent from Virginia for three years, he was planning to spend the next winter in Philadelphia; he was looking forward to the prospect of a season of "close reading" and "agreeable and even instructive society."[37] In April, having altered his plans to include Kitty Floyd, he was expecting to be in Virginia in August. Then, after Kitty disengaged herself, he once more thought of carrying out his earlier plan. He had been urged to visit his sickly mother, but he thought he would be able to "decline a visit" to Virginia or "speedily get away from it" if Jefferson and the Congress were to be in Philadelphia during the winter. Jefferson was elected delegate to the Congress, but the Congress failed to return to Philadelphia. Madison then decided to return to Virginia. His last recorded vote in Congress was on October 22. He was in Philadelphia until the last week in November, when he accompanied Jefferson to Annapolis. He was back in Orange County by December 10.[38]

CHAPTER IV

Merging American and Virginia Interests

MADISON RETURNED TO VIRGINIA WITH NO CERTAIN PLANS for his future, except to do what he had hoped to do at Philadelphia during the winter. He lost no time getting started on his program of reading. Interruptions by visiting neighbors, which he at first thought would be impossible to guard against, proved to be fewer than he had "presupposed." During his mornings he read law; in the afternoon "works of a philosophical cast." Among the latter were the volumes of Buffon on natural history, which he supplemented by his own observations and measurements of animals from the nearby countryside.[1]

Jefferson, at his request, bought books for him in Philadelphia and Paris. In January, 1786, two trunks sent by Jefferson brought him a "literary cargo" from France. There were encyclopedias; dictionaries; memoirs; letters; histories of Mexico, China, Spain, and ancient empires; treatises on agriculture, botany, Anglo-Norman customs, public finance in France, and the philosophy of morals and politics. As editors or authors appeared the names of Trevoux, De Solis, Burlamaqui, Mirabeau, Neckar, Mably, Voltaire, Lannaeus, Clayton, Diderot, Wolff, Paget, Buffon, Pascal, Valin, and Mariana.[2]

Madison used some of the books sent by Jefferson to make a systematic investigation of European confederations. From his studies, carried out in 1786 and early 1787, he concluded that other confederations, in their dependence upon member states for enforcement of confederation legislation, suffered from the same fundamental weakness as the American Union. For his own use he prepared a compendium on "Ancient and Modern Confederacies" which he drew upon when he later wrote number eighteen, nineteen, and twenty of *The Federalists*.[3]

Madison was usually away from his home in Orange County during the last four months of each year during the mid-1780's. In the early fall or late summer, he made visits to Philadelphia and New York for business and "for exercise after a sedentary period." In September and October, 1784, traveling with La

Fayette to Fort Stanwix, he found the landscape of the Mohawk Valley charming and foresaw a prosperous future for that area.[4] He had "long had a curiosity to see" the Eastern states and was disappointed in both 1784 and 1785 when he was unable to extend his "ramble" into that region.[5]

Madison never expressed a desire to see the Western country, any part of the United States south of Richmond, or Europe. In December, 1784, Jefferson invited him to come to France for a visit, which, at a cost of two hundred guineas, would bring him "the knowledge of another world." While this invitation was on the way to Virginia, he learned that Madison had been nominated minister to Spain. On March 18, 1785, Jefferson wrote: "I need not tell you how much I shall be pleased with such an event. Yet it has it's displeasing sides also. I want you in the Virginia Assembly and also in Congress yet we cannot have you everywhere. We must therefore be contented to have you where you chuse."[6] Madison declined to go to either France or Spain. He was afraid for his health and afraid he might never again have such a convenient time for the course of reading he was then pursuing.[7]

When away from home, Madison expressed no nostalgia for his home in Orange County and, when considering choices for moneymaking, place of residence was never mentioned. He wrote to an old college friend living in the "wilderness" of Kentucky that he had "no Local partialities which can keep me from any place which promises the greatest real advantages."[8] Yet he always came back to Orange County.

Not even Jefferson could entice him to move to nearby Albemarle County. In a letter of February 20, 1784, Jefferson urged him to acquire "a little farm of 140 acres" two miles from Monticello, where, with William Short and James Monroe as neighbors, they could form the kind of "rational society" which "informs the mind, sweetens the temper, cheers our spirits, and promotes health." Madison's reply was profusely noncommittal: "I know not my dear Sir what to reply to the affectionate invitation which closes your letter. I feel the attractions of the particular situation you point out to me; I can not altogether renounce the prospect; still less can I as yet embrace it. It is far from being improbable that a few years more may prepare me for giving such a destiny to my future life; in which case the same or some equally convenient spot may be commanded by a little augmentation of price. But wherever my final lot may fix me be assured that I shall ever remain with the sincerest affection & esteem Yr. friend and servant."[9]

At age thirty-four, Madison was still undecided about his own means of earning a living. Perhaps he had thoughts of becoming a lawyer when he began to read law in December, 1783; if so, he found in time that his youthful aversion to the practice of law could not be overcome. On July 26, 1785, he wrote to Edmund Randolph: "I keep up my attention as far as I can command my time, to the course of reading which I have of late pursued & shall continue to do so. I am however far from being determined ever to make a professional use of it. My wish is if possible to provide a decent & independent subsistence, without encountering the difficulties I foresee in that line."[10]

In August, 1784, his father gave him a tract of five hundred and sixty acres, but he was also disinclined to become a farmer. "Another of my wishes [he wrote to Randolph] is to depend as little as possible on the labor of slaves."[11] Farming and slave-holding were inextricably linked in his mind; tilling the soil with his own hands was unthinkable to a man of his upbringing. "The difficulty of reconciling these views," he explained, "has brought into my thoughts several projects from which advantage seemed attainable. I have in concert with a friend here, one at present on the Anvil which we think cannot fail to yield a decent reward for our trouble." He forebore "to particularize," but his letter to Randolph seems to have forecast a venture in land speculation.[12]

On the way back from Philadelphia in October, 1785, he talked with Washington about land speculation in the Mohawk Valley. The General "intimated that if he had money to spare and was disposed to deal in land, this is the very spot which his fancy had selected of all the U.S." In March, 1786, Madison "cheerfully" joined with Monroe in the purchase of nine hundred acres located about ten miles from Fort Stanwix.[13]

No foreseeable rise in land values could bring financial independence for two men from this small amount of land. After consultation in New York in August, 1786, they decided to buy a much larger tract if the money could be obtained in France. Both wrote Jefferson seeking his assistance. Madison described the area and quoted Washington's opinion, but he said nothing about the personal gratification he expected from the venture. Monroe, less reticent, wrote from New York: "Mr. Madison and myself have been desirous if possible of forming an engagement of land in this State which *would hereafter put us at ease.*" The italicized clause was written in code.[14]

Money from France was not forthcoming. Jefferson reported

that moneyed men in that country could get better returns lending to the government than in backing land speculations in America. Thus ended Madison's last attempt to escape the bondage to slavery. The effort, however, did produce a nice profit when he sold the small tract ten years later.[15]

Madison's devotion to his studies and his search for an independent income did not mean that he desired to retire from public life. His correspondence continued at all times to be that of a man engaged in public affairs. He jealously guarded his time for study, but he always approached this study as preparation for public service. He never contrasted the pleasures of private life with the pains of public duty.

Jefferson could think of reading, study, and philosophical conversation as very pleasurable substitutes for the burdens of public office. The "rational society" which he envisioned when he invited Madison to live near Monticello was a rural retreat of detached philosophers, not a headquarters for plotting political strategy. "With such a society [he wrote] I could once more venture home and lay myself up for the residue of life, quitting all its contentions which grow daily more and more insupportable."[16] No such thought was ever put on paper by his friend Madison.

In April, 1784, Madison was once again elected from Orange County to the House of Delegates. When he went to Richmond in May, he took with him a reputation that immediately placed him at the front of a new generation of leaders. On May 14, William Short wrote to Jefferson: "The Assembly have not yet proceeded to active Business. They have formed great Hopes of Mr. Madison, and those who know him best think he will not disappoint their most sanguine Expectations." The next day, Edmund Randolph wrote that Madison would become the leader of a new group of members who were unattached to the older factions led by Patrick Henry and Richard Henry Lee. These "children of the revolution," he predicted, "will want a general, to enable them to make head against those of the other parties, who will not fail to impeach them with an affectation of novelty, when they only press the result of liberality and reflection. This renders it probable, that our friend of Orange will step earlier into the heat of battle, than his modesty would otherwise permit. For he is already resorted to, as a general, of whom much has been preconceived to his advantage."[17]

In the legislatures of 1784, 1785, and 1786, he was brought to deal again with some of the strictly state issues that he had encountered in Williamsburg eight years before. The issue of church-state relations came before each of the sessions he attended during these years. In 1784 the House of Delegates postponed the third reading of a bill which levied a tax which the payer could assign to teachers of religion of his choice or to a county school. In 1785, the Episcopalians continued to support the bill, but the adverse reaction among the laity of other churches was so great that it was not even brought to a vote when the legislature met in the fall of that year.[18]

Madison spoke against the "assessment" bill in November, 1784. His arguments of this speech received a wide dissemination during the next summer when he put them into his "Remonstrance and Memorial," an anonymous document which he prepared for circulation among petitioners opposed to the bill.[19]

Economic conditions in Virginia in 1785 may have been responsible in part for a favorable reception of the "Remonstrance." A growing scarcity of specie and declining agricultural prices were leading to demands for postponing the collection of all taxes. A new tax, for whatever purpose, would have been highly unpopular that year.[20]

Ironically, the same depression which spawned demands for tax- and debt-relief measures repugnant to Madison may have contributed indirectly to passage of an act which he believed had "extinguished for ever the ambitious hope of making laws for the human mind."[21] Knowing that opponents of tax support for religion were in the majority in the legislature of 1785, Madison proceeded in January, 1786, to obtain enactment of Virginia's famed Statute of Religious Freedom. With only minor verbal alterations, this act was the same as a bill which Jefferson had drafted in 1777. It had been included among 126 bills recommended to the legislature in 1779 by a council of revisors which had been appointed to submit a reformed legal code for the new state of Virginia and which included Jefferson as one of its most active members.[22]

Only a few of the bills recommended in 1779 had been enacted before 1784. Under Madison's management, the legislatures of 1785 and 1786 devoted perhaps half their time to these bills, enacting many, revising or replacing some, and discarding a few. Most of the bills were passed, Jefferson wrote in his autobiography, "by the unwearied exertions of Mr. Madison, in opposition to the endless quibbles, chicaneries, perversions, vexations and delays of lawyers and demi-lawyers."[23]

Despite the fact that he was not a practicing lawyer, Madison was chairman of committees which brought forward several bills for the reorganization of the courts of the state. One of the most important of these passed in 1784 but was repealed before it went into effect.[24]

Madison was also active in framing legislation designed to develop and regulate commerce in Virginia. He advocated and obtained approval for legislation chartering corporations to improve navigation on the James and Potomac Rivers, providing surveys of routes for roads, and appointment of commissioners to meet with representatives of Maryland to negotiate uniform regulations for Chesapeake Bay and the Potomac. Arguing that Virginia farmers would be able to buy more cheaply if there were a large port city like Baltimore or Philadelphia in the state, he also obtained approval for an act concentrating all foreign trade at selected ports; in his judgment, however, the number of ports finally designated by the legislature was too great to achieve his main purpose of building at least one large commercial city.[25]

The disadvantages of state regulation of commerce were demonstrated in the Virginia legislature during these years. Establishment of uniform regulations on waterways such as the Potomac and Chesapeake Bay by means of interstate compacts was legally permissible but in practice difficult to institute. The power of states to enact navigation laws could not be used effectively to support negotiation of commercial concessions from the European powers. If one state discriminated against Great Britain, as Virginia did in a law of January, 1786, British ships might simply be diverted to the ports of a state where the terms of entry were more favorable.

Negotiation of commercial treaties by the Confederation was also handicapped by the fact that states could with impunity enact laws in conflict with treaties. Virginia, for example, by a law of 1782, barred from its courts suits for the recovery of pre-Revolutionary debts owed to British creditors. Congress, fulfilling its obligation under the peace treaty, recommended repeal of such laws. Madison strongly urged compliance with this recommendation, but was frustrated in his efforts. In January, 1785, a bill which he supported failed to pass only because several members whose presence was necessary for it to become enrolled were prevented by a storm from getting into Richmond before adjournment.[26]

Virginia, too, was one of the states, much to Madison's chagrin, which failed to comply with Congressional requisitions for money.[27] It thus contributed to the failure of the states to provide funds for redeeming the national debt. Creditors of the United States were among those who had substantial reasons to be dissatisfied with the handling of economic and financial problems by the states during the mid-1780's.

At the same time that legislatures were failing to provide uniform commercial regulation and revenue to pay the creditors of the United States, an economic depression in 1785 and 1786 was breeding contention and turmoil within the states. As specie flowed out of the country to purchase British imports and agricultural prices fell, farmers were unable to pay their taxes and their debts. In state after state they sought relief in the form of laws issuing paper money (bills of credit), making taxes commutable in produce, or postponing the payment of taxes and private debts. In some states, where the legislatures were controlled by majorities adverse to such measures, debtors resorted to direct action to stop court enforcement of contracts. In Massachusetts, such direct action led in turn to use of state troops against rebellious debtors under the leadership of Daniel Shays. Despite a lack of power in the Articles, a majority of the delegates in Congress were prepared to send U.S. soldiers to help the constituted authorities of Massachusetts to suppress "Shays' Rebellion."

Confederation diplomacy and arms were also sources of dissatisfaction in the mid-1780's. The British declined to open their colonies in the West Indies to American shipping, retained troops on American soil at several posts along the St. Lawrence and Great Lakes, and neglected to return slaves taken away when they evacuated New York. Spain occupied posts claimed by the United States and closed the lower Mississippi to American traffic. Nothing could be done diplomatically to satisfy complaints of American frontiersmen that the British and Spanish incited Indian depredations against their settlements. Militarily, the tiny Confederation army was able to do little in the Northwest and nothing in the Southwest to keep the peace between whites and Indians. Treaties were negotiated for cessions of land by the Indians, but peaceful execution of them was difficult against tribes that often disputed their validity. In the trans-Appalachian West, sale of public lands was delayed and political discontent was engendered by the failures of American diplomats and soldiers.

Everyone of these interrelated diplomatic and economic issues was debated in Virginia during the years 1783–86. Divisions in the legislature were determined by the degree to which each member believed that Virginia could deal with these problems by its own actions. A great majority agreed with Madison that some degree of cooperation with the other states, either through interstate compacts or Congressional legislation, was essential. This great majority, however, split into rival factions when considering the terms and extent of Congressional legislation and interstate agreements, the kinds and methods of collecting taxes, and the advisability of extending Confederation jurisdiction to permit restrictions on state legislation.

Although no man in the legislature was more convinced than Madison that Virginia alone could not provide for its future economic growth and overcome its immediate financial difficulties, he did not, before 1787, advocate drastic changes in the Confederation. He supported amendments to the Articles to empower Congress to tax imports, to fix sums requisitioned from the states in proportion to population, to coerce delinquent states, to enact navigation laws, and to regulate foreign and interstate commerce.[28] But a special national convention for revising the Articles, which was proposed at different times by the legislatures of New York and Massachusetts, received only a passive and private endorsement from him.[29]

Before 1787, Madison evinced no special predilection for designing model constitutions. He criticized the Virginia constitution of 1776 in a speech of June, 1784, but, unlike Jefferson, he did not draft a substitute for it and did not persist in his efforts for revision. Only in a letter of August 23, 1785, in reply to the request of a friend for his views on a state constitution suitable for Kentucky, did he expound his basic constitutional beliefs.[30]

Nor did he present a systematic statement of his views on all features of the Confederation. His comments, although frequent, were scattered and fragmentary and were concentrated exclusively upon the powers of Congress. He said nothing about the organization of the executive, the possible role of a federal judiciary, the basis of representation in Congress, or the payment, tenure, qualifications, and method of selecting federal officers.

At the close of the session of 1785 he achieved passage of a resolution calling for a convention of the states to consider a uniform system in their commercial regulations. The support he gave to this resolution illustrated his well-documented tendency to settle for something rather than nothing, whenever he was convinced that something was better than nothing and the most that could be obtained. Previously in the session he had failed to obtain passage of a satisfactory resolution calling for Congressional regulation of commerce.[31]

Throughout the first eight months of 1786, Madison was pessimistic about what was happening in Virginia and the Union. He saw a worsening economic situation in Virginia; believed that the "political evils" of the country stemmed from "commercial" conditions; and forecast a doubtful future for the Union. He expected little to be accomplished by the commercial convention which he was to attend as a delegate in September.[32]

On August 12, 1786, about a month before the convention was to assemble at Annapolis, he wrote to Jefferson: "Gentlemen both within and without Congress wish to make this meeting subservient to a plenipotentiary convention for amending the Confederation. Tho' my wishes are in favor of such an event, yet I despair so much of its accomplishment at the present crisis that I do not extend my views beyond a Commercial Reform. To speak the truth I almost despair even of this."[33]

Rufus King, who talked to Madison in New York before his departure for Annapolis, wrote on September 3: "He does not discover or propose any other plan than that of investing Congress with full powers for the regulation of commerce foreign and domestic."[34]

What Madison expected the Annapolis convention to do is easier to document than what he wanted it to do. He who assumes that his true desires in 1786 were frankly expressed in 1787 necessarily concludes that he wanted much more than he thought the convention would approve. He did, of course, intimate that he would support changes other than those which he had already publicly advocated, but he never specified what these changes should be, and he never estimated their comparative importance. Not even in coded letters to his friend in faraway France did he suggest what changes he wanted beyond those which he had publicly advocated.

Only Virginia, Delaware, New Jersey, Pennsylvania, and New York were represented at Annapolis in mid-September. Discarding their instructions, the delegates proceeded to approve an address to all the states proposing another convention to meet in Philadelphia in May for purposes that went beyond commercial regulation to include any matter of importance to the Union.

Madison's attitude toward general revision of the Articles changed abruptly when he returned to the Virginia legislature in October. He no longer thought, as he had between 1780 and 1785, that the state legislatures would refuse to support a convention to revise the Articles. No longer did he presume, as he had throughout the first eight months of 1786, that opponents of a general revision would dominate a convention called by the states. He came to the legislative session of 1786 with a determination and hope that contrasted sharply with the resigned discouragement that characterized his thinking at the end of the session of 1785.

CHAPTER V

Making the United States Constitution

IN THE FALL OF 1786 MADISON WAS APPREHENSIVE ABOUT what was happening outside Virginia. The "folly" of paper money in several states and civil commotion in Massachusetts were disquieting. He was bothered too that support in Congress for sanctioning a Spanish order preventing Americans from navigating the lower Mississippi was arousing distrust of the Union in the Kentucky counties.[1]

The course taken by the Virginia legislature, however, was reassuring. Quick and unanimous approval was given to the recommendation of the Annapolis Convention. A delegation generally sympathetic to the purposes of the men who urged the convention was selected. Madison himself was to be one of the delegates. His friend Edmund Randolph was elected governor, and, as such, had authority to appoint replacements for delegates who declined to go to Philadelphia. General Washington did not immediately accept his appointment but at least was prevailed upon to postpone a negative decision.[2]

The legislature defended navigation on the Mississippi "with as much zeal" as Madison wished. Instructions to the Virginia delegation in Congress which he drafted were adopted unanimously, and he was elected delegate to the next Congress, where he hoped to combat the political harm of this issue to the movement to revise the Articles. Also returned with him to Congress was Joseph Jones, an old friend with whom he had been closely associated in 1780 and 1781.[3]

His anxiety of the past two years about paper money in Virginia was relieved, at least temporarily, by a vote taken on November 1. The House of Delegates, by a vote of 85 to 17, approved a resolution which declared paper money to be "unjust, impolitic, destructive of public and private confidence, and of that virtue which is the basis of Republican Government."[4]

Despite his successes in the Virginia legislature, Madison, in the early months of 1787, was once again as fearful of the future as he had been throughout most of 1786. The Union, he thought, still faced a great crisis. On the one hand, majorities in the Congress and the state legislatures seemed willing to legislate without regard to justice for minorities; on the other hand, minorities, defeated in their attempts to obtain passage of tax- and debt-relief measures, were seeking redress outside the law.[5]

In 1787, however, the sequel to collapse of the Union appeared even more foreboding than it had been in 1786. Then he seems to have assumed that republican governments would continue in the states, which might or might not combine into several smaller confederacies and which might or might not enter into alliances with Spain or Britain. In 1787, in the wake of Shays' Rebellion in Massachusetts, he expressed fears that there might be a reaction against popular rule in the states.[6]

Also, although pleased that opponents of mob violence and paper money were being aroused to give strong support to the Philadelphia convention, he was afraid that some of these same people might want to go too far in curbing the republican principle in a revised constitution. A move to incorporate monarchical features into both the national and state governments, it seemed to him, might result from the reaction against Shays' Rebellion.[7]

In early 1787 Madison defined the problem facing the revisers of the Articles not merely in terms of adding powers to Congress but also in terms of protecting minorities in the exercise of legislative powers. Revision of the Articles came to be viewed as a means of protecting minorities in the states against the kind of legislation which he had hitherto assumed belonged exclusively to state jurisdictions.

Madison believed that fears about state legislation contributed more than Confederation failures in bringing forth the Convention of 1787. On June 6, at Philadelphia, he said that interference with private rights and "the steady dispensation of justice" in the states were "evils which had more perhaps than anything else, produced the convention." Again, on June 19, he said that there was "great reason to believe" that unsatisfactory state laws "had a full share in the motives which produced the present convention." In a letter to Jefferson, October 24, 1787, he said that state encroachments on individual rights "contributed more to that uneasiness which produced the Convention" than "inadequacy" of the Confederation in achieving its national objects.[8]

Even without a change of representation, Madison trusted the Congress more than the state legislatures to protect the interests of the creditors. To Washington he wrote on April 16, 1787: "There has not been any moment since the peace at which the representatives of the Union would have given assent to paper money or any other measure of a kindred nature."[9]

In an essay entitled "Vices of the Political System of the United States," he systematized much of what he had written in the previous six years as to the inadequacies and failures of the Congress and state legislatures. His proposed solution, however, was no longer the same. Now he argued that Congress, if it represented varied interests, could be trusted more than state legislatures to enact just legislation. The implication was that there should be a new principle of representation and that some intrastate matters previously under state jurisdictions should be placed under the national Congress.[10]

In letters written to Jefferson on March 19, to Randolph on April 8, and to Washington on April 16 he made clear what change in representation he wanted and what means should be employed by the national government to protect minorities in the states: he proposed representation for each state in proportion to its population, and he proposed that Congress have the power to veto any state law whatsoever.[11]

To Jefferson, he explained the need for a Congressional veto of state laws: "Without this defensive power experience and reflection have satisfied me that however ample the federal powers may be made, or however clearly their boundaries may be delineated, on paper, they will be easily and continually baffled by the Legislative sovereignties of the States. The effects of this provision would be not only to guard the national rights and interests against invasion, but also to restrain the States from thwarting and molesting each other, and even from oppressing the minority within themselves by paper money and other unrighteous measures which favor the interest of the majority."[12]

Before this letter to Jefferson, Madison had given no hint of wanting a national veto of state laws. The idea was suggested to him, he wrote many years later, "by the negative in the head of the British Empire, which prevented collisions between the parts and the whole, and between the parts themselves. It was supposed that the substitution of an elective and responsible authority, for an hereditary and irresponsible one, would avoid the appearance even of a departure from Republicanism."[13]

The letters to Randolph and Washington in April were written with the expectation that the Virginia delegation would present to the convention "some leading propositions." They summarized to these two prospective delegates his own opinions as to what these propositions should embody. In addition to the Congressional veto of state laws and proportionate representation, he proposed the establishment of a national executive and national judiciary, and division of the legislative branch into two houses.

The Philadelphia Convention was scheduled to start on May 14. Since February 12, Madison had been in New York attending the Confederation Congress. In order to have plenty of time for consultation with the other Virginia delegates, he departed for Philadelphia as early as May 2. But not until May 17, when Mason arrived, did the delegates begin the daily discussions from which emerged a set of propositions subsequently known as the Virginia Plan of Union. Since Washington was expected to serve as presiding officer for the convention, Governor Randolph was designated to introduce the Virginia propositions.[14]

On May 25, for the first time, representation of the states was sufficient to begin official proceedings. On that date, twenty-nine delegates were present. This was about the average daily attendance during the convention, although at one time or another a total of fifty-five men representing twelve states were present.[15]

Although Madison was thirty-six in the summer of 1787, his age was only six years below the average for all the delegates. Experienced in state and national politics, learned in political history and theory, student of the law, and owner of landed property, he had much in common with the other fifty-four delegates. However, there were some financial and occupational differences. Unlike thirty-one of the delegates, he never practiced law; unlike thirty, he owned no public securities; unlike fifteen he had no connection with mercantile business; unlike thirteen, he was not in debt for any large amount of money; unlike twelve, he held no undeveloped land for speculative purposes; and unlike twelve, he neither owned bank stock nor held interest-bearing loans. Judged by his own earnings and value of property held in his own name, he was one of the least wealthy of the delegates.[16]

There is no evidence that differences of opinion between Madison and the other delegates corresponded with these financial and occupational differences. As in the past, Madison often supported measures favorable to interests with which he had no personal association. Neither a creditor nor a debtor, he generally spoke for the creditor point of view. Not a lawyer, he favored a strong national judiciary. Not a merchant, he would make possible legislation favorable to shippers and merchants engaged in overseas and interstate commerce. An exporter of tobacco, he would make possible taxes on exports. Not a land speculator, he was favorable to Western expansion and navigation on the Mississippi. Not a banker, he would have empowered Congress to charter banks.

No delegate was more exempt from the imputation of self-interested motivation of opinion than the leading exponent of the economic interpretation of politics at the convention. Adhering to a vow that he made at the beginning of his political career, Madison never permitted himself "to deal in public property, lands, debts or money, whilst a member of the body whose proceedings might influence these transactions."[17]

Undoubtedly, some of the other delegates hoped to be direct beneficiaries of what they advocated; but the exact number of delegates, the exact amount of influence, and the exact parts of the Constitution affected by expectation of personal gain cannot be determined. Madison himself, always ready to stress the influence of economic purposes in bringing about the movement to revise the Articles, denied that the delegates expected personal gain from what they did at Philadelphia. There "never was an assembly of men," he wrote toward the end of his life, "who were more pure in their motives, or more exclusively or anxiously devoted to the object committed to them, than were the members of the Federal Convention of 1787."[18]

In April, as he had learned the names of the men who would be coming to Philadelphia, he had been pleased with the caliber of men being sent by the states. He was already personally acquainted with many of them. He was on friendly terms with all the Virginia delegates, having known most of them for a decade at least; three, Blair, Randolph, and Mason, had served with him in the Virginia Convention of 1776. Twenty-one of the delegates from other states had served with him in the Confederation Congress, either between 1780 and 1783 or more recently in the spring of 1787. Seven graduates of Princeton (one of whom had been in attendance with Madison) were represented on five other delegations. Even as the convention began, he had what he later described as "a familiarity with the style and train of observation and reasoning which characterized the principal speakers."[19]

The Virginia Plan resolutions were presented to the convention on May 29. Until June 14, they were the sole text for debate in the convention. From the very beginning of the debates, the Virginia delegates felt perfectly free to propose or accept amendments to the Plan. The resolutions had been introduced "with an understanding that they left all the Deputies entirely open to the lights of discussion, and free to concur in any alteration or modifications which their reflections and judgments might approve."[20]

A rule adopted by the convention on May 29 encouraged a tentative approach to the Plan among all the delegates. In order "to secure unbiased discussion within doors, and to prevent misconceptions and misconstructions without," the convention agreed that "nothing spoke in the House be printed, or otherwise published, or communicated without leave."[21]

Many years later Madison believed that no constitution would have been adopted if the debates had been publicized. "Had the members commited themselves publicly at first," he explained to Jared Sparks, "they would have afterwards supposed consistency required them to maintain their ground, whereas by secret discussion no man felt himself obliged to retain his opinions any longer than he was satisfied of their propriety and truth, and was open to the force of argument."[22]

The Virginia Plan resembled closely what Madison had proposed in letters to Randolph and Washington. The other members of the delegation had overruled him only in the scope of the Congressional veto of state laws; rather than permit it in all cases whatsoever, they confined it to constitutional issues. The Plan called for a bicameral legislature, an executive selected by Congress, and a national judiciary. Representation for each state in both houses was to be in proportion to "quotas of contribution" or "the number of free inhabitants." One house was to be selected by the people of the states; the other was to be selected by the first house from a list of nominees submitted by state legislatures. To the enumerated powers of Congress under the Articles were to be added the power to coerce delinquent states, to guarantee to the states their territory and a republican form of government, and to veto state laws in conflict with the Constitution of the United States. The Congress was also to have a general grant of power to "legislate in all cases to which the separate states are incompetent, or in which the harmony of the United States may be interrupted by the exercise of individual Legislation." A council of revision, composed of the executive and national judges, was to have the power to veto legislation approved by Congress. The constitution was to include provisions for admitting new states, amending the constitution, obligating state officials to uphold the Federal Constitution, and ratifying the document approved at Philadelphia by special assemblies in the states chosen by the people. The word national was repeatedly used in the resolutions.[23]

In the debates on the Virginia Plan during the first two weeks, Madison was able to combine dozens of specific provisions into a pattern consistent with three guiding principles. Of these, most fundamental was the aim of establishing a powerful government for the Union. In every part of the Constitution he sought to provide additional powers for the national government and to make it independent of the states in its operations. He proposed that the extensive legislative powers in the Virginia Plan be further enlarged to permit Congress to veto all state laws. He sought in many ways to make the national government independent of the states in its legal and electoral processes. He favored the establishment of inferior national courts, exclusion of state legislatures and executives from the procedures for electing and removing national officers, national regulation of national elections, payment of national officers from the national treasury, and ratification of the constitution by special assemblies elected by the people instead of by state legislatures. He was pleased to delete from the Virginia Plan the specific provision for coercion of states, leaving implicit the idea that national law would be enforceable directly upon individuals without the agency of state governments.[24]

A second guiding principle that permeated the positions he took during the first two weeks was the aim of establishing a republican government for the Union. Representation of the people, the essence of the republican principle to him, was defended as an autonomous value cherished by the American people and as a means for promoting the power and independence of the national government. Popular election of at least one branch of a legislative body was essential to every plan of free government, he argued, and had the practical advantage "of avoiding too great an agency of the State Governments in the General One."[25]

Popular election of national legislators, he also argued, was a means of promoting legislative justice in Congress; and, if they possessed the power to veto state laws, justice in the state legislatures. In a speech on June 6, he explained why he thought a national legislature representing the people was more likely to be just than a state legislature. It was the same argument that he first formulated in his "Vices of the Political System of the United States" and which he was to make again in *Federalist* Number 10 and in a long letter to Jefferson on October 24, 1787. His theorizing on this theme was his most distinctive contribution to political theory in the convention; it was perhaps the most unusual theorizing done by any delegate at Philadelphia. Madison himself seems to have been captivated by the way it could be used to justify the practicability of a republican form of government for a large country and the merits of a veto of state laws by the national Congress.

A national Congress selected by the people, he argued, would be more likely than a state legislature to represent numerous and varied interests. On any given issue the probability would therefore be greater that some of the legislators would be impartial. The impartial legislators, possessing a balance of power between self-seeking minorities, would determine the formation of each new majority by joining with whatever minority came nearest to the just position. Underlying his whole argument were the assumptions that legislators would vote according to the interests of their constituents without regard to justice for minorities and that legislators who represented constituencies having nothing to gain or lose from a given piece of legislation would be impartial in their judgments. The validity of his argument depended upon the universality of these assumptions.

The one blemish in Madison's coherent and consistent system of philosophical thought was the one deviation from the republican principle which he sanctioned in apportioning the number of congressmen to each state. In approving a resolution that permitted three-fifths of the slaves and all unqualified voters to be counted in apportioning legislators, he was assigning to the Southern voter a greater weight than the Northern voter. Such a discrimination was hardly in harmony with the republican principle as he himself expounded it.

The positions that he took in behalf of national power and the republican principle were generally advantageous to the large states. His own state, with about 20 per cent of the population of the nation, was then the largest in the Union and to the extent that Virginia's share of influence in controlling a new government was commensurate with its size, it would have a good reason not to fear strong national powers. To the extent that proportionate representation and popular elections helped to insure Virginia's obtaining an influence in the national government that corresponded with its size, a Virginia delegate could easily afford to support such measures. "We cannot err," Madison wrote later, in supposing that the large states "would contend for a participation in the government, fully proportioned to their superior wealth and importance."[26]

A third guiding principle for Madison was stability in national and state legislation. In the national government, he mainly supported long terms of office to achieve this end. He advocated a three-year term for members of the House, seven years for senators, seven years for the President, and life tenure contingent upon good behavior for judges. To promote stability of state legislation, he relied on the national legislative veto.[27]

Madison's closest allies during the first two weeks were from the two largest Northern states, Pennsylvania and Massachusetts, and from North Carolina, South Carolina, and Georgia. Wilson of Pennsylvania, King of Massachusetts, and Charles Pinckney of South Carolina were among the speakers who frequently agreed with him.

He did not, of course, get his way on all issues during the first two weeks. His biggest defeats were in the approval given to selection of senators by state legislatures and rejection of his proposal to expand the national veto of state laws. One other which caused some disappointment was elimination of the Council of Revision from the Virginia Plan.[28]

Far more significant than the few cases in which the convention majority went against him were those in which he was supported. Most important was the overwhelming endorsement given to the strong legislative powers in the Virginia Plan, acceptance of proportionate representation in both houses, and popular election of the lower House.

A constitution based on the Virginia Plan as amended prior to June 19 would have been satisfactory to Madison; indeed, no other delegate could have been more pleased. Nevertheless, from his standpoint, there was uncertainty as to whether the convention would in the end produce such a constitution. He was afraid that some of the delegates from the six states that had voted against equality of representation in the Senate might be willing to consider concessions on this point in order to prevent secession of delegates from the convention or subsequent opposition to ratification. Compromise-minded delegates among supporters of the Virginia Plan might be impressed by the threat posed on June 9 by William Paterson of New Jersey, who had vowed that he would lead an opposition if a constitution based on proportional representation were submitted for ratification.[29]

Madison, on June 12, urged the majority of the delegates to draw up the constitution which they themselves considered the best. The "opinions of the people" could not be taken as their guide, he said, since no one really knew what the opinions of their constituents were at that time. He expressed confidence that a constitution based on what they considered "right and necessary in itself for the attainment of a proper Government" would be given active support by "the most enlightened & respectable citizens" and would not be opposed by "the unreflecting multitude."

Two delegates thought that there might be a compromise on the issue of legislative apportionment. Dickinson of Delaware on June 2 and Sherman of Connecticut on June 11 suggested that equality in one house and proportionate representation in the other might become the eventual basis of a compromise. On June 11, the Connecticut delegation voted for equality in one house and proportionate representation in the other.

Neither the delegates from New Jersey nor those who voted against equality in the Senate on June 11, however, gave any overt sign prior to June 29 that such a compromise might become acceptable. Indeed, the delegates from New Jersey, in cooperation with several delegates from other states that had been defeated on apportionment, proceeded to draw up a plan that offered no compromise to the big states. In the New Jersey Plan of Union, presented to the convention on June 15, the unicameral structure of Congress and equality of representation for each state continued as under the Articles of Confederation. In his speech of June 16 defending the New Jersey Plan, William Paterson said that the only acceptable alternative to equality of representation in the Congress was abolition of the existing states and the division of the United States into thirteen equal districts.

Just how many delegates among the advocates of equality in the Senate would have agreed to a division of the nation into new states of equal size is uncertain. One other delegate from

New Jersey, David Brearly, had made the same proposition on June 9. In a letter to Jefferson, October 24, 1787, Madison said that the "little states insisted on retaining their equality in both branches, unless a compleat abolition of the State Governments should take place." His statement would seem to intimate that Paterson's and Brearly's view was shared by other delegates from the small states.

There was little response to Brearly's and Paterson's suggested alternative to equality of representation. In a long speech on June 19, in which he analyzed the defects of the New Jersey Plan, Madison rejected the idea as impracticable, because of "dissimilarities existing in the rules of property, as well as in the manners, habits and prejudices of the different States." Leaving the small states free to combine with adjacent states, he said, would accomplish the same purpose without obtruding an arrangement that would be "obnoxious to many of the States."

While the New Jersey Plan, by retaining the basis of representation in the Confederation Congress, conceded nothing to the big states on apportionment, the revisions of the Articles that it did propose were hardly satisfactory to Madison and many other delegates who had already voted for quite different provisions in the Virginia Plan. Under the New Jersey Plan, the Congress was to have fewer powers than in the Virginia Plan, the executive was to be plural, and there were to be no national courts below one Supreme Court.

After three days of debate, on June 19, the New Jersey Plan was rejected in favor of the amended Virginia Plan. Seven states (Massachusetts, Connecticut, Pennsylvania, Virginia, North Carolina, South Carolina, Georgia) voted affirmatively, three (New York, New Jersey, Delaware) voted negatively, and one (Maryland) was divided.

At this point, taking the proceedings of the convention at face value, it appeared that neither the majority nor the minority was willing to take a middle position acceptable to both sides. Nevertheless, supporters of the New Jersey Plan stayed at Philadelphia—for reasons which remained obscure for many days after June 19. Were they staying because they intended to acquiesce in the verdict of the majority? Did they still hope to win over at least three states that had voted against the New Jersey Plan on June 19? Or did they really intend to compromise with the majority by accepting proportionate representation in one house? And if they were privately intending to compromise, were they confident that the states which had voted against equality in the Senate on June 11 would reverse their position for the sake of compromise?

As late as three weeks after defeat of the New Jersey Plan, it appeared that the minority was less inclined than the majority to consider a middle ground acceptable to both sides. The three states that had voted for the New Jersey Plan on June 19 continued to vote for equality of representation in both houses and to reject all proposals for compromise. As late as July 2 New Jersey and Delaware voted against a motion to form a special committee to report a compromise.

Connecticut, unlike the other states that voted against the New Jersey Plan on June 19, supported equality in both houses on June 29 and July 2. However, on June 29, two delegates from Connecticut, Johnson and Ellsworth, advocated the compromise which had been suggested earlier by Dickinson and Sherman; and on July 2, the Connecticut delegation voted for the special committee to report a compromise.

Madison and Wilson were against such a compromise and spoke against the special committee formed on July 2. They were not, however, able to convince the majority in a single delegation that had voted for the Virginia Plan on June 19; even Virginia and Pennsylvania voted for the committee. Manifestly some of the delegates who had voted with Madison against the New Jersey Plan were also rejecting his plea of June 12 that the majority frame whatever constitution it deemed best without regard to the desires of the minority.

The compromise advocated by Dickinson, Sherman, Johnson, and Ellsworth was the core of the report that Elbridge Gerry submitted for the special committee on July 5. In addition, it proposed (1) that the exact number of Representatives for each state be the total population used for apportionment purposes divided by forty thousand; and (2) that the Senate should have no power to originate, alter, or amend bills for raising or appropriating money.

On July 7, equality of representation for each state in the Senate was tentatively approved by six states, opposed by three, and two were divided. Although this vote was subject to reversal later, when a vote was to be taken on the committee report in its entirety, the debate on House apportionment that followed was very much shaped by the presumption that equality in the Senate would prevail.

In the debate on House apportionment that took place be-

tween July 9 and 13, delegates that had been in agreement
before July 7, apparently anticipating drastic losses in the Senate, seemed very much concerned to bargain for advantages
that they had not sought before. Now they scrutinized carefully
the implications to their own states and sections of the exact
number of Representatives to be allocated to each state in the
first Congress; of the size of the House of Representatives; of
delegating to future congresses the time and criteria for reap-
portionments; of counting all, a fraction, or none of the slaves
in apportioning Representatives; of counting other forms of
wealth or tax contributions in apportionments.

In discussing these issues of apportionment, the conflicting
and competing economic interests among the big states were
stressed by their spokesmen. Already, in trying to convince the
small states that they had no reason to fear a combination of the
large states against them in a Senate based on population, Madison had pointed out that the interests of the large states con-
flicted more than the small states. In their manners, religion,
and "other circumstances which sometimes beget affection between different communities," he had said on June 28, Massachusetts, Pennsylvania, and Virginia were not more assimilated
than the other states; and in their staple productions, fish, flour,
and tobacco, they were as "dissimilar as any three other States
in the Union." On June 30 he had contended that

> the States were divided into different interests not by their difference
> of size, but by other circumstances; the most material of which resulted
> from climate, but principally from the effects of their having or not
> having slaves. These two causes concurred in forming the great division
> of interests in the U. States. It did not lie between the large & small
> States: it lay between the Northern & Southern and if any defensive
> power were necessary, it ought to be mutually given to these two inter-
> ests.

On July 14, he said:

> It seemed now to be pretty well understood that the real difference
> of interests lay, not between the large & small but between the N. &
> Southn. States. The institution of slavery & its consequences formed the
> line of discrimination.

Madison was unwilling to support any major departure from
representation in both houses in proportion to population. On
July 9 he "suggested as a proper ground of compromise, that in

the first branch the States should be represented according to their number of free inhabitants; and in the second ... according to the whole number, including slaves." For Virginia, this proposal would have meant a slight reduction in the House below what had been approved on June 19, since no slaves were to be counted; and a slight increase in the Senate above what had been approved, since all slaves would be counted. It suggests that equality in the Senate was especially obnoxious to him. The special powers of the Senate as distinguished from those of the House had not been debated in the convention, but discussion of the term of office for senators, the lengthy term already approved, and Madison's own motion, approved on June 13, that the Senate appoint judges of the Supreme Tribunal, were enough to indicate that the Senate was expected to have powers, influence, and prestige in excess of the House. His proposal of July 9 showed that if there were to be any differences between the two houses he preferred Virginia's share to be greater in the Senate than in the House.

Madison offered his proposal as a "compromise," but it clearly was not a compromise on the issue between the large and small states. His offer was a compromise between the Southern states and the large Northern states. He was asking the large Northern states to accept an augmentation of their representation in the House in return for their refusal to accept state equality in the Senate. He was offering each section a strong defensive position in one house, on the condition that the large states concede considerably less than what advocates of equality in the Senate were demanding.

State equality was much more of a blow to Virginia than to the South as a whole. Madison had more reason to be dissatisfied with Virginia's share than the Southern share. On the other hand, in seeking proportionate representation in both houses in June, he was not proposing a Southern share less than would come from Senate equality. Indeed, if the plan of representation approved in June had been retained, the bloc of states between Maryland and Georgia would have had more representation than it had with Senate equality.

He unabashedly refused to entertain any compromise that might concede equality of representation in the Senate. Speaking against the "Great Compromise" proposed by the committee report of July 5, he contended

... that the Convention was reduced to the alternative of either departing from justice in order to conciliate the smaller States, and the minority of the people of the U. S. or of displeasing these by justly gratifying the larger States and the majority of the people. He could not himself hesitate as to the option he ought to make. The convention with justice & the majority of the people on their side, had nothing to fear. With injustice and the minority on their side they had everything to fear. . . . The merits of the System alone can finally & effectually obtain the public suffrage. He was not apprehensive that the people of the small States would obstinately refuse to accede to a Govt. founded on just principles, and promising them substantial protection . . . if the principal States comprehending a majority of the people of the U.S. should concur in a just & judicious plan, he had the firmest hopes, that all the other States should [by degrees] accede to it.

Madison's bold appeal failed. "The Great Compromise" passed on July 16.

Until the next day, several of the delegates from the large states clung to the hope that they might bring about a reconsideration of equal representation in the Senate. They still believed that the minority should concede to the majority, would have stood firmly in opposition to the small states, and, if eventually necessary, would have agreed to "a separate recommendation." They found, however, on the morning of July 17, that other delegates who disliked state equality differed with them as "to the importance of that point" and as to the advisability of risking failure "by inflexibly opposing it."[30]

The first two weeks of July shattered the June bloc beyond reconstitution. Of the delegates who had stood with the Virginia delegation in June, only those of Pennsylvania, South Carolina, and Georgia were willing to take the same risks that Madison called for. Delegates from North Carolina and Massachusetts accepted what they had rejected on June 11 and June 19. Connecticut, which had favored state equality in the Senate on June 11 but had voted against the New Jersey Plan on June 19, now had the combination of parts from both plans that it wanted. New York was not represented on July 16.

After approval of Senate equality on July 16, the convention resumed debate on the Report of June 19 (the Virginia Plan as amended prior to that date). A Report of July 26 incorporated all amendments made to the Report of June 19. The Report of July 26 was then turned over to a Committee of Detail for use in preparing the first draft of a constitution.

For the Committee of Detail, John Rutledge submitted the draft of a constitution on August 6. This document was the text

for debate until September 11. In twenty-three articles the constitution of August 6 amalgamated the Report of July 26 and the
Articles of Confederation. In form, notably in the articles
enumerating and restricting legislative powers, it resembled the
Articles of Confederation. In content, the affirmative powers of
the national Congress were to be considerably greater than
under the Articles of Confederation but seemingly less than the
maximum permissible under the Report of July 26. Specific restrictions on state governments were somewhat greater than under the Articles of Confederation. Sections in the articles
dealing with territorial and land disputes and legal reciprocity
among the states resembled similar sections in the Articles of
Confederation. Sections that prescribed basic rules governing
the qualifications and internal operations of the national Congress contained much that was in neither the Report of July 26
nor the Articles of Confederation and which had not yet been
debated by the convention.

Throughout July and August Madison continued to adhere to
the same basic position on total national powers that he had
advocated during June. He and other big-state nationalists, contrary to his apprehensive warning of July 7, did not show any
disposition to reduce national powers because of the loss of
representation in the Senate. Instead, Madison's strategy after
July 16 was to transfer powers from the Senate to the executive,
judiciary, or electorate.

Virginia's loss of representation produced an abrupt desire to
put into practice Montesquieu's theoretical principles about
separation of powers. In the thirty-seventh *Federalist* Madison
explained that the compromise on representation "produced a
fresh struggle between the same parties, to give such a turn to
the organization of the government, and to the distribution of
its powers, as would increase the importance of the branches,
in forming which they had respectively obtained the greatest
share of influence."

The day after the convention approved "The Great Compromise" Madison for the first time expressed apprehension about
"a tendency to throw all power into the Legislative Vortex."
Again, on July 21, he said: "Experience in all the States had
evinced a powerful tendency in the Legislature to absorb all
power into its vortex. This was the real source of danger to the
American Constitutions." He did not mention the fact that the
Virginia Plan of Union was the most recent example of the
dangerous tendency he now discovered.

On June 5, Madison had said that he was "not satisfied with referring the appointment of judges to the executive" and on June 13 had proposed that the appointment should be made by the Senate. Two days after the "Great Compromise," however, he spoke for nominations by the executive with concurrence of the Senate. The Senate, now "very differently consituted," he said, should share this power with "a national officer acting for and equally sympathizing with every part of the United States." In a letter to Jared Sparks, June 27, 1831, Madison explained his change in position: "After the compromise which allowed an equality of votes in the Senate, that consideration, with the smaller number and longer tenure of its members, will account for the abridgment of its powers by associating the Executive in the exercise of them."[31]

Madison continued in August to support reductions in the power and influence of the Senate. He objected to the Senate voting as a separate body, if the national Congress were to elect the President or Treasurer of the United States, and he sought to eliminate from the constitution of August 6 the exclusive power of the Senate to make treaties.[32]

After July 16, Madison also championed measures that would render the executive less dependent on the legislative body. When, on July 17, ineligibility for re-election was stricken from the Report of June 19, in order to given emphasis to his belief that either ineligibility for re-election or a long term was essential if the President were to be selected by the legislative branch, he even condoned consideration of a proposal to permit the President to serve "during good behavior." He asked the convention to hear the case for this proposition "until a less objectionable expedient should be applied for guarding against a dangerous union of the Legislative and Executive departments."[33]

His heightened interest in executive independence after the Great Compromise was also voiced repeatedly in debates on the method of selecting the President. Although the Virginia Plan of May 29 had called for election of the executive by the national Congress and the convention had retained this method by a vote of eight states to two on June 2, he no longer supported this provision on July 19. Now he was disposed to think that election by the legislature endangered "a fundamental principle of free government." If the executive were "appointable from time to time by the legislature," he would not be a free agent.[34]

Madison now preferred that the executive be elected by "the people" or by "the qualified part of them, at large." He was willing, however, to accept election of the President by electors apportioned on the same basis as he had advocated for Congress. He admitted that the Southern states would prefer a system of electors to popular election at large, if unqualified whites and slaves were given weight in apportioning electors to each state.[35]

Madison also introduced the issue of legislative domination when he attempted on July 21 to gain support for a Council of Revision. He now stressed the contribution that such an arrangement would make to the independence of the executive and judiciary. He did not think, he said, that a Council of Revision would tend to give too much strength to either the executive or the judiciary. Notwithstanding the cooperation of the executive and the judiciary which such a council called for, it was much more to be apprehended that "the Legislature should still be an overmatch for them."

After the convention once more rejected his Council of Revision, he proposed other ways of strengthening the veto power of the executive and judiciary. In August he advocated giving to a supreme court the power to veto bills approved by the President and he proposed that three-fourths of each house be necessary to enact legislation vetoed by both the executive and the supreme court.[36]

Madison's strategy after Virginia lost proportionate representation in the Senate of redistributing powers among the three branches of the federal government was a total failure throughout July and August. The convention persisted in retaining what it had approved in June.

Ironically, the one case in which there was an important shift of power from the legislative branch was the one which he strenuously opposed. On July 17, the convention eliminated from the Report of June 19 the power of Congress to veto state laws in conflict with the constitution, acts of Congress, or treaties. In debating with Morris and Sherman as to the merits of a legislative veto, he agreed that the courts would exercise a veto but questioned its probable efficacy in comparison with a Congressional veto. Invalidation by the "National Tribunals," he argued, would give the states time enough to "accomplish their injurious objects" before the negative was registered; invalidation of state courts would be uncertain because they were too much dependent on the state legislatures to serve "as guardians of the National authority and interests."[37]

Two articles in the constitution of August 6, numbered XII and XIII, were intended to accomplish the threefold aims of Madison's proposed national legislative veto of state laws: prevent encroachments by state governments on (1) the legislative and treaty powers of the national government, (2) other states, and (3) private property rights.[38] They correspond to the general veto advocated by Madison in the same way that the enumerated Congressional powers corresponded to the general grant of legislative power in the Report of July 26. Article XII, in addition to specifying denials, differed from Madison's proposed national veto in that the negative would be exercised in the courts rather than in Congress. Article XIII, also specific rather than general in its denials of powers, provided a procedure that came close to being a legislative veto; it listed powers that state governments could exercise only with the consent of Congress.

No delegate at the Philadelphia Convention placed more stress than Madison upon the desirability of a national veto of state legislation. Yet he evinced no enthusiasm for the ingenious substitute for a general legislative veto that the Committee of Detail put into the Constitution of August 6. To be sure he supported the denials of power recommended by the committee, spoke favorably of adding a restriction on the state laws interfering with private contracts, and offered a motion to add embargoes to the list of specified denials; but he continued to declare his preference for a general veto power lodged in the national legislature. He remained convinced that state legislatures would devise ways of getting around court decisions interpreting the specified constitutional prohibitions.[39]

He made no comment upon the fact that article XIII requiring Congressional consent for the exercise of certain powers by the states could function as a negative of a sort, even if not termed a veto, and he made no proposals to transfer denials in article XII to article XIII. Indeed the only transfer he proposed was the reverse: he advocated moving from XIII to XII the prohibition of imposts.[40] Also, the restrictions on embargoes and state legislation affecting contracts which he desired to add to the constitution of August 6 were to go into article XII.[41] He seems to have taken for granted that specification of denials, in article XIII as well as in article XII, must necessarily give to the courts the ultimate negative.

Although persistent in his preference for a general power of Congress to veto state legislation, he was easily reconciled to eliminating a general statement of the affirmative powers of Congress. Early in the convention, on May 31, he had declared that he was biased in favor of an enumeration but had "doubts concerning its practicability." He did not, however, raise the issue of practicability when the Committee of Detail replaced the general statement in the Report of July 26 with an enumeration of the affirmative powers of Congress.

Nor did he protest against the circumscribed set of specific powers that the Committee of Detail put into the constitution of August 6, despite the great amount of power bestowed upon Congress by the Report of July 26. Instead, he disclosed his dissatisfaction implicitly by proposing and supporting amendments adding to the list of specified powers. He spoke for taxation of exports, for stating Congress's power to fulfill the engagements which had been entered into by the Confederation Congress, for national regulation of state militias, for national appointment of general officers for the state militias, for calling forth the militias to suppress insurrections against the United States as well as against states, for a broader definition of treason, and for the establishment of offices necessary and proper for carrying into execution the specified powers.[42] On August 18, he submitted a list of nine amendatory clauses providing for the power to dispose of the unappropriated lands of the United States, institute temporary governments for new states, regulate Indian affairs, govern a capital district, grant charters of incorporation, grant copyrights, establish a university, encourage the advancement of useful knowledge and discoveries by "premiums & provisions," and to authorize executive procurement of landed property for the use of forts, magazines, and other necessary buildings.

Madison, unlike his colleague Mason, made no attempts to protect the special interests of Virginia in the section of the constitution distributing powers between the states and Congress. And he consistently opposed special constitutional prohibitions and restrictions sought by other Southern delegates, such as restraints upon the power of Congress to levy export taxes, pass navigation laws, and prohibit the importation of slaves.[43] He preferred to prevent legislation adverse to Virginia by means of presidential and Congressional apportionments favorable to the large states and by depriving the Senate of special powers.

In the debates on taxing and regulating foreign trade that occurred between August 16 and August 31, Madison was conciliatory toward the shipping and mercantile interests. These debates tended to provoke disagreements among the big states similar to those that had been expressed during the debates on House apportionment, and Madison, as he had between July 9 and July 13, tried to mediate between the Southern states, with their interests in slavery, Western lands, and agricultural exports, and the big Northern states of Pennsylvania and Massachusetts, with their interests in fishing, shipping, and the marketing of American imports and exports. He preferred to strike out of the constitution of August 6 the requirement of a two-thirds vote in each house to enact navigation laws and the denial of a Congressional power to tax exports and to prohibit or tax "the migration or importation of such [enslaved] persons as the several States shall think proper to admit."[44] To promote a compromise of sectional differences, however, he was willing to support a two-thirds vote for levying export taxes and postponement of authority to ban the slave trade to 1800.[45]

Madison served on a special committee appointed to report a compromise on the issues of the slave trade and navigation laws.[46] Its report of August 24 recommended eliminating the two-thirds requirement to enact navigation laws, allowance of a tax on imported slaves, and postponement of authority to abolish the foreign slave trade until 1800.

Permission of slave importations until 1800 was repugnant to Madison but tolerated for the sake of conciliating Georgia, South Carolina, and North Carolina. This concession was rendered even less palatable to him when the convention approved a motion to substitute 1808 for 1800. Virginia, Delaware, Pennsylvania, and New Jersey voted against this change in the committee report. Just before the vote was taken, Madison said: "Twenty years will produce all the mischief that can be apprehended from the liberty to import slaves. So long a term will be more dishonorable to the National Character than to say nothing about it in the Constitution."[47]

On August 31 the convention approved a motion to refer such parts of the constitution as had been postponed and such parts of reports as had not been acted upon to a committee composed of one delegate from each state. The probabilities were considerable, when the balloting to select this vitally important committee began, that the Virginia delegate would be either Mason, Randolph, or Madison. The active role played by these three men had led to their having been chosen to several committees in July and August. Mason and Randolph had been appointed to three committees; Madison to two. Mason had served on the committee that proposed "The Great Compromise." Randolph had served on the Committee of Detail, which reported the constitution of August 6. This time, perhaps because his turn had come, perhaps because he seemed less intractable than Mason and Randolph, the convention chose Madison to represent Virginia.

Madison had been on the losing side many times since June 11, when the convention had approved election of senators by state legislatures. Each series of revisions of the basic texts before the convention, despite numerous alterations and additions which he favored, had culminated in a draft, which, from his standpoint, was worse than its predecessor. The Report of June 19 had dropped from the Virginia Plan of May 29 the method of electing senators and a Council of Revision to exercise the veto power over bills passed by the Congress. The Report of July 26 had dropped from the Report of June 19 proportional representation in the Senate and the Congressional veto of state laws, and had given to the Senate the power to appoint judges and ambassadors and to make treaties. The constitution of August 6, as introduced by the Committee of Detail, had reduced Congressional powers below what was allowable in the Report of July 26. The enlargement of Congressional powers and national restrictions on the states approved between August 16 and August 31 fell short of what he had advocated; the additional powers proposed in his list of August 18 had not yet been debated. Furthermore, he had continued to be frustrated in his attempts to have the executive and judiciary share the appointing and treaty-making powers with the Senate and to take from the Congress the selection of the executive.

If Madison ever expressed bitterness or despair at the repeated rejections of his proposals and arguments, he never recorded them for posterity, in his journal or in his correspondence. Whatever resentment he may have felt subjectively never led him to withdraw from the struggle, sulk, or issue ultimatums. Day after day, he patiently sought revisions that would rectify what he considered shortcomings and defects of previously approved resolutions while at the same time trying to shape the new decisions to conform to his basic objectives and criteria.

By the close of August, Randolph and Mason, unlike Madison, were registering complaints against an "accumulation of obnoxious ingredients." On August 29, Randolph said there were features so odious in the constitution as it then stood that "he doubted whether he could agree to it." On August 31, Mason said "that he would sooner chop off his right hand than put it to the Constitution" as it then stood.

Much of what Madison had sought in vain since July 16 was endorsed by reports submitted by David Brearly for the committee selected on August 31. On September 4 and 5, six new legislative powers, four of which had been on Madison's list of August 18, were recommended. The eighth on Madison's list was not included, but science and the useful arts were to be promoted by protecting the exclusive rights of inventors who made new discoveries. Approval of the committee recommendation meant that fewer than three of the powers on Madison's list of August 18 had not been accepted by September 5, namely, to establish a university, to grant charters of incorporation, and to encourage the advancement of useful knowledge and discoveries by "premiums." Of these three, one or more might be construed as necessary and proper for carrying out the specified powers. All might become the beneficiaries of a new clause, recommended and accepted on September 4, which provided taxes for the common defense and general welfare.

Recommendations on the treaty-making and appointing powers of the Senate in the report of September 4 agreed with what Madison had advocated on July 18 and August 23. When debated on September 7 and 8, no objections were made to having the executive share in appointing judges and ambassadors and in making treaties. Criticisms centered on whether consent of the Senate to treaties should be by a number greater or smaller than two-thirds of the members present. Several motions to amend this provision were defeated, and on September 8 the committee recommendation was approved by all states except Pennsylvania, New Jersey, and Georgia.

The report of September 4 also proposed a method of selecting the executive in accord with the position taken by Madison after July 16. It proposed that an electoral college, with electors apportioned to each state according to its total number of senators and representatives, should elect the President.

The only part of the report of September 4 that was sharply contested was the contingent role of the Senate in electing the

President and Vice President. It recommended that the Senate choose the President from five candidates who had the largest number of votes, whenever no one candidate received a majority in the electoral college. The Senate also was to make the choice between candidates whose votes equally entitled them to be elected Vice President.

Critics of the Senatorial role were convinced that the electors would only rarely elect a candidate. Since the electors were to cast their votes separately in their own states rather than at a general convocation and would tend to support men known in their own state or region, they reasoned that the total cast would be divided among many candidates with the result that no single candidate would receive a majority. They further assumed that a majority of the electors would not reach an informal agreement through concerted negotiations to support some one candidate prior to the official casting of ballots. The probable effect, therefore, of the committee recommendation would be to give the small states an even greater role in selecting the President than if selected by the Congress.

Rather than substitute Congress for the Senate, Madison preferred to increase the probabilities of selection by the electoral college. Retention of some threat of election by the Senate, if selection by the electors was rendered somewhat easier, he thought would be an inducement for a "concerted effort" to achieve election in the electoral college. To render selection by the electors more probable, he supported proposals to reduce the number of candidates from which the Senate was to make a choice, for excluding non-voting electors in calculating the number necessary to elect, and for giving the choice to the Senate only if the highest number of votes received by a candidate was less than one-third of the total number of electoral votes cast.[48]

Much less satisfactory to him was Sherman's proposal to replace the Senate with the House of Representatives, each state delegation voting as a unit. However, when Mason, a sharp critic of the plan recommended by the committee, expressed a liking for Sherman's proposal "as lessening the aristocratic influence of the Senate," he joined the majority of delegates in approving it.[49]

A part of the committee report of September 5 to which Madison objected in debate also pertained to a special power of the Senate. The committee recommended continuation of a provision in the constitution of August 6 which gave to the

Senate the power to try an impeached President. Madison argued that the power of Congress to remove the President made him "improperly dependent" on that body. He preferred that the trial be by the Supreme Court of a special tribunal partly composed of the Supreme Court. But when he moved to strike out trial "by the Senate," only Virginia and Pennsylvania voted affirmatively.[50]

Such defeats, however, were few. The four days in September devoted to the Brearly reports brought acceptance of most of the revisions which Madison had strongly desired since July 16. After September 8, he seems not to have been eager to seek reconsideration of other decisions that had gone against him in August. Most of all, he would have liked for the convention to reconsider elimination of the Congressional veto of state laws, but he was resigned to the fact that the majority in the convention clearly preferred the judicial veto. On September 12 he noted that he had been "overruled" in his desire for a legislative veto, which, none the less, he was still convinced would be a better "source of redress" than the Supreme Court, whenever state laws violated provisions in the Constitution or acts of Congress.

In a letter to Jefferson dated September 6, Madison lifted the veil of secrecy enough to summarize the main features of the proposed constitution. At this time his forecast for its future was pessimistic:

These are the outlines. The extent of them may suprize you. I hazard an opinion nevertheless that the plan should it be adopted will neither effectually answer its national object nor prevent the local mischiefs which every where excite disgusts against the state governments.[51]

Madison initiated only a few motions after September 8, but he was as active as ever in supporting and opposing changes proposed by others. By September 17, the last day of the convention, he had compiled a record for continuous attendance and participation unexcelled by any other delegate. According to his own testimony, he "was not absent a single day, nor more than a casual fraction of an hour in any day."[52] His own journal records him as speaking on 71 out of 86 days.

Madison was able to perform the remarkable feat of keeping a full record of debates in which he participated. Taught the difficulties presented by scarce records when making his recent studies of past confederacies, he came to Philadelphia determined to provide posterity for the first time with a complete record of the establishment of a new government. He was especially eager to provide information about "the process, the principles, the reasons, & the anticipations" which prevailed in the formation of the new constitution. "In pursuance of the task I had assumed," he wrote later, "I chose a seat in front of the presiding member, with the other members on my right & left hands. In this favorable position for hearing all that passed, I noted in terms legible & in abbreviation & marks unintelligible to myself what was read from the Chair or spoken by the members; and losing not a moment unnecessarily between the adjournment & reassembling of the Convention I was enabled to write out my daily notes during the session, or within a few finishing days after its close, in the extent and form preserved in my own hand on my files."[53]

His reports of the convention debates were first published in 1840. They are still the main source of information for what was actually said by the various delegates.

Madison never claimed any special influence in shaping the contents of the Constitution of 1787. To William Cogswell he wrote when he was in his eighty-fourth year: "You give me credit to which I have no claim, in calling me '*the* writer of the Constitution of the U. S.' This was not, like the fabled Goddess of Wisdom, the offspring of a single brain. It ought to be regarded as the work of many heads & many hands."[54]

His denial of fatherhood of the Constitution was good history not false modesty. No one delegate had a pervasive influence upon the Constitution; and of the men who first introduced proposals subsequently adopted by the convention or who were most active in debate, perhaps a dozen in number, no one can be cited as significantly more successful or convincing than the others. Only by including his contributions to ratification, to adoption of the first ten amendments, to passage of basic legislation in the first Congress, and to the historiography of the convention can it be said that he had a place of singular preeminence among the Fathers of the Constitution.

Madison failed to place his imprint upon several basic features of the Constitution. He failed to obtain proportionate representation in both houses, failed to prevent election of senators by state legislatures, failed to have the judiciary share with the executive the power to veto acts of Congress, and failed to obtain his much-cherished Congressional veto of state laws. There is no reason to suppose that he had any role in the decision of the Committee of Detail to enumerate the affirmative powers of Congress and the specific denials of certain powers to Congress and the state legislatures. The most crucial decision made at Philadelphia—"The Great Compromise"—was made in the face of his opposition. The two most novel features of the new Constitution came from the initiative of others. Judicial review of state laws, which came in time to be thought of as a unique innovation of the Constitution of the United States, he thought of dubious practicality. The idea of an electoral college to select the President should probably be credited to Wilson.[55]

The finished Constitution fell short of what Madison had advocated in the convention, but it more than fulfilled what he had proposed before March, 1787. The same can be said for Hamilton, another delegate who signed a constitution which was far different from what he had advocated in the convention. In September, 1786, both men would have praised the Philadelphia constitution, as they were soon to do during the ratification struggle. Madison's and Hamilton's readiness to sign and defend the constitution framed at Philadelphia is easily understood if they are placed in the perspective of the six years before 1787.

Madison and Hamilton were not the only delegates who had failed to get approval for provisions they considered important. For all who had continued to prefer parts of the Virginia and New Jersey plans discarded by the convention, the constitution was somewhat of a disappointment. Nevertheless, for the great majority of these men the finished Constitution was a great improvement upon the Articles of Confederation, and they did not believe that further consideration, either by this convention or another, would produce a better one. Therefore, with the exception of Gerry of Massachusetts and Mason and Randolph of Virginia, all of the forty-two delegates present on September 17 signed the Constitution in the form in which it was submitted to the states for ratification.[56]

CHAPTER VI

Making a Federal Republic

AT THE END OF SEPTEMBER, MADISON WENT TO NEW YORK City to take part in the proceedings of the Confederation Congress, to which Washington, as presiding officer of the convention, had transmitted the Constitution with the recommendation that it be forwarded to the states for ratification by special state conventions. While in New York, at the invitation of Alexander Hamilton and John Jay, he collaborated in writing for New York newspapers a series of articles that expounded the meaning and merits of the proposed Constitution. The first written by Madison, number ten in the series, appeared in *The Daily Advertiser* on November 22, 1787; his twenty-ninth and last, number sixty-three in the series, appeared in *The Independent Journal; or the General Advertiser* on March 1, 1788. In the newspapers the three authors used the pseudonym Publius. When two volumes of the essays were published in book form in March and May, 1788, the title used was *The Federalist.*[1]

In March, 1788, Madison returned to Orange County to campaign for his selection as delegate to the Virginia ratifying convention. In June he was in Richmond, where, despite poor health and fatigue, he was a persuasive speaker in the convention that ratified the Constitution by a vote of 89 to 79. From July to October, 1788, he was back in New York, serving as delegate to the expiring Confederation Congress. In November, the same legislature that re-elected him to the Confederation Congress failed to select him as U. S. Senator under the new Constitution. In December, 1788, he returned to Virginia to campaign for his election (February 2, 1789) to the U. S. House of Representatives. From March to September, 1789, he was once more in New York, where he had a leading role in drafting and passing the legislation enacted by the first session of Congress.

The records for Madison's thoughts and activities during the two-year period between September, 1787, and September, 1789, are perhaps the fullest we have for portraying the perfect blend of theoretical philosopher and practical politician in his leadership.[2] In his New York writings and his Richmond speeches, he acted as though philosophical argumentation and analysis had some capacity to persuade; as though some of the delegates would be influenced by their estimation of the anticipated consequences of the Constitution to the long-term and collective interests of the United States, and not merely by what they thought to be its impingement upon their own immediate interests. He made a highly rational argument that took seriously the arguments of the other side; he dealt with his opponents as though they were informed, intelligent, and honorable men. Never did he speak or write as if civic and patriotic exhortation were sufficient to persuade men to change their minds.

Viewed from the angle of practical politics, the timelessness of *The Federalist* is astonishing. Despite the fact that the essays were propaganda designed to influence a particular decision in a particular place at a particular time, they deliberately avoided appeals to the special prejudices and interests of the people that they sought to influence. Written by two New Yorkers and a Virginian primarily for the purpose of influencing opinion in one state, the great marvel is the scarcity of arguments aimed at the special reasons existing in that state for opposing ratification. The historian could never determine, from internal evidence alone, the immediate political function they were intended to fulfill.

Madison's collaboration with Hamilton and Jay was based on a division of labor rather than joint authorship of all the essays. "Though carried on in concert," Madison wrote to Jefferson, August 10, 1788, "the writers are not mutually answerable for all ideas of each other, there being seldom time for even a perusal of the pieces by any but the writer before they were wanted at the press, and sometimes hardly by the writer himself."[3]

The assignment of topics among the three authors of *The Federalist* reflected their background, previous experiences, and special interests. Jay's five essays were on foreign relations. Hamilton wrote on the executive and the judiciary. Madison wrote on the Congress and the relationship of the state and central governments.

Madison, like Hamilton, wrote several general essays. Numbers 18, 19, and 20 dealt with the weaknesses of ancient and modern confederations. Number 14 argued that a representative republic was suitable to the vast geographical extent of the United States. Number 10 argued that a legislative body representing an extensive republic would settle factional disputes more justly than small republics or pure democracies. Number 40 defended the authority of the convention to draw up a new constitution rather than merely revise the Articles of Confederation. Number 39 argued that the Constitution would establish a republic containing a mixture of national and federal features.

In all his essays, Madison maintained the pose of a person who had reliable information about what had transpired at the convention, although at no point did he admit that he had been present. His language therefore often stated as inference what had been in fact his own observation at the convention. He wrote as if he represented the point of view of a Northern, middle-ground compromiser at the convention; only when discussing those features in the Constitution that he had advocated at Philadelphia did he repeat what he had already said.

Some positions that he had supported without debate at Philadelphia received exposition in *The Federalist*. In Number 44 he explained the "necessary-and-proper" clause. In Number 54, he made a defense, somewhat contrived it seems, for counting three-fifths of the slaves in apportioning members of the House to each state. In this essay he did not write as if totally convinced of the justice of this provision; he placed in quotation marks the case which a pretended Southerner would make and then observed: "Such is the reasoning which an advocate for the Southern interests might employ on this subject; and although it may appear to be a little strained in some points, yet, on the whole, I must confess that it fully reconciles me to the scale of representation which the convention have established."

In one essay he cursorily referred to provisions that he had strongly opposed during the convention. In Number 62 he said that election of senators by state legislatures and equality of representation in the Senate did "not call for much discussion." Of equality of representation he merely said that it was "evidently the result of compromise between the opposite pretensions of the large and small States." In two sentences, he defended election of senators by state legislatures, using the arguments that his opponents had used at Philadelphia.

Madison made no references to omissions which had displeased him. He made no allusion to a national legislative veto and council of revision. His discussion of restrictions on the states in Number 44, unlike his statements in the convention and a letter of October 24 to Jefferson, said nothing about the difficulties in adjudicating Section 10 of Article I.

Because of the tactful and attorney-like case for the Constitution that Madison made for strategic reasons, *The Federalist* essays yield no autobiographical attestations. Yet they do indirectly tell us something about the man. Aside from the obvious erudition and analytic powers displayed, his suppression of views which he had ardently championed at Philadelphia demonstrated his remarkable capacity for restraining his own ego in pursuit of goals which he deemed of utmost public importance.

A scanning of Madison's speeches at the Virginia ratifying convention of June, 1788, may give the impression that he merely repeated what he had already written in *The Federalist*, as indeed he did.[4] But in his convention speeches, proportions, emphases, and tone were different. At Richmond he was obliged to make rebuttals to anti-ratification speeches that were much influenced by fears and objections that were especially strong in Virginia. The defense of the taxing power occupied a larger part of the total argument than in *The Federalist*. In Virginia, too, he had to pay special attention to the treaty-making power, because of fears, especially in the Kentucky counties, that the Eastern states would be able to barter away American navigation of the Mississippi in Spanish territory in return for commercial concessions. Also, he had to take more pains to assure critics of the Constitution that a continuation of state governments was essential to the total scheme of government and that none of the powers delegated to the central government would authorize an infringement upon individual liberties.

Madison's practicality was not confined to adjusting the contents of his speeches so as to concentrate his defenses upon those provisions which were claimed to be most vulnerable by the opposition. He saw that the opposition, or at least a part of it, would have to be persuaded, perhaps as much by private discussion as public debate, that certain interests in Virginia would not be harmed by putting the new Constitution in effect.

As a keen observer of the realities of political behavior, he knew that public debate does not always reflect the total reasoning of the contestants. Some arguments never make their appearance in the public debates, and some are brought forward on a scale that is small in proportion to their importance in private and confidential discussion. He knew perfectly well that some delegates were as much influenced by judgments of the probable impact of the new federal government on the immediate interests of certain Virginians as they were by arguments that portrayed it as the closest approach yet made by mankind to a model federal republic. Would Virginians who had received land confiscated by the state during the Revolution or who held land once claimed by companies chartered in other states find their titles jeopardized by suits in federal courts? Would British creditors be able to use the new federal courts to collect pre-Revolutionary debts owed by Virginians? Would the treaty power be employed so as to make it impossible for Americans to navigate the lower Mississippi and thus sacrifice the interests of those who lived or owned land in the Kentucky counties?

In his private correspondence, Madison said that the presumed adverse impingement of the Constitution on certain interests constituted a major obstacle to ratification. To Washington, he wrote on June 13, 1788: "British debts, the Indiana claim, and the Mississippi are the principal topics of private discussion & intrigue, as well as of public declamation." To Jefferson, he wrote on October 17, 1788: "The little pamphlet herewith inclosed will give you a collective view of the alterations which have been proposed for the new Constitution. Various and numerous as they appear they certainly omit many of the true grounds of opposition. The article relating to Treaties, to paper money, and to contracts, created more enemies than all the errors in the System positive & negative put together."[5]

Another facet of Madison the practical politician during the ratification struggle was his concern for devising a strategy based upon a discriminating assessment of the sources and distribution of popular opposition to the Constitution and of the characteristics and motives of leaders. He sought information about the course of events and situations in other states and he transmitted reports to Virginia. He did not make the mistake of viewing the opposition as a monolith. He knew that the proportions of support varied in different states and that the sooner the strongly pro-Constitution states ratified the better it would be for those states where the opposition was the strongest.

Long before the Virginia convention met, he knew that the outcome was in doubt.[6] But he also knew that the opposition in Virginia was composed of two groups whose views of the Union were fundamentally different. One group, under the leadership of Patrick Henry, was irreconcilably opposed to ratification, because at heart they had no great fears of the dissolution of the Union and would have accepted independent statehood or a Southern confederacy almost as readily as they would accept a Federal Union under the proposed Constitution. Another group, smaller in number, in reality wanted to preserve the Union and to have a central government stronger and more effective than the Confederation, but had certain reservations about the particular constitutional provisions proposed by the Philadelphia Convention. The course preferred by this second group was a new national convention that would revise the document adopted in September, 1787, in the light of amendments proposed by the various ratifying conventions. If this choice were not available, however, Madison assumed that men in the latter group would choose the Philadelphia document rather than run the risk of leaving Virginia in political isolation from the rest of the Union.

A major objective of Madison's strategy therefore was to prevent the Virginia convention from calling for a new national convention to consider a revision of the Philadelphia document or to give some form of conditional approval such as an automatic revocation of ratification if certain amendments were not adopted within a stipulated period of time. Several arguments were used in an attempt to persuade the amicable critics of the new Constitution to avoid a postponement of ratification. They were shown that other opponents of ratification desired a consitution that would be even less satisfactory to them than the Philadelphia document and that a compromise with them in a new national convention would necessarily produce a weaker central government than they truly desired. They were told that the amending process provided by the Constitution itself would be the surest means of revising the Constitution without impairing its national powers. And, after nine states had ratified, they were told that Virginia had only two choices: (1) unconditional ratification accompanied by recommendations to the first Congress of whatever amendments that were thought desirable, or (2) independent statehood outside the new Union.

Argumentation, whether to influence public opinion in general or to sway delegates to align themselves with the unconditional advocates of ratification, was not the sole approach employed by the pro-Constitution "Federalists" in Virginia. Madison and his associates knew that in some cases that the personal characteristics or public reputation of the candidates would be a factor in the election of delegates. They were anxious that the most respected leaders who favored ratification should become candidates for membership in the convention, for they knew that the personal prestige of individuals in some counties would be as important as their views on constitutional issues. Reported endorsements by venerable men who were not delegates were also circulated, the most notable and influential being those of Washington and Jefferson. They also knew that the manner of presenting their arguments would have some influence on certain personalities. The lettters of Madison to Governor Randolph record the artful adaptation of argumentation to the temperament of an important leader whose doubts about the new Constitution placed him temporarily in the camp of the opposition to ratification.

Madison's approach to the issue of a bill of rights further illustrates the methods by which his discriminating mind worked in behalf of theoretical and philosophical principles of government. Personally, he remained skeptical about a federal bill of rights, partly because of his doubts about the feasibility of enforcing such constitutional provisions against majority opinion by any representative government and partly because he thought such prohibitions of power to the federal government were superfluous in a government of delegated powers.[7] He came to see, however, the political liability of an uncompromising opposition to a federal bill of rights, since some of those who were most insistent upon a bill of rights, such as his friend Jefferson, had no desire to shift any of the proposed federal powers back to the states. By giving satisfaction to those whose fears of the federal government were based on their concern for individual liberties rather than a loss of state powers he would be able to deprive the State Righters of indispensable allies.

At Richmond he indicated his willingness to have the first Congress propose amendments; and when he campaigned for Congress against Monroe in January, 1789, he gave an unequivocal endorsement to a federal bill of rights in order to counteract the damaging reports that he was totally opposed to any changes in the Constitution.[8] In the first session of the first Congress (April 6–September 29, 1789), he fulfilled his pledge by proposing nine formal amendments, none of which, however, gave comfort to the advocates of State Rights, except one that embodied a declaration of doctrine that subtracted nothing definite from the delegated powers of Congress (ratified as the Tenth Amendment). Nothing could have made clearer his distinction between amendments that aimed to protect individual liberties and those that aimed to diminish or impede the exercise of the delegated powers of Congress than his proposal to amend Section 10 of Article I so as to use federal power to protect the civil rights of individuals: he proposed that "No state shall violate the equal rights of conscience, or the freedom of press, or the trial by jury in criminal cases."[9]

This amendment was an exceptional contribution from the imagination of one man; none of the ratifying conventions that submitted recommendations had included such a proposal.[10] Without any prompting by circumstances or current opinion, Madison had come to believe, only two years subsequent to the Philadelphia convention, that individual civil rights just as well as economic interests might be endangered by majorities in state legislatures. He "considered this to be the most valuable amendment in the whole list."

The Senate failed to approve Madison's proposed amendment to Section 10 of Article I; and, until the Fourteenth Amendment was adopted in 1868 it was destined to remain nothing more than an obscure historical curio.

Madison ignored most of the amendments recommended by the state ratifying conventions that sought to change the structure and powers of the national government. He opposed all attempts to diminish or further circumscribe the delegated powers of Congress. Only two of the amendments that he proposed on June 8, one dealing with the size of the House and the other with the timing of pay raises for Congress, would have necessitated governmental changes. Several merely declared principles that were implicit in the Constitution.[11]

Madison was more pre-eminent as a leader in the first session of the House of Representatives than he had been in the framing and ratifying of the Constitution. His influence on the basic legislation of the session was substantial and pervasive. In addition to his role in proposing amendments, he took a leading part in shaping the legislation that provided the first taxes and established the several executive departments and the federal court system. Also, in arriving at the etiquette of procedures dealing with the Senate and the President, he gave no support to forms and language that might imply aristocratic features in the Senate or monarchical features in the Presidency.[12]

What Madison said in the debates of the first session of Con-

gress was consistent with positions he had taken in the Philadelphia convention after July 16. He continued to argue that
the legislative branch was the strongest of the three and most
to be feared as an usurper or abuser of power.[13] He argued for
giving the President an exclusive power to remove officers
whose appointments required Senate consent.[14] He supported
the establishment of inferior federal courts. As at Philadelphia,
he assumed that the courts would exercise the power of judicial
review but cautioned that each of the other branches had an
authority equal to that of the courts in defining the limits of its
own powers.[15]

Madison had said little about the taxing power at Philadelphia. In *The Federalist* and at the Richmond ratifying convention he had defended the necessity of the taxing powers
granted in the Constitution, but had said little as to what he
would favor as tax policies once the Constitution began to operate. In the first session, he took the position that duties should
be levied mainly for the purpose of raising revenue with the
incidence falling as nearly as possible on all parts of the Union
equally.

He expressed a theoretical preference for the economic theories of Adam Smith:

I own myself the friend to a very free system of commerce, and hold
it as a truth that commercial shackles are generally unjust, oppressive
and impolitic; it is also a truth that if industry and labor are left to take
their own course, they will generally be directed to those objects which
are the most productive, and this in a more certain and direct manner
than the wisdom of the most enlightened legislature could point out.[16]

Madison, however, ran into the same difficulties that others
in his era encountered when they tried to apply the doctrine of
international free trade to a system of competitive national
states; in order to bargain for the removal of protective duties
levied by other countries, they had to violate the doctrine of
free trade by advocating retaliatory duties as a weapon of diplomacy. In the first session, Madison advocated tonnage duties
that discriminated in favor of American shippers and to a lesser
degree in favor of shippers from countries that had commercial
treaties with the United States. Also he was willing to provide
incidental protection to domestic manufactures by making sure
that competitive imports should not escape taxation.[17] The
House approved but the Senate rejected discriminatory duties

that favored countries with which the United States had commercial treaties.

Madison's proposal to discriminate against countries lacking commercial treaties was aimed primarily at Great Britain. As early as April 29, 1789, Phineas Bond, British consul at Philadelphia, criticized Madison's lack of understanding of commercial relations between the United States and Britain. George Beckwith, unofficial observer for the British government in New York, told Hamilton in October, 1789, that he had been surprised by Madison's anti-British stand in Congress. Hamilton confessed that he, too, was surprised.[18]

Madison accomplished more in the first session of the House than in any legislative body that he ever served, but not because the difficulties were less. The session was almost over when he wrote to Edmund Pendleton: "The difficulty of uniting minds of men accustomed to think and act differently can only be conceived by those who have witnessed it." Earlier, on July 5, he had written to his father: "The business [of Congress] goes on still very slowly. We are in a wilderness, without a single footstep to guide us. It is consequently necessary to explore the way with great labor and caution. Those who may follow will have an easier task."[19]

Madison had been an indefatigable worker in the several legislative bodies in which he had served since 1776. Yet, in this first session of the House he may have worked even harder than before. "I never had less time that I could truly call my own" he wrote to Edmund Randolph on May 31.[20] For Madison, who rarely alluded to the burdens of public office, such a statement, although hardly a wailing complaint, was exceptional.

In the midst of the busiest legislative session of his career, Madison also served as a confidential assistant to the President. He helped to prepare the inaugural address, and, when the House sent a reply to the President which he himself wrote, he was asked by Washington to compose a brief response. He advised the President on matters of form, ceremony, social etiquette, and procedures for communicating with the Congress. He gave advice on presidential appointments and served as intermediary to persuade Jefferson to come into the cabinet as Secretary of State.[21] By September, the President was apologetic about calling upon him for further assistance. Asking to be excused for being "very troublesome," Washington concluded a letter with this testimonial of his regard for Madison: "Ascribe it to friendship and confidence, and you will do justice to my motives."22

About two weeks before the adjournment of Congress, Alexander Hamilton assumed his duties as Secretary of Treasury. He had been in New York during the session, but there is no evidence of consultation between the erstwhile authors of *The Federalist*. Having failed to talk to Madison before he departed for Orange County, Secretary Hamilton wrote a letter of October 12 seeking his views on additional taxes and provisions for the debt. In his reply, dated November 19, Madison suggested a tax on distilleries, an increase of the tax on imported liquors, a land tax, and a stamp tax on the proceedings of federal courts. His ideas on the public debt were less specific. The Western lands, he thought, might aid in redemption of the debt. He asserted that the foreign debt should "be put on the most satisfactory footing" and that the whole debt be put "in a manifest course of extinguishment."23

Neither Hamilton's letter of October 12 nor Madison's letter of November 19 referred directly to issues that were to divide them during the second session. During the year 1789, the only recorded dissatisfaction expressed by either man toward the policies of the other was Hamilton's statement to Beckwith about Madison's commercial policy. Hamilton predicted to Madison that there would be disagreements about the exact items to be taxed but he did not link expected disputes about import duties with commercial policy and funding of the national debt. In subsequent years dependence upon British imports for revenue to fund the national debt was clearly seen. Although the two men in 1789 expressed no disagreement about tax and debt policies and made no connection between commercial policy toward Britain and the national debt, Madison's views on commercial policy toward Great Britain would have probably brought him into conflict with Hamilton eventually, even if he had accepted all of Hamilton's proposals for funding the debt in 1790.

CHAPTER VII

Leader of the Opposition

IN CONGRESS IN 1789 MADISON PLACED GREAT VALUE UPON the meaning given to the Constitution by the men who had the first opportunities to interpret it. In a speech of May 19 he said: "I look upon every Constitutional question, whatever its nature may be, as of great importance." On June 17, speaking about the President's power to remove executive officers, he said: "The decision that is at this time to be made, will become the permanent exposition of the Constitution; and on a permanent exposition of the Constitution will depend the genius and character of the whole Government."[1]

In the first session, in line with the positions he had begun to take at the Philadelphia convention after July 16, he expounded a broad interpretation of executive and judicial powers. During the next seven years in Congress, he was to be engaged in several constitutional debates, but they were quite different in content from those which had preoccupied his attention during the late eighties; except for Senatorial powers, none were about the issues which had seemed of utmost importance to him at Philadelphia. Equality of representation in the Senate was universally accepted as not amendable; and no one, not even Madison, proposed that the Constitution be amended to give Congress the power to veto state laws.

Because of improved economic conditions and specific restrictions on the states in Article I of the Constitution, the issues which had made Madison so distrustful of state legislatures in the 1780's were absent in the 1790's. With no threat of state encroachments on federal authority and private property rights, he no longer saw the same need for a national veto of state laws. If there had been state encroachments on national authority or private rights, judicial review was available to accomplish the purposes of a Congressional veto.

In the 1780's, of course, he had not simply looked upon national powers in their role of restricting the states. He had been just as ready to expand the affirmative powers of Congress. At no time did he express fear that a national Congress might enact legislation objectionable to him. He probably did not foresee then that he would oppose the policies which he began to oppose in 1790. One fact is indisputable: at Philadelphia he was willing to give to Congress all the powers which it did in fact exercise during Washington's presidency.

In the second and third session of the first Congress, Madison strongly protested against legislation recommended by Hamilton. Beginning in mid-February, 1790, he took a leading part in speaking against parts of the report submitted by the Secretary of Treasury to the House on January 14. First, he advocated a modification of Hamilton's plan for funding the domestic national debt in order that the original creditors, some of whom had been unpaid soldiers, might receive a partial indemnity for losses resulting from transfers of ownership at a time when the market price of their holdings was drastically depreciated. He explained in his memoirs:

His opinion ... in favour of dividing the payment of the public debt between the original holders, and the purchasers, grew out of the enormous gain of the latter, particularly out of Soldiers Certificates, and the sacrifice of these, to whom the public faith had not been fulfilled. Whilst the case of this class of Creditors was less in view he had opposed any discrimination; as in the Congress of 1782. Prior to the final settlement with the Army in the address drawn by him recommending the plan providing for the debt, until indeed the subject came close into view & the sacrifice of the soldiers was brought home to reflection, he had not sufficiently scanned and felt the magnitude of the evil. Hence in a hasty answer to a letter from the Secretary of Treasury which followed him after the adjournment, he did not suggest the idea of discrimination as one of the ingredients in the funding system. It grew rapidly on him on his return to Congress as the subject unfolded itself; and the outrageous speculations the floating paper pressed on the attention. Such was the spirit which was stimulated by the prospect of converting the depreciated paper into par value, that it seized members of Congress who did not shrink from the practice of purchasing thro' Brokers the certificates at little price, and contributing by these at the same moment to transmute them into the value of the precious metals.[2]

Later in the second session he opposed federal assumption of state war debts. In the third session, he opposed a Congressional charter for the first Bank of the United States. In February, 1791, he prepared a veto message for Washington, whose reasons for hesitating to sign the bank bill included his respect for Madison's authoritative opposition to its constitutionality.[3]

The President and the Congress ultimately supported Hamilton on all these issues. Only in his opposition to federal assumption of state debts did Madison almost win. Backers of assumption in the House, at first defeated by a vote of 31 to 29, were able to gain a majority only by agreeing to locate the capital district on the Potomac.[4]

Hamilton felt that Madison's opposition was out of harmony with the constitutional position he had taken in 1789 and inconsistent with views that he had earlier expressed on issues of financial and economic legislation. In the Philadelphia Convention he had proposed that Congress be delegated the power to charter corporations. In the Confederation Congress he had acquiesced in chartering the Bank of North America, had supported a plan for redeeming the national debt which had made no special allowance for losses suffered by the original holders of the debt, and had favored the Union assuming the war debts of the states. According to Hamilton, Madison had told him in private conversation at Philadelphia in the summer of 1787 that he favored national assumption of state debts, and in his letter of November 19, 1789, there was "not a lisp of his new system."[5]

Madison's change was puzzling to Hamilton. In a letter to Edward Carrington, he mentioned "a spirit of rivalship, or some other cause," for Madison's becoming "personally unfriendly." He said that Madison was left "a very discontented and chagrined man by the course of this [public-debt] business and a variety of circumstances." He was not certain whether "any peculiar opinions of Mr. Jefferson's concerning the public debt wrought a change in the sentiments of Mr. Madison ... or whether Mr. Madison, seduced by the expectation of popularity, and possibly by the calculation of advantage to the State of Virginia, was led to change his own opinion." He implied that the change was a manifestation of a complex personality: "The opinion I once entertained of the candor and simplicity and fairness of Mr. Madison's character, has, I acknowledge, given way to a decided opinion that it is one of a peculiarly artificial and complicated kind."[6]

President Washington never recorded his opinion of Madison's leadership of the opposition to Hamilton's policies. One can safely surmise, however, that he was displeased. After February, 1790, his requests for Madison's assistance were reduced in number and altered in kind. On only two occasions did he ask for help in composing a public address or official state paper. He asked for comments upon a preliminary draft of the message which he submitted to Congress on October 25, 1791; and in May, 1792, he asked Madison to prepare the draft of a "Farewell Address" to his countrymen. In May, 1792, he also asked Madison's advice as to the timing and method of announcing his retirement from public office.[7] His other requests for advice after February, 1790, were confined to constitutional questions. In February, 1791, he had several conversations with Madison about the bank bill and asked him to draft a veto message. Although the bank bill received the presidential signature, Madison's advice was decisive in causing Washington to veto an apportionment bill presented to the President on May 26, 1792. In October, 1793, Washington asked for and accepted Madison's opinion that the President lacked constitutional authority to call the next session of Congress to meet in some place other than Philadelphia, where a terrible epidemic of yellow fever was then raging.[8]

Madison was as reluctant to criticize the President as Washington was to criticize the leader of the Congressional opposition. Not only did he respond promptly and cordially to all of Washington's requests for assistance, but he also refrained from placing the blame for Hamilton's policies on the President. In May, 1792, he urged Washington to serve another term.[9]

If Madison uttered any criticism of Washington during his first term, it was oblique and confined to confidential conversations with trusted friends. In March, 1790, he told Jefferson that Washington was being victimized by apers after royalty. Three years later Jefferson recalled a conversation in which Madison had observed "that the satellites and sycophants" who surrounded Washington "had wound up the ceremonials of the government to a pitch of stateliness which nothing but his personal character could have supported, and which no character after him could maintain."[10]

As his opposition to Hamilton's policies placed increasing strains upon his friendship with Washington, so did it at the same time and for the same reasons produce a close political collaboration with his good friend Jefferson. By the close of the first Congress (March, 1791), his contacts with Jefferson were becoming frequent, intimate, confidential, and as viewed by their political enemies, conspiratorial.

For about a month, in May and June, 1791, the two men made a vacation tour along the shores of the Hudson, Lake George, Lake Champlain, and the Connecticut River. Traveling leisurely, they observed with careful attention and delight the wildlife, topography, soils, forests, vegetation, landscapes, and battlefields. Writing many years later about his friendship with Jefferson, Madison remembered this trip as "among the occasions" which "made us immediate companions."[11]

For Madison, the objects of the tour were "health, recreation & curiosity." The "scenes and subjects which had occurred during the session of Congress which had just terminated" entered into their conversations;[12] but there is no evidence in the extant records to support contemporary speculations that the purpose of the tour was to organize a party in New York and New England in opposition to Hamilton, or, as the British consul in New York believed, "to proselyte, as far as they are able to a commercial war with Great Britain."[13]

After their northern tour ended in mid-June, 1791, Madison stayed in New York City for about two months. While there he undertook to persuade his Princeton classmate Philip Freneau to edit a newspaper to combat the support given to Hamilton's policies by John Fenno's *Gazette of the United States.* Since February, Madison, Henry Lee, and Jefferson had been seeking Freneau's services for such a purpose. As an inducement for his undertaking the venture, they had held out the prospects of his paper printing public notices and documents for the State Department and had offered him a paying job in the department which would require little time for his official duties.[14]

In August, Freneau was at last persuaded to come to Philadelphia, to which the capital had moved in December, 1790. He accepted a clerkship for foreign languages in the State Department and by the last day of October was able to publish the first edition of a new newspaper called the *National Gazette.* About a year later, in a letter to Edmund Randolph, Madison justified the part he had played in helping Freneau to establish a paper in Philadelphia. He wrote on September 13, 1792:

That I wished & recommended Mr. Freneau to be appd. to his present Clerkship is certain. But the Department of State was not the only, nor as I recollect the first one to which I mentioned his name & character. I was governed in these recommendations by an acquaintance of long standing, by a respect for his talents, & by a knowledge of his merit & sufferings in the course of the revolution. Had I been less abstemious in my practice from solicitations in behalf of my friends, I should probably have been more early in thinking of Mr. F. . . . That with others of Mr. Freneau's particular acquaintainces I wished & advised him to establish a press at Philadelphia instead of one meditated by him in N Jersey, is also certain. I advised the change because I thought his interest would be advanced by it, & because as a friend I was desirous that his interest should be advanced. This was my primary & governing motive. That as a consequential one, I entertained hopes that a free paper meant for general circulation, and edited by a man of genius of republican principles, & a friend to the Constitution, would be some antidote to the doctrines & discourses circulated in favour of Monarchy and Aristocracy & would be an acceptable vehicle of public information in many places not sufficiently supplied with it, this also is a certain truth; but it is a truth which I never could be tempted to conceal, or wish to be concealed. If there be a temptation in the case, it would be to make a merit of it.[15]

Madison and Jefferson desired that the *National Gazette* should be designed to circulate in all the states. In 1791 and 1792 Madison contributed seventeen essays to the paper, all of which discussed general principles that transcended local and sectional interests. Jefferson did not write for Freneau's *Gazette*, but he joined with Madison in soliciting subscriptions among their friends in Virginia.[16]

Madison and Jefferson were together in Philadelphia during the first session of the second Congress (October 24, 1791–May 8, 1792). Since there were no occasions for the two men to write letters to each other, there are no documentary records from which their collaboration during this period can be reconstructed. Except for what others said about the relationship of the two men, there were only a few recorded instances of their joint activities. Right before the session, Washington met them at Georgetown and sought their advice on the message he was to submit to Congress. On April 5, 1792, upon Washington's request, Randolph and Jefferson met with Madison to obtain his concurrence in a veto of the apportionment bill that had been presented to the President on March 26.[17]

In the first session of the second Congress, two groups in the House consistently voted on opposite sides. About one quarter of the House membership voted with Madison and another quarter voted against him. About one-half of the members neither supported nor opposed him consistently. The strongest support for his positions came from the delegations of Virginia, North Carolina, and Georgia; the least support came from the New England states. Maryland was evenly divided. Federalists and Anti-Federalists of 1787 were present in both fixed extremes and the fluid group.[18]

Madison was contributing three or four essays a month to the *National Gazette* during this session of Congress, but he was an

infrequent speaker in the House. Hamilton surmised nevertheless, on the basis of "his votes and a variety of little movements
and appearances," that he was active behind the scenes in
prompting those "who were the open instruments of the opposition."

He was also convinced that Madison was cooperating with
Jefferson. During this session, he "became unequivocally convinced of the following truth: 'that Mr. Madison, co-operating
with Mr. Jefferson, is at the head of a faction decidedly hostile
to me and my administration; and actuated by views, in my
judgment, subversive of the principles of good government and
dangerous to the Union, peace, and happiness of the country.' "19

In a long letter of May 26, 1792, to Edward Carrington of
Virginia, Hamilton reviewed Madison's role as a leader of the
opposition. According to this letter, Hamilton had been "ap-
prised that it was Mr. Madison's intention to oppose" his plan
for refunding the public debts and had conversed with him
about his report before the debate began in the House. While
the debate was going on and afterward, he had received "repeated intimations" that Madison was "personally unfriendly,"
but he continued to suspend judgment until late in the first
session of the second Congress. On March 7, 1792, Madison
opposed a House resolution that directed the Secretary of Treasury to report his opinion of the best mode for raising the additional supplies requisite for a new army expedition in the
Northwest Territory. Thereupon Hamilton, for the first time,
"declared openly" his determination to consider him a "political enemy."20

Hamilton's letter to Carrington referred to several other
points of disagreement: "Womanish attachment to France and
a womanish resentment" against Great Britain; attempts "to
produce a commercial warfare with Great Britain"; bounties to
the fisheries; the militia bill; the mint; weights and measures;
legislation fixing the presidential succession after the vice-
presidency; and his negotiations to bring Freneau to Philadelphia.

When Hamilton wrote his letter to Carrington, Madison appeared to him as a consistent defender of a strict interpretation
of the Constitution: "In almost all the questions, great and small,
which have arisen since the first session of Congress, Mr. Jefferson and Mr. Madison have been found among those who are
disposed to narrow the federal authority."

By May, 1792, it is quite possible that a doctrine of constitutional interpretation may have begun to have a guiding influence on Madison's attitudes toward specific economic issues. It is most doubtful, however, that a doctrinal outlook shaped Madison's opinions on policies in the first Congress. The records seem to indicate that Madison's views on specific policies came first and that the constitutional argument was derivative and secondary. A strict interpretation of the Constitution does not appear to have been a self-contained political value but an instrumentality for blocking undesirable federal legislation.

Nor does it appear that Madison's positions in the first Congress were determined by a general philosophy about governmental forms and principles. During the second Congress he came to equate his own positions with the defense of republican liberties, but it does not appear that the initial grounds for opposing Hamiltonian policies rested on fears about their ultimate consequences for forms of government and philosophical principles. Madison's original opposition appears to have stemmed from economic and ethical objections, some of which were personal to himself and some of which reflected a general attitude of his constituents. At first each separate policy was judged on its own merits, with his arguments stressing immediate origins and immediate consequences. Subsequently, each policy was viewed as related to others as parts of a greater whole and as having ultimate consequences to basic principles of republican and federal government.

The first two Congresses demonstrated the incapacity of a variety of interests and neutral blocs to guarantee the kind of justice that Madison had been seeking in legislative bodies in 1787. There can be no doubt that some of the votes that enacted Hamilton's program came from members who hoped to profit personally or who were closely associated with constituents who had selfish interests in it. Madison and other leaders of the opposition complained of legislators who enriched themselves with their own votes in Congress, but they never charged that a majority of the votes came from self-interested congressmen. The large number of members who had no self-interests in the funding scheme or the national bank who voted with those who did must have been a bitter pill for the author of *Federalist* Number 10.

The first two Congresses revealed the basic weaknesses in the approach to legislative justice advocated by Madison in *Federalist* Number 10. A large number of neutrals on a specific legislative issue is no guarantee of action in behalf of justice. The neutrals may be ignorant, they may make errors of judgment, they may be indifferent, or they may deliberately abstain from voting in order to avoid entangling alliances. Furthermore, and most important of all, the legislator who has no direct interest in a given bill may fail to act impartially because of a desire to recruit votes for another bill in which he does have a direct interest. That is, he may engage in what the political scientist calls "logrolling," a classic example being the exchange of votes that made possible passage of the bills that provided federal assumption of state debts and location of the District of Columbia on the Potomac.

Logrolling is nothing more than a temporary alliance in a legislative body for a limited and immediate purpose. Exactly the same motives that produce logrolling may, however, produce permanent alliances in the form of political parties. Both temporary alliances in the form of logrolling agreements and permanent alliances in the form of political parties operate to counteract what Madison had presumed in *Federalist* Number 10 to be the beneficent effect of a variety of interests, for in both temporary and permanent alliances each member essentially agrees that he will relinquish his own independent judgment when considering matters of direct and primary interest to his allies with the expectation that they in turn will do the same in matters that affect his own.

In Number 10, Madison had said that factions were inevitable but had failed to take account of the tendency of factions to form alliances and thus to make it possible for a combination of interests to comprise a majority, even when no one interest constituted a majority. He had placed his hopes on the expectation that no one factional interest would be able to constitute a majority in a legislative body that represented numerous and varied interests. He had said that factions were inevitable wherever there was freedom for superior abilities to acquire property; and, in free republics based upon majority rule the best safeguard for preventing injustice and oppression was to arrange the representation in the legislative body in such a way that no one interest would be a majority. He had said nothing about the possibility of logrolling as a technique by which selfish minorities could create temporary majorities. And he said nothing about political parties combining varied interests so that logrolling in effect would become organized and institutionalized as a permanent influence on legislation. Logically his thesis had implied that virtually every majority on a bill would represent a new combination of factions.

In his unsigned essays in *The National Gazette* in 1792, Madison implicitly abandoned the basic tenets of *Federalist* Number 10.[21] In these essays he came to his final philosophical position as to the best means for guaranteeing liberty, federalism, republicanism, and legislative justice to economic interests. In them he showed that he had come to believe that only a national public opinion that cherished these values could insure their protection.

In 1787 Madison had believed that men could employ government merely to give assistance to a natural equilibrium of selfish interests. In 1792 he professed to have little confidence in any kind of equilibrium theory. The state governments, to be sure, were given more attention as possible counterweights to federal power, but even they were looked upon essentially as fortresses to which retreating armies could escape temporarily in order to avoid total defeat. His view in 1792 was the simple one that has prevailed throughout most of our national history in the realm of practical politics: he would seek to protect and propagate his political values by winning a national majority to their support. Active political organization and political education on a national basis, not a natural or artificial balancing of interests, were the only sure way to safeguard individual liberty, republican and federal principles of government, and economic justice in legislation. Political parties were accepted as inevitable and their positive benefits justified.

Little that Madison wrote in 1792 was in harmony with *Federalist* Number 10. In addition to replacing an equilibrium theory with advocacy of organization and propaganda, he abandoned his fatalism about the ability of government to influence the causes of faction. In Number 10 he had written that nothing could be done about the causes of factional conflicts in a free government; the only solution was to control their evil effects. In the *National Gazette*, however, he broached the possibility of governmental power being used to influence the distribution of wealth, both by adopting measures that would provide positive assistance to the poor and by avoiding measures that would further enrich the very wealthy. In Number 10 inequalities and diversity were linked together as inevitable products of inequalities and diversity of talents and were not looked upon with disfavor. In the *National Gazette* he wrote about uniformity of opinion as possible and desirable in a republic.

Just about all that was left of Number 10 by 1792 was Madison's continued acceptance of economic motives as important determinants of opinion. But the weight of the economic factor was reduced in his thinking and its manifestations even more complex. Idealistic motives were placed on a par with materialistic motives, and the economic motives did not always express themselves in the form of specific factions or interest groups. Economic motives might influence the average citizen without regard to economic groupings; the cost of government, for example, was of general interest and was linked to no particular economic interest.

Madison's theory of 1792 was a reflection of practice. For two years, as an active leader in the House of Representatives, he showed no signs whatever of putting his trust in a passive acceptance of the beneficent operations of an automatic equilibrium.

Quite the contrary. He worked for a system of collective security in domestic politics by means of a grand alliance of republicans. In Congress he negotiated with leaders in an attempt to form a working coalition of interests. But he also appealed to public opinion as though it might be an entity distinguishable from an aggregation of opinions congruent with the separate interests making up a Congressional coalition; he appealed to voters as though they might be influenced by arguments that had no perceptible or obvious relationship to their vocational activities or economic status. His writings for the *National Gazette* had this practical political purpose, and they constituted the best example of his technique of general appeals.

When Madison was in his thirties and forties, he achieved greatness in statesmanship as a practical intellectual. A student of ideas, he never became, during this creative stage of his career, the prisoner of fixed ideas and doctrinaire opinions. He studied and learned from books about the past and about contemporary governments in Europe; and he learned what the great political philosophers and theorists of all ages said about political ethics and causation. These studies, of course, functioned in part to provide him with rationalizations and illustrations for opinions which were in fact generated by current controversies; but to a degree unusual in the history of politics they stimulated his mind to perceive what others overlooked, warned him against false steps that others were ready to take, enabled him to profit from mistakes that had been made by others in similar situations, added perspective to the commanding present moment, provided mental exercises for his imaginatively logical mind, and helped him to sharpen and clarify his own categories and distinctions.

In using the ideas and experiences of others as they were recorded in books, he looked to no one philosopher as an infallible authority and to no one government as a model for imitation. Whatever he read in books was well digested. Ingredients borrowed from others were put into a new blend and became indistinguishable from those that originated in his own observations and perceptions of events.

His studies and his writings were made in the context of political controversy and were motivated by a desire to solve immediate practical problems. In the late 1780's they were so closely linked to current problems that it is not possible to disentangle them from his own experiences as a practical politician. He never ceased to seek an intellectual understanding and exposition of politics, but his thinking in the 1790's was almost exclusively the result of his own activities as an officeholder and party leader. The simple truth is that the first two Congresses under the Constitution demonstrated the shortcomings of his previous views, and being a man who was more interested in achieving practical results than in justifying his own pet theories, he discarded them. Changes that he made in his earlier theories did not come from scholarly studies but from his own observations of events and his own logical imagination.

In "A Candid State of Parties," published in *The National Gazette* of September 26, 1792, Madison classified political parties since the Revolution in terms of basic beliefs about government. Since 1789, he said, the division had been between the republican and anti-republican parties. The "republican party," supported by the great majority in the country, consisted of those who hated hereditary government, believed that mankind was capable of governing itself, and supported measures that appealed to the understanding and general interest of the community. The anti-republicans, he said, were a small minority in the country who believed that government could be conducted only by "the pageantry of rank, the influence of money and emoluments, and the terror of military force." Through administration, they hoped that the government by degrees would come under the control of fewer hands and would eventually approximate to an hereditary form. Their public measures were "more partial to the opulent than to the other classes of society."

In this essay on parties, and in another which he had published early in the year, Madison dealt with general principles of government and broad classes of people. He made no attempt to correlate the division of parties which he described with divisions in the Congress on issues of specific public policies, and he made no effort to correlate "the few" with any specific interest group in the country. The reader of his essays who identified "the republican party" with the group that supported Madison in opposition to Hamilton's financial policies would have had to do so by a process of inference.

By the summer of 1792, the opposition led by Madison and Jefferson was being referred to as a party. As that word had been used previously in the eighteenth century, the two Virginians were indeed leaders of a party. It is doubtful, however, that they yet visualized the kind of national organization that was to triumph in the election of Jefferson to the presidency in 1800. Madison was not self conscious that he was participating in the establishment of "the party system."

In a small way, however, even if he lacked awareness that he was becoming the founder of a new political institution, he was in fact a national party leader in 1792. The small bloc with which he was associated in Congress, although strongly centered in Virginia, included men from other states. In association with Senator James Monroe and the clerk of the House of Representatives John Beckley, he kept himself informed about elections in several states, and he participated in negotiations to unite a nationwide slate of electors behind George Clinton as vice presidential candidate in opposition to John Adams. In the *National Gazette* he was writing essays designed to have a national appeal.[22]

On July 25, 1792, Hamilton began to publish in a series of pseudonymous letters in the *Gazette of the United States* the same complaints which he had uttered in his long letter to Edward Carrington. Unlike the author of the private letter of May 26, however, the author who signed himself "T.L.," "American," and "Catullus" concentrated his attacks upon Jefferson alone. He mentioned Madison only when he quoted what he had said in the Richmond ratifying convention about Jefferson's views on the Constitution. When dealing with the Freneau episode, he alluded to "a very powerful, influential, and confidential friend and associate" of Jefferson but did not give Madison's name.[23]

Madison in turn made no public attacks upon Hamilton during the summer and fall of 1792, despite his belief that Jefferson was the victim of unjustified calumny. The main task of defending Jefferson he left to their mutual friend James Monroe.[24]

By September, Madison knew that Hamilton was talking about him as a "personal and political enemy."[25] He considered replying to Hamilton's account of the role that Jefferson's "particular friend" had in the negotiations with Freneau, but, since he had not been named, decided instead to explain his own part in the establishment of *The National Gazette* to Edmund Randolph, in the letter of September 13 already quoted. Freneau, however, was defended; with the assistance of Monroe, he wrote a laudatory article for publication on October 20 in the *American Daily Advertiser*. Also, in order to rectify what he considered Hamilton's misinterpretation of what he had said at the Richmond ratifying convention, he permitted Monroe to publish letters received in 1788 in which Jefferson had commented favorably on the Constitution.[26]

Jefferson was pleased with the outcome of the Congressional elections of 1792. On December 3, 1792, he wrote to Thomas Pinckney: "The elections for Congress have produced a decided majority in favor of the republican interest. . . . I think we may consider the tide of this government as now at the fullest, and that it will, from the commencement of the next session of Congress, retire and subside into the true principles of the Constitution."[27]

Jefferson wrote this letter to Pinckney during the expiring session of the second Congress. With the prospects better for the next Congress, postponement of legislative decisions in this session was highly desirable.[28] And in fact, the Madison group was remarkably effective in postponing or defeating new legislation endorsed by Hamilton. After first rejecting (December 26) amendments to a bill incorporating Hamilton's proposal of a new loan to pay off two million dollars owed to the Bank of the United States, the House later (February 27) accepted Madison's motion to pay only the installment due, that is, two hundred thousand dollars. A bill that would have provided a supplementary assumption of state debts passed the House by the vote of the Speaker but was defeated in the Senate. The House failed to act upon Hamilton's report of November 30 which presented his plan for redemption of the public debt by means of designated revenues to be derived from dividends on bank stock and new taxes.[29]

In January of this session, Fisher Ames, who in 1789 had thought Madison "too timid in his politics," bewailed his domineering leadership of the opposition:

Virginia moves in a solid column, and the discipline of the party is as severe as the Prussian. Deserters are not spared. Madison is become a desperate party leader, and I am not sure of his stopping at any ordinary point of extremity.[30]

Madison was able to get support in this session against Hamiltonian legislative measures which he was not able to get on resolutions designed to discredit his management of the Treasury Department and debt-funding operations. A set of resolutions introduced by William B. Giles on February 27 which censured Hamilton for allegedly exceeding Congressional and Presidential authority and for failing to keep the House informed of certain unauthorized transactions were overwhelmingly defeated when voted upon on March 1, 1793.[31] The strongest support for the resolutions of censure came from the Virginia and North Carolina delegations, but even in these states a solid majority was lacking. No support came from the seaboard states north of Pennsylvania and Maryland; and Pennsylvania came close to voting unanimously against them.

Giles's resolutions of February 27, 1793 supposedly were based upon Hamilton's failure to give satisfactory explanations to questions raised in resolutions introduced by Josiah Parker on December 24 and by Giles on December 27 and January 23. Hamilton's replies to these resolutions of inquiry had been made in five written reports submitted to the House between January 4 and February 19.[32]

Madison was one of only five men who voted for all the resolutions of censure. Biographers and historians have freely surmised that Madison and Jefferson were the instigators of Giles's resolutions of inquiry and censure, but in actual fact there are no records describing the relationships of these three men during the session. Indeed, not much is known about Madison's attitude toward the resolutions of inquiry until late in the session; not until Hamilton had made his reports to the House in January and February do we have any trustworthy indications of Madison's opinions of the investigations. To Edmund Pendleton he wrote on February 23 that "a pretty interesting scrutiny" had been "started into the administration of the Treasury Department," that there had been "at least a very lamentable irregularity & secrecy in some particulars," and that "many appearances" required explanation.[33]

Madison put himself publicly on the record on March 1, 1793, one day before the adjournment of Congress, when he spoke in support of the resolutions of censure. His whole speech was legalistic and cautious. His charges against Hamilton were concerned with the Congressional and presidential authority of the Secretary's acts and his obligations to keep the House informed, especially if there were any departures from legislative authorizations. He voiced no innuendoes that might suggest that Hamilton had been corruptly influenced, that he had been guilty of favoritism, or even that the country had suffered material losses from his transactions. The harm to the nation at large, Madison implied, came from his failure to preserve "order in the public finance," and to show "a proper respect for the authority of the laws."[34]

The House investigations of the Treasury Department by this session of Congress were viewed by Hamilton and his friends as an attempt to drive him from office, just as Jefferson's friends had thought Hamilton's newspaper attacks had as their purpose the driving of Jefferson from the State Department. If the resolutions had passed, said William Smith of South Carolina, "the Secretary would have been removed, disgraced, and ruined forever."[35]

Madison himself, of course, never admitted, privately or publicly, to a plan to investigate the Treasury head for the purpose of driving Hamilton from office. Yet, there can be little doubt that he expected the Giles resolutions would have an adverse effect on public opinion and perhaps upon President Washington's estimate of his Secretary of Treasury. William Smith said that Madison had "observed" that defeat of the Giles resolutions "would not change the truth of facts, and that the public would ultimately decide whether the Secretary's conduct was criminal or not." To Jefferson, Madison wrote on April 12, 1793: "I suspect the President may not be satisfied with the aspect under which that and other parts of the fiscal administration have been left."[36]

What effect the inquiries had upon the reluctance of this session to approve new legislation is necessarily speculative but not to be ignored in assessing the failure of Madison and Giles to discredit Hamilton's management of fiscal affairs. Perhaps they made a majority in the Congress wary about approving new legislation until they were sure of the outcome of the inquiries. By the time the outcome was known, there was too little time to act upon Hamilton's proposals. If the House inquiries and Hamilton's reports had come during the first two months of the session instead of the last two months and if debate on Hamilton's proposals had come after the overwhelming vindication of the Secretary's management of fiscal affairs, the legislative record of the session conceivably might have been different. Whatever their intent, Giles's resolutions probably tended to delay action and raise doubts about legislation pertaining to the public debt and the bank.[37]

CHAPTER VIII

Vanquished by the Venerable

THE END OF THE SECOND CONGRESS MARKED THE END OF the first phase of Madison's leadership of the opposition. For three years his opposition had centered on the domestic policies of Alexander Hamilton. In the next two Congresses he was to lead the opposition to Washington's foreign policy.

When war in Europe brought new issues to the foreground during Washington's second term, Madison merely adapted long-held beliefs about foreign policy to recently acquired opinions about public finance and party politics. Long before the French Revolution he had been pro-French and anti-British; a predilection against Britain was undoubtedly the most consistent attitude maintained by him throughout his public career. During the American Revolution he had appreciated the value of the French alliance and he had anticipated a strategy of seeking French assistance in future negotiations with Spain and Britain. Long before the first French Republic, he had been an unqualified adherent of republicanism; he had never seen the same virtues in the British monarchy that John Adams and Hamilton had seen. Several years before the British began confiscating American cargoes and impressing American sailors into the Royal Navy, he had advocated economic retaliation as a weapon of diplomacy.

Madison thought that his views on policy toward Great Britain were the most consistent of his career. On January 29, 1794, he told the House of Representatives

that if in any instance of his public life he was free from the charge of inconsistency, it was on the subject of vindicating our national interest against the policy of Great Britain towards us; that in all the public stations with which he had been honored since the peace, and on every occasion which had occurred, his conduct had been marked by an adherence to this principle.[1]

In the year 1792, France was at war with Austria and Prussia after April and the monarchy was overthrown in September;

but, prior to the adjournment of the second Congress, Madison gave little thought to the implications of these events to the future of American politics. Displeased when Hamilton objected to paying installments on the French debt to the new republic on the grounds that it might soon be overthrown, he nevertheless had concentrated his criticisms of the last session on past transactions and new proposals connected with the debt and the bank. What he expected the next session of Congress to do is unknown; presumably he would have had it continue to block new proposals emanating from Hamilton and investigate his managerial practices. On February 23, 1793, he had written to Edmund Pendleton that the next session would "form a crucial epoch in our political History."[2]

Jefferson, writing to Madison on August 11, 1793, proposed that the next Congress divide the Treasury Department into two departments, adopt resolutions proclaiming the unconstitutionality of the Bank, and censure "censurable things."[3] Such references to the issues that dominated the second Congress were, however, scarce in the numerous letters that Jefferson and Madison exchanged between March and November, 1793. The entrance of the British navy into the European war and the arrival of a minister representing the new French Republic presented President Washington with the necessity to seek advice from the two men in his cabinet who had so sharply opposed each other during his first term. The differences in views between Jefferson and Hamilton on these issues of foreign policy pre-empted the correspondence of Jefferson and Madison between the two sessions of Congress.

From the beginning of the revolutionary movement of 1789 Madison and Jefferson had expressed their sincere and enthusiastic support and confidence in the changes taking place in France. When England came into the war in February, 1793, both were benevolently sympathetic toward France and willing to be as helpful as a neutral country could be without becoming an active belligerent and without provoking the belligerency of the less favored country. Both assumed that the treaty of 1778 was still in effect despite the termination of the monarchy, and both thought the debts owed to France were neither suspended nor canceled by the Revolution. Both favored diplomatic recognition of the French Republic and hoped for a warm reception for its representative, Edmond Charles Genêt.[4]

Although Washington rejected Hamilton's views on the alliance, debts, and recognition of the new republic, his strict

interpretation of neutrality, his issuance of a proclamation announcing a policy of impartiality, and his icy reception of
Genêt were disappointing to Jefferson and Madison. Omission
of the word neutrality in the President's proclamation of April
22, 1793, did not propitiate Madison. On June 19, he wrote to
Jefferson:

> The proclamation was, in truth, a most unfortunate error. It wounds
> the national honor, by seeming to disregard the stipulated duties to
> France. It wounds popular feelings, by seeming indifference to liberty.
> And it seems to violate the forms and spirit of the Constitution, by
> making the Executive Magistrate the organ of the disposition, the duty,
> and the interests of the nation in relation to war and peace—subjects
> appropriate to other departments of the Government.[5]

Hamilton, using the pseudonym Pacificus, defended the
proclamation and a broad interpretation of the executive's diplomatic powers in a series of eight public letters. Jefferson, in
a letter of July 7, implored Madison to reply to them: "For
God's sake, my dear Sir, take up your pen, select the most
striking heresies and cut them to pieces in the face of the
public. There is nobody else who can & will enter the lists
against him."[6]

Madison was reluctant to accede to Jefferson's request. At
this time his disposition was "perfectly alienated from such
things." He felt that he lacked information that would enable
him to make a solid and prudent reply. He was afraid he could
not avoid "vulnerable assertions or suppositions which might
give occasion to triumphant replies," and he knew that the
pertinacity of Hamilton would not allow "the business to be
terminated by a single fire." Nevertheless, with lingering misgivings, he did at length write five essays under the pseudonym
Helvidius which appeared in the *Gazette of the United States*
between August 24 and September 18.[7]

Their composition was the "most grating" task he had yet
experienced. He had no taste for the subject. At every step he
found "the want of counsel on some points of delicacy as well
as of information as to sundry matters of fact," and he worried
about "turning the controversy too much into the wilderness of
Books." As he wrote, he suffered from a "distressing lassitude"
brought on by "the excessive & continued heat of the season."[8]

The letters of Helvidius analyzed the war-making and treaty-
making powers of the President. They argued that Hamilton's
interpretation of presidential powers and obligations was not

exemplified by the President's proclamation of April 22; that the proclamation was nothing more than a public notification of war in Europe and of the obligations of the American people so long as the United States was at peace; that it implied no particular decision as to whether the United States should remain at peace in the future and no particular interpretation of the French treaty; and that the President lacked the prerogative of deciding whether there was a cause for war in the obligation of states. They were largely a finespun legalistic argument. One of them, however, included this moralistic statement:

In no part of the constitution is more wisdom to be found, than in the clause which confides the question of war or peace to the legislature, and not to the executive department. Beside the objection to such a mixture to heterogeneous powers, the trust and the temptation would be too great for any one man; not such as nature may offer as the prodigy of many centuries, but such as may be expected in the ordinary successions of magistracy. War is in fact the true nurse of executive aggrandizement. In war, a physical force is to be created; and it is the executive will, which is to direct it. In war, the public treasures are to be unlocked; and it is the executive hand which is to dispense them. In war, the honours and emoluments of office are to be multiplied; and it is the executive patronage under which they are to be enjoyed. It is in war, finally, that laurels are to be gathered; and it is the executive brow they are to encircle. The strongest passions and most dangerous weaknesses of the human breast; ambition, avarice, vanity, the honourable or venial love of fame, are all in conspiracy against the desire and duty of peace.

Hence it has grown into an axiom that the executive is the department of power most distinguished by its propensity to war: hence it is the practice of all states, in proportion as they are free, to disarm this propensity of its influence.[9]

By the time Madison had completed the first of his Helvidius letters, the President had decided to ask for the recall of Genêt, who, in his judgment, violated and improperly criticized his policy of neutrality. In May, Madison had "anxiously" wished that the reception of Genêt would testify to "the real affections of the people" for France. By August, however, he was distressed by the audacity of this "mad man" and annoyed that his declining popularity was becoming a liability to the party opposed to Hamilton. Steps should be taken, he thought, to counteract any political advantages that the anti-French party might seek to exploit from the popular reaction against Genêt; to Jefferson he suggested that they should avoid blaming the revolutionary French nation for his mistakes. Madison himself drafted resolutions which he hoped would be approved in substance in several forthcoming county meetings in Virginia; they expressed the good will of the American people for the cause of liberty and republican government in France.[10]

Even before the reaction against Genêt occurred in the United States, Jefferson and Madison were aware that some Americans had been repelled by the bloody massacres that accompanied the downfall of the monarchy in September, 1792, by the imprisonment of prominent men who had served the American cause during the Revolutionary War, and by the beheading of King Louis in January, 1793. Nevertheless, Jefferson thought that the violence in France was a small price to pay for putting an end to despotism. True republicans, he wrote to Madison, would realize that the cause of liberty in France was the cause of liberty everywhere and that the defeat of France by the European monarchies would put the cause of liberty on the defensive in the United States. Critics of Revolutionary France, he averred, were the "fashionable circles of Philadelphia, New York, Boston and Charleston," merchants trading on British capital, "paper men," and generally the secret admirers of monarchy.[11]

Madison in May and June had written that the country people of Virginia "universally and warmly" sympathized with "Liberty and France." At the beginning of September, after the reaction against Genêt was known, he described the "sense of the people" as fundamentally unchanged:

> They are attached to the Constitution. They are attached to the President. They are attached to the French Nation and Revolution. They are attached to peace as long as it can be honorably preserved. They are averse to Monarchy and to a political connection with that of Great Britain and will readily protest against any known or supposed danger that may have this change in their situation for their object.[12]

Comforting as were such reports of opinion from rural Virginia, Jefferson was dissatisfied as Secretary of State. He was discouraged by the President's tough-minded and coldhearted attitude toward France, by the embarrassments that Genêt created for supporters of the French cause, and by complaints from both the French and British ministers about enforcement of neutrality.

Madison strongly urged him to make a further sacrifice of his "longings for the repose of Monticello," but Jefferson protested at great length that he had fully paid the debt of service he owed his fellow citizens.[13] On August 11 he notified Washington that he would remain as Secretary of State no longer than the end of the year.

Before he left office, Jefferson at last complied with a request made by the House of Representatives in February, 1791: on December 16, 1793, he submitted a report summarizing the barriers placed upon American exports and shipping by Britain and six continental countries. He included in this report recommendations for retaliatory measures against countries which placed barriers against American trade which were excessive in comparison with those which their own trade was then encountering in the United States.

On January 5, 1794, Jefferson departed from Philadelphia for his beloved Monticello. Two days before, Madison introduced a set of resolutions proposing discriminatory duties and restrictions along the lines proposed by the report of December 16. In the House on January 29, he praised that report and eulogized its author. He confidently declared

that the Report would be regarded by all discerning and unprejudiced judges as one of the many monuments which its author had left behind him, of the zeal, the talents, and the patriotism with which he had discharged the duties of his station; and that he had carried with him into retirement a purity, both in his public and private name, which nothing that could be said within or without the walls of Congress could tarnish.[14]

The damage done to the Republican cause by the reaction against France in 1793 was apparent in this first session (December 3, 1793–June 9, 1794) of the third Congress. It probably would have been even greater, if reports of British interference with American trade had not been received in increasing numbers as the session progressed. As early as September 15 Madison had said that British interception of non-contraband articles bound for unblockaded ports would probably continue and in time bring on a crisis with the United States.[15] Nevertheless, in their correspondence in August and September, Jefferson and Madison had been primarily concerned with devising a defense for their French policy.

When the Congress actually met, increasing reports of British seizures of American cargoes enabled them to shift over to an attack on Great Britain. On March 12, 1794, Madison wrote to Jefferson: "The merchants, particularly of New England have had a terrible *slam* in the West Indies. About a hundred vessels have been seized by the British for condemnation."[16] At the same time other complaints were being voiced. The British were suspected of complicity with the Algerine pirates, and an address of the governor-general of Canada seemed to encourage Indian warfare in the Northwest.[17]

Madison's resolutions of January 3 were debated between January 13 and February 3. Madison himself delivered major speeches on January 14 and January 29.[18] As in the first Congress, he admitted a theoretical preference for free trade. In a system of competing national states, however, in which each of the European powers discriminated in favor of its own commerce, he argued, the United States would have to retaliate in order to obtain commercial concessions. In his speeches, unlike his resolutions, he named Great Britain as the main target of his proposals. He argued that Great Britain was particularly vulnerable to economic coercion. Essentially, he said that Great Britain needed American trade more than the United States needed British trade. Britain and her colonies in the West Indies needed American crops and materials for survival; the United States merely needed British manufactures for comfort and convenience. He seems to have thought that deprivation of American exports, especially in the West Indies, would constitute a devastating blow against Britain. Also, he argued that loss of American markets would hurt British manufactures and merchants.

Madison was convinced that economic measures would be more effective than war against Great Britain. More vulnerable in her commerce than in her fleets and armies, Britain feared loss of American trade more than American frigates and militia. American arms, "though invincible in defence," would not be formidable in an offensive war against Britain. The costs to the United States of seizing Canada he thought would be immense. Furthermore, the loss of Canada to Britain would be "trifling" compared to a branch of its commerce which fed one part of its dominions and sent annually to the other a balance in specie of more than ten millions of dollars.[19]

Madison also believed that war should be the last resort of all countries with republican institutions. In April, 1795, he wrote:

Of all the enemies to public liberty war is, perhaps, the most to be dreaded because it comprises and develops the germ of every other. War is the parent of armies; from these proceed debts and taxes; and armies, and debts, and taxes are the known instruments for bringing the many under the domination of the few. In war, too, the discretionary power of the Executive is extended; its influence in dealing out offices, honors, and emoluments is multiplied; and all the means of seducing the minds, are added to those of subduing the force, of the people. The same malignant aspect in republicanism may be traced in the inequality of fortunes, and the opportunities of fraud, growing out of a state of war, and in the degeneracy of manners and of morals, engendered by both. No nation could preserve its freedom in the midst of continual warfare. Those truths are well established. They are read in every page which records the progression from a less arbitrary to a more arbitrary government, or the transition from a popular government to an aristocracy or a monarchy.[20]

Some of Madison's critics maintained that economic reprisals would provoke war rather than prove to be a substitute for it; that is, that Britain would go to war rather than make the concessions necessary to retain American trade. Madison was sure that Britain would not go to war against the United States. He did not interpret the havoc inflicted upon American trade in the West Indies as signifying a design to force war with the United States. Her aim was to destroy American trade that benefited her enemy while profiting from it herself; war would tend to have the opposite effect. Furthermore, Britain was too occupied in waging war against France to want to add another enemy. The British, he argued, would push her aggressions no further than the United States would tolerate.[21]

The strategy of exploiting the troubles of Europe was in Madison's thinking a second alternative to war and preparations for war. His correspondence was filled with observations on the course of the war in Europe which showed his belief that the bargaining power of the United States was directly correlated with French victories on land and sea. Madison, like the other Founding Fathers, was quite aware that sailors and soldiers fighting in Europe were sailors and soldiers unavailable for service in North America. Like the others, too, he was always ready to make the most of such situations in the conduct of American diplomacy.

Unlike Washington, Madison believed that economic retaliation and exploiting the wartime troubles of Europe were mutually supporting strategies. At a time when the European powers were at war, they would be more effective and less risky. Loss of American markets at a time when markets were being lost to the enemy in Europe would hurt British interests more than in peacetime, and there would be no danger that trade losses would provoke the British to declare war against the United States. While the war against France remained unsuccessful, he argued, the United States was in no danger from the powers engaged in it.[22]

The idea of some form of economic retaliation against Britain temporarily gained strong support in the House, but Madison's resolutions were never adopted. By March 14, the last day they were debated, anger against Britain was aroused to such a fury that Republicans and many Federalists alike were ready for much stronger measures. On March 9 Madison wrote to Jefferson that friends of his resolutions were beginning to say that "more vigorous measures" were necessary because of "the progress of British outrages." On March 26, he reported that the constituents of the Eastern members "were growing clamorous under their losses in the W. Indies." Hamilton's collaborator William Smith, who had made the first rebuttal to his resolutions in the House, had thought them needlessly provocative when he spoke on January 13. Two months later he said that the resolutions, considering the critical state of affairs produced by recent British "aggressions," were "not only too inefficient" but would be "too tardy in their operation."[23]

On March 25 and April 17 the House of Representatives, with the subsequent concurrence of the Senate, adopted embargoes which detained all foreign-bound vessels in U. S. ports until May 25. On April 7, Abraham Clark of New Jersey introduced a bill which would have discontinued the importation of British products so long as Americans were not compensated for losses resulting from seizures by armed vessels violating the rights of neutrals and so long as the British retained posts within the United States on the Northern frontier. On April 21, the House amended Clark's bill by approving Madison's motion not to specify the terms upon which commerce would be restored.

During the second week of April, while the House was debating embargoes and non-importation, President Washington came to a decision to send a special emissary to Britain—a move favored by Hamilton and his friends in Congress who had recently been supporting embargoes and urging preparations for war. Washington selected Chief Justice Jay, who made clear his opposition to the pending non-importation bill before accepting the appointment. Jay was confirmed by the Senate on April 19 by a vote of 18 to 8.

On April 25, the House sent to the Senate Clark's amended non-importation bill. The House had approved the bill by a vote of 58 to 34, but it was defeated in the Senate by the casting vote of Vice President Adams. Madison explained to his father that the bill was killed by senators who were "determined to rely on the extraordinary mission of Jay to sue for satisfaction."[24]

For Madison, there was no inconsistency between his own resolutions and the special mission. Indeed, he was sure that Jay's bargaining power would have been increased if they had been adopted. Although disappointed in rejection of his commercial resolutions and the non-importation bill, he still believed that the support which had been demonstrated in Congress for such measures constituted a warning to the British which helped Jay as he carried out his negotiations. A threat that such measures might be approved if Jay's mission failed, coupled with the actuality of French victories in the campaigns of 1794, from Madison's point of view, placed Jay in a strong position to obtain concessions.[25]

Toward the close of the session, despite the support given to presidential embargoes by Hamilton's friends, Madison was pessimistic about Congressional support for economic retaliation. "Measures of this sort are not the fashion," he wrote to Jefferson on May 25. "To supplicate for peace, and under the uncertainty of success, to prepare for war by taxes & troops is the policy which now triumphs under the patronage of the Executive. Every attack on G. B. thro' her commerce is at once discomfited; & all the taxes, that is to say excise, stamps, & c. are carried by decided majorities."[26]

On balance, the first session of the third Congress was less favorable to Madison's positions than the previous session. His own commercial propositions were passed over for stronger measures of economic retaliation; but non-importation, the one measure that commanded the greatest support from him and other Republicans, was defeated in the Senate. The only form of economic coercion that survived to the end of the session was the discretionary power to levy embargoes given to a President who gave no signs that he intended to use it. New excise taxes that Madison opposed, notably those on tobacco and carriages, were adopted. A stamp tax was defeated in the House only by a maneuver that "poisoned" it for some Federalists—it was amended to apply to sales of public securities.[27] Large increases of the regular army were defeated in the House; but a bill was enacted providing for the construction of six new frigates. The House turned to a special committee rather than the Treasury Department for recommendations as to the need and sources for new revenue; but the composition of this committee, despite Madison's membership in it, was such that Hamilton was able to get his own views into its report.[28] Another investigation of the Treasury Department, which the Secretary himself had called for on December 16 and which was conducted by a special committee dominated by men unfriendly to Hamilton, quietly submitted an exonerative report at the close of the session.[29] Because the House approved an amendment moved by Madison, the Neutrality Act of June, 1794 did not include a section forbidding sales in the United States of prizes taken by foreign (i.e., French) ships; but the Senate defeated a House bill that would have permitted payment of advances on the French debt.[30] Madison's friend Monroe was selected by Washington to be the new minister to France; but Jay, whose bias for Britain equalled Monroe's for France, had been selected for the special mission to London.

Madison saw Washington as a major obstacle to the Republicans. On May 25 he wrote to Jefferson: "The influence of the Ex. on events, the use made of them, and the public confidence in the P. are an overmatch for all the efforts Republicanism can make. The party of that sentiment in the Senate is compleatly wrecked; and in the H. of Reps in a much worse condition than at an earlier period in the Session." Reviewing the session a year later, he said that the "popularity" of Washington's "great and venerable name" was often invoked to gain support for "unpalatable measures."[31]

While Madison was away from Philadelphia between the sessions of Congress, President Washington received fresh reports of increasing troubles in collecting the excise tax on whiskey in western Pennsylvania. In October, he sent about fifteen thousand militiamen from Pennsylvania, Virginia, Maryland, and New Jersey to assist the tax collectors.

Madison seems to have taken very little interest in this "Whiskey Rebellion" until he returned to Philadelphia in mid-October. His mind had been on matters more personal; on September 15, he married Dolly Payne Todd, with whom he had become acquainted during the spring of this year. Perhaps, too, he received little information about public events during the summer. Certainly he no longer had the kind of information about the President and his cabinet which he had obtained when Jefferson was Secretary of State. Randolph, Jefferson's successor, was not the frequent and confidential correspondent he had been for fourteen years, and as a mediator between Hamilton's point of view and that of his critics in the opposition party, he was less inclined to detail complaints or provide full expositions of cabinet discussions.

Madison had no sympathy for the "real authors" of the resistance to federal tax collectors. Like Daniel Shays, they were "doing the business of Despotism," because of "the general tendency of insurrections to increase the momentum of power."[32] At the same time, he was worried that Hamilton and his friends were exploiting the troubles in Pennsylvania for their own political advantage. The "whiskey rebels" he found were functioning somewhat the way Genêt had a year before. Just as Genêt's supporters agreed with Madison on matters of domestic and foreign policy, so did the "whiskey rebels" and their sympathizers. But just as Genêt's transgressions and improprieties alienated those who placed value upon constituted authorities and established proprieties, so did the resisters to tax collections alienate those who placed value upon law, order, and majority rule.

Madison was especially annoyed at the attempts that were being made to link rebellious taxpayers in Pennsylvania to various political clubs that had been organized recently to propagate principles of government similar to those he himself had championed in his essays in the *National Gazette*.[33] One of these clubs in South Carolina was known as The Madisonian Society;[34] generally they were known as Democratic or Republican Societies. Madison never joined or contributed to the financial support of any of these societies, but he agreed with their basic beliefs and resented vilification of their members by those who viewed them as Jacobin terrorists or as unqualified to form voluntary associations because they were mere shopkeepers and mechanics. Washington's reprimand of "certain self-created societies" in his message to Congress on November 19, Madison wrote to Monroe, was "the greatest error of his political life."[35]

Not only were these societies being unfairly linked with the tax troubles in Pennsylvania, but attempts were being made in turn to link them with the Republican opposition in Congress. "The game was," Madison explained to Monroe, "to connect the Republicans in Congs with those Societies—to put the P. ostensibly at the head of the other party, in opposition to both, and by these means prolong the illusions in the North, & try a new experiment on the South."[36]

Madison's strategy to defeat those who were trying to link the Republicans to the Whiskey Rebellion was to minimize public differences between them and the President. He expressed no sympathy for those who disobeyed the law and made no condemnation of the President's sending an armed force into the disaffected areas of Pennsylvania. He praised the use of state militias and cited the expedition as evidence of the ability to enforce the laws without the use of the regular army. He also minimized the role of the administration in the success of the operation by praising the ready support given by the American people to law enforcement.[37]

As a member of a three-man committee to compose a reply to the President's message, Madison favored silence on the subject of "self-created societies."[38] He undoubtedly assumed that his own privately expressed views on this subject could not command majority support in the House and believed that silence was preferable to a statement expressing approbation of the President's remarks. He said little during five days of acrimonious debate on the committee text. On the fourth day of the debate, in a brief statement, he took a position similar to that which had been voiced in the Virginia Statute of Religious Freedom: governments should neither censure nor punish people for their opinions.[39] The reply finally approved by the House, although not exactly what he had recommended, was, he reported to Jefferson, considered a Republican victory by those who voted against it.[40]

From the beginning of the session, Madison had been bothered that an attempt would be made to sanction employment of the army in law enforcement. When he first came back to Philadelphia in mid-October he had found that "conversation ran high for a standing army to enforce the laws." The attempt might have been made, he wrote to Monroe, if the President had supported it, if the insurrection had not been suppressed by the several state militias, and "if the temper of N. England had not been dreaded on this point."[41]

Neither Madison nor his opponents ever came to the point of demanding an explicit affirmation or denial of presidential use of the army for law enforcement. Madison merely attempted to specify positively the purposes for which the army should be used. He was not successful. On February 13, he obtained only 26 votes for his motion to confine the army to frontier defense.

On the same day, he voted for a motion—defeated by a vote of 44 to 36—which stated that the purposes of the army were protection against foreign invasion and Indian tribes.[42]

In February, 1795, need for the army was less than a year before. The threat of war with Great Britain had subsided, and the Indians of the Northwest had been subdued since Wayne's army defeated them at Fallen Timbers in August, 1794. Nevertheless, the army was not reduced in size. On the same day that the House rejected motions specifying the purposes of the army, it also rejected by a vote of 58 to 25 a motion to reduce the army to twenty-five hundred men whenever there was peace with the Indians. Commenting upon the several motions defeated on February 13, Madison wrote to Jefferson: "I am extremely sorry to remark a growing apathy to the evil and danger of standing armies."[43]

This second session of the third Congress was the last that received reports and recommendations from Hamilton. On January 19, 1795, the Secretary of Treasury submitted to the House a record of past revenue acts and provisions for funding the debt together with recommendations for additional measures to extinguish the principal of the national debt within the next thirty years. On February 2, he submitted a report for the improvement and management of the public revenues.

Madison made no analysis of these reports in the House. What he had to say about the debt and taxes was put into a speech delivered three days before the first of Hamilton's reports came to Congress. Privately, to Jefferson, he described the "valedictory" report of January 19 as "arrogant," but the objections which he offered to its recommendations were perfunctory in tone.[44]

For five years, Madison had been a persistent critic of the outgoing Secretary of Treasury. He had been a pertinacious critic of his plan for funding the public debts, tax proposals, banking policies, and management of debt-funding transactions. He had also come into conflict with Hamilton's views on the diplomatic powers of the President, French and British policy, the European war, employment of economic measures as a weapon of diplomacy, the worth and nature of revolutionary changes taking place in France, and the formation of societies in the United States to proclaim republican principles of government and sympathy for the French Republic.

A systematic review of Madison's responses to Hamiltonian policies is a convenient framework for summarizing the story of

Madison's leadership of the opposition in the House during these five years. Such a review, however, should not be permitted to leave an impression that his opposition was directed against Hamilton personally. If Madison was motivated by a personal dislike of Hamilton to criticize the policies of the Secretary, he succeeded almost completely in sublimating his hostility in his public speeches and his private correspondence. Usually his statements condemning Hamilton's policies failed to discriminate between the Secretary of Treasury and men in Congress and the executive branch who supported them. When he expressed fear or disgust with these policies, he rarely mentioned Hamilton by name.

It should be noted, too, that he was seldom alone in his criticisms of Hamilton's policies. On most issues, there were perhaps a dozen men who were just as ready as he was to speak out against Hamilton's recommendations and practices. The conflict between Madison and Hamilton appears to have been entirely a conflict of policies. Each man was the spokesman for a point of view that had strong support in different segments of the electorate and the government. A large majority of Virginia's congressmen and state legislators agreed with Madison's positions. This same basic conflict of course was also central to the differences between Hamilton and Jefferson, but in the latter relationship one can easily perceive a readiness on the part of each man to express his personal distaste for the temperament, personality, and methods of the other.

After February, 1795, with Hamilton no longer in the cabinet, Madison's criticisms of administration policies necessarily had to take on the appearance of opposing Washington alone. In his private correspondence, since 1793, he had not been inclined to excuse the President for approving Hamilton's policies. Indeed, he had placed upon Washington the main responsibility for their acceptance by the public and the Congress. Publicly, however, he had not yet criticized the President directly. Within a few months the great debate on Jay's Treaty was to be the occasion for severe attacks in the press upon Washington, but Madison even then remained reluctant to say publicly what many of his journalistic friends were saying.

After the "fatiguing" session that ended March 3, 1795, Madison wrote an anonymous pamphlet entitled *Political Observations* in which he defended the foreign policy and tax measures which he had advocated in the third Congress. Largely an exposition of the economic-reprisal measures proposed in the first session, he argued that events since the spring of 1794 had completely vindicated his policies. He did not yet have authoritative details as to the terms of the treaty signed by Jay on November 19, 1794, but its expected benefits he attributed to British fears caused by the Congressional threat of economic retaliation and by French military victories in 1794.

Madison wrote his *Observations* in response to the urgings of his political friends. He wrote the pamphlet while on the way home, at a time when he was impatient to be with his family but with the advantage of having the whole subject fresh in his memory and familiar to his "reflections."[45]

Looking at the pamphlet thirty-two years later, he felt apologetic about its prevailing "tone," which he said could "be explained if not excused by the epoch which gave birth to it."[46] As a matter of fact, in comparison with other political polemics of that epoch, his *Observations* were devoid of malice and only mildly partisan. He asserted that supporters of the commercial propositions were the most vigorous champions and defenders of republican liberty, but he made no direct charges that their opponents were monarchists or aristocrats. He introduced the essay as a refutation of fallacious charges made "against the Southern members of Congress in general, and particularly against the Representatives of Virginia." He did not report and interpret the proceedings of the third Congress as a contest between Federalists and Republicans.

An official text of Jay's Treaty arrived in Philadelphia on March 7, four days after the third Congress adjourned. Not until June 8 did the President submit the treaty to a special session of the Senate, and not until June 28 did the Senate, after excluding article twelve dealing with the West India trade, give its approval by the narrow margin of one vote. Even then Washington hesitated to put his signature to the final ratification. He had had serious doubts about the merits of the treaty even as he had submitted it to the Senate; he was bombarded with protests against the treaty; he was uncertain as to the procedure to follow when the Senate struck out part of a treaty; and he was advised by Secretary Randolph not to sign at a time when reports were being received that British ships continued to seize American grain as contraband. Not until August 18, after he thought he had evidence which suggested that Randolph's motives for withholding ratification were deviously and treacherously connected with the French minister Fâuchet, did he finally sign.[47]

Assuming that he could have no influence with the President, Madison had refrained from speaking to him about the treaty.[48] He also had no desire to debate the subject in the press, as Hamilton was doing under the pseudonym Camillus.

"Hamilton is really a colossus to the anti-republican party," Jefferson wrote to him. "Without numbers, he is an host within himself. ... We have only middling performances to oppose him. In truth, when he comes forward, there is nobody but yourself can meet him."[49]

Madison did not, as he had done two summers before, yield to his friend's plea. He made a detailed analysis of the treaty, and he was no less vehement in his denunciations of it than he had been of the presidential proclamation of 1793, but this time he preferred to disseminate his arguments through his private correspondence. His first public critique was presented in the next session of Congress.[50]

Madison was well informed about the great furor aroused by the treaty. At no time after August, 1795, did he doubt that majority opinion in the country supported his own position. He was not sure, however, that approval by the Senate and President could be annulled in the House of Representatives. Throughout the first session of the fourth Congress (December 7, 1795–June 1, 1796) he was keenly aware of latent advantages favorable to those who were giving support to what Jay and Washington had done. He knew that complaints against Britain were not so great as they had been when Jay's mission had been initiated; that defenders of Jay were carrying out a vigorous campaign of propaganda and applying financial pressures to sway doubters in the mercantile communities of the cities; that specific terms in the treaty would be overlooked by advocates of peace who were persuaded that it was the only alternative to war; that the country was enjoying economic prosperity produced by the great boom in exports and shipping which accompanied the war in Europe; and that many who had doubts still had great trust in President Washington. He was perplexed as to the best strategy for counteracting these factors and vexed by the difficulties in uniting the opponents of the treaty in support of a single course of action.[51]

President Washington transmitted the treaty to both houses of Congress on March 1, 1796, the day after he proclaimed it in effect. Then, for the first time, the House had an official copy for consideration.

Debate on the subject of Jay's Treaty and the constitutional powers of the House with respect to treaties generally occupied the House in March and April. On April 6, Madison made a long speech in which he defended House jurisdiction over treaties insofar as an exercise of the delegated powers of Congress was required to put them into effect. He also argued for the right of the House to obtain information and documents from the executive without specifying a purpose. On the same day, by large majorities, the House approved resolutions which embodied his positions.[52]

On April 14 debate began on a resolution for carrying into effect Jay's Treaty. Madison spoke on April 15. In a letter to Jefferson three days later he was somewhat optimistic about defeating the treaty by a majority nearly the same as had asserted House jurisdiction over treaties. By April 23, however, he was reporting that his earlier estimate of a majority of 20 had dwindled to 8 or 9. Within the next week, his expected majority dwindled further. By April 30, it was no longer a majority at all; by a vote of 51 to 48, the House approved a resolution asserting the expediency of making "necessary appropriations for carrying the Treaty with Great Britain into effect."[53]

Madison explained this final outcome as the result of those factors which he all along had feared might bring about victory for the "treaty party."[54] His outlook was gloomy as he commented upon the political scene to his friends Jefferson and Monroe. On May 22 he wrote:

A crisis, which ought to have been so arranged as to fortify the Republican cause, has left it in a very crippled condition; from which its recovery will be the more difficult, as the elections in N. York, Massachusetts, and other States, where the prospects were favorable, have taken a wrong turn under the impression of the moment. Nothing but auspicious contingencies abroad or at home, can regain the lost ground. Peace in Europe would have a most salutary influence, and accounts just received from France revive in some degree hope of it with the Emperor, which will hasten, of course, a peace with England. On the other hand, a scene rather gloomy is presented by a letter I have just received from Col. Monroe.[55]

Madison received numerous, lengthy, and confidential reports from Monroe on political developments within France and on the course of the European war.[56] Since the summer of 1795, he had received several letters telling of the angry indignation of French officials against Jay's Treaty, which they thought incompatible with the letter and spirit of the treaties of 1778. The gloomy letter which he had just received when he wrote to Jefferson on May 22, 1796, was dated February 27. It told of his efforts, barely successful, to persuade the French government not to send an envoy extraordinary to the United States. Monroe was convinced that such a mission at that time would fail and might lead to war between the two countries.[57]

Hopes that the strong opposition to Jay's Treaty in the United States might lead to a repudiation of the treaty in the House of Representatives or in the next presidential election tended to postpone ultimatums and retaliatory measures by the French. In his letters to Monroe, Madison reported on public and Congressional opinion. He was, we may presume, willing for such reports to influence the French to hope for a change of policy at Philadelphia, but he never explicitly pointed to the opposition as a reason for them to withhold retaliatory measures against the United States. He was careful not to say anything that might suggest a political cooperation between Republicans in the United States and the French government.

Madison never sought political help from French officials. Because of his known sentiments toward France, he was necessarily brought into personal contact with the French minister in Philadelphia and other agents of the French government, but he never said or did anything that might embarrass him if reported in the press. He gave no encouragement to French officials to propagandize in the United States for candidates and measures which he approved. When correspondence between the Secretary of State and the French minister was published by the latter in 1796 in an attempt to influence the election, he sensed that the Republicans would lose support among those who agreed with Washington that foreign governments should stay out of American domestic politics.[58]

He was also sensitive to the possibilities of exploiting reports from Monroe that inadvertently reflected upon the cause of republicanism. He called Monroe's attention to the way some of his adverse comments upon the Jacobins had been taken from his dispatches and published in the press for the purpose of discrediting the Democratic societies in the United States.[59]

In 1794, 1795, and 1796, Madison said little about internal changes in France and the fate of the Revolution. In his *Observations* of April, 1795, he wrote that "splendid objects" were still visible "through the gloom of revolution" and termed the French Revolution "a blessing to mankind and bulwark to their own," but he said as much about the value of French commerce and French military victories to the United States.[60] In his letters to Monroe he was much more inquisitive about the course of the war than the course of the Revolution. He continued to express a hope for French victories because he realized that French successes placed the United States in a more favorable bargaining position with regard to the English.

The forthcoming presidential election was a subject of discussion in the exchange of letters between Madison and Monroe in 1796. Madison as early as February 26 predicted that Washington would not serve another term and said that the Republicans, "knowing that Jefferson alone can be started with hope of success, mean to push him." Monroe, writing on July 5, forecast an improvement in French relations if there were a change of administration; he "earnestly" hoped for the election of Jefferson and his consent to serve.[61]

In February, Madison feared that Jefferson might "mar the project and ensure the adverse election by a peremtory and public protest." He knew that Jefferson had continued to express his determination to remain in private life. As late as December, 1796, Jefferson was still protesting his lack of interest in the presidency, but at no time did he "mar the project" by announcing his refusal to serve if elected. In the late summer and fall Madison avoided Jefferson in order to give him no opportunity "of protesting to his friends against being embarked in the contest."[62]

While justifying his own retirement from public office at great length, Jefferson did not hesitate to urge Madison to stay in Congress and become a candidate for the presidency. On December 28, 1794, he wrote: "I do not see, in the minds of those with whom I converse, a greater affliction than the fear of your retirement; but this must not be, unless to a more splendid and more efficacious post. There I should rejoice to see you. I have long had much in mind to say to you on that subject. But double delicacies have kept me silent." On April 27, 1795, he wrote: " . . . I expressed my hope of the only change of position I ever wished to see you make, and I expressed it with entire sincerity, because there is not another person in the United States, who being placed at the helm of our affairs, my mind would be so completely at rest for the fortune of our political bark. The wish, too, was pure, and unmixed with anything respecting myself personally." On December 17, 1796, he wrote: "The first wish of my heart was, that you should have been proposed for the administration of the government."[63]

In reply to Jefferson's letter of December 28, 1794, Madison said that "reasons of *every kind*, and some of them of the most insuperable as well as *obvious kind*, shut my mind against the admission of any idea such as you seem to glance at." Anything further on the subject of the presidential election, he said, should be said in private conversation.[64]

What the two men wrote to each other about the presidential election is easier to document than what they said to other people. The presumption must be that Madison worked actively to achieve Jefferson's election. While he was in Philadelphia during the session of Congress that ended on June 1, 1796, he was in a position to speak with other Republicans in behalf of Jefferson and judging from allusions in his correspondence with Monroe and John Beckley one may safely surmise that he did so.[65] Jefferson, on the other hand, at Monticello, would have had to advocate Madison's candidacy by mail. He seems not to have done so; his strong desire that Madison become President was not expressed in writing to other Republicans.

When Madison returned to Philadelphia for the last session of the fourth Congress (December 5, 1796–March 3, 1797), the outcome of the presidential election was still in doubt. On December 19 he wrote to Jefferson telling him that he must be prepared to accept the vice presidency. Later, in January, he also strongly implied that Jefferson should maintain a position of aloofness toward President-elect Adams; he advised against sending a letter in which Jefferson would have made friendly overtures to the incoming President. Madison was more skeptical than Jefferson about Adams' following an acceptable course as President. The Republicans would probably have to oppose his administration he said, and such a letter in the possession of the President might become an embarrassment to them.[66]

Washington and Madison faced this last session of the fourth Congress with the knowledge that they would not be in public office when the next Congress met. This prospect seems to have had little effect on the public conduct of either man. The irritations that Washington expressed privately about the opposition party and that Madison expressed about the President were not vented on the eve of their retirement from politics. As in December, 1794 and 1795, so in 1796, Madison continued to follow a course of avoiding both damnation and laudation of Washington.

Once again in this session Madison was a member of the committee that composed a first draft of the House reply to the

President's address to Congress. Passages in the committee draft commendatory of Washington were sharply attacked by William B. Giles. Madison took no part in the debate on the text but voted for retention of a sentence which expressed an earnest wish that Washington's example should guide his successors. Madison voted with fifty-three members of the House for retention of the sentence, but only three other men from Washington's home state voted as he did. Eight of twenty-four votes cast for deletion of the sentence came from Virginia; seven members of the delegation did not vote.[67]

Neither in the House debates of this session nor in his private correspondence did Madison make a retrospective evaluation of Washington's presidency. His remarks about Washington, as they had invariably been in the past, appeared in a discussion of current policy. In this last session of the fourth Congress it was the growing friction with France that worried him. How would Washington respond to reports of recent French seizures of American ships in the West Indies? The President's statements to Congress in this session were not unsatisfactory, but he feared that Washington might be influenced by his close advisers to adopt a more belligerent policy toward France before his term expired.[68]

Madison also failed to leave us a retrospective view of his own career in the House of Representatives. If he had done so, it surely would have been an account of repeated frustrations and failures. Except for the first session of the first Congress, he had failed in every major attempt to shape constitutional interpretation, domestic legislation, and foreign policy. His role of leadership in organizing the opposition party was recognized by his colleagues in Congress, but in the end this leadership had been in vain.

The opposition was never able to overcome four advantages of the administration party: (1) Washington's popularity; (2) a constitutional apportionment that rendered the opposition weaker in the Senate than in the House; (3) a constitutional grant of power that gave the Senate greater control than the House over foreign affairs; and (4) a reluctance in Congress to risk policies that might jeopardize the booming prosperity that came to the United States from expanding its trade with both sides in the European war.

Historians of the distant future were to assign to him a significant role in history as one of the founders of the two-party system. Madison himself was not conscious of his role in creating a new political institution. And there is nothing to indicate that he ever expected to gain subsequent fame from his leadership of the opposition party in the 1790's. In his octogenarian memoir he recalled that

He had become wearied with public life, and longed for a return to a state in which he could indulge his relish for the intellectual pleasures of the closet, and the pursuits of rural life, the only resource of his future support. He had also in the year 1794 entered the married state, with a partner who favoured these views, and added every happiness to his life which female merit could impart. In retiring from the public service at that juncture, he had the example of Geo. Washington and his testimony of the prosperous condition of the Country.[69]

CHAPTER IX

Winning a National Majority

MADISON'S FUTURE POLITICAL PLANS WERE NOT DISCLOSED to his correspondents upon his retirement from Congress; whether he thought of himself as retiring permanently from politics he did not make known. For some indeterminate period, at least, he had apparently resolved to be free of public office. Even the thought of a month or two in Richmond was distasteful to him as he ended his service in Philadelphia. To his father he wrote on March 12, 1797, that he was "sincere and inflexible" in his determination not to become a candidate for the legislature: "If Mr. Jefferson should call & say anything to counteract my determination I hope it will be regarded as merely expressive of his own wishes on the subject, & that it will not be allowed to have the least effect."[1]

He was also averse to writing for the press. He felt justified in leaving this task to others because his time was taken up by "a crowd and weight of indispensable occupations" which would be "very tedious to explain."[2]

Jefferson, of the opinion that certain letters appearing in the press under the pseudonym Marcellus required rebuttal and ascribing them to Hamilton, made the same flattering plea that he had made in his letters of July 7, 1793 and September 21, 1795. He wrote to Madison on April 5, 1798: "You must, my dear Sir, take up your pen against this champion. You know the ingenuity of his talents; and there is not a person but yourself who can foil him. For heaven's sake, then, take up your pen, and do not desert the public cause altogether."[3]

Madison took a different view of the letters. They seemed less "threatening" to him than to Jefferson, and they did not have the marks of Hamilton's style. If they must be answered, Madison replied, others were more favorably situated than he to do so "with advantage & effect."[4]

His refusal to serve in the legislature and to write for the press did not mean that he was closing his mind to the issues of politics. His correspondence with Jefferson continued as it had in the years since 1793. Now however the roles of the two men were reversed. Jefferson provided news from the capital, while Madison reported on opinion and conditions in Virginia.

Madison had been less sanguine than Jefferson about the incoming Adams administration, and he continued to be distrustful throughout 1797. He doubted the sincerity and seriousness of negotiations with France. "Nothing but the most cordial dispositions on both sides," he believed, could overcome the difficulties which Jay's Treaty had placed in the way of an adjustment between the United States and France.[5]

The second year of Adams' presidency was even more deplorable to Madison. All that had caused him anxiety for the future during the last Congress under Washington seemed to be coming to fruition: military and naval preparations for war, severance of commercial relations with France, the equating of a friendly or peaceful disposition toward France with sedition, accusations that the opposition party was secretly in league with the French government against the government of the United States, land taxes for new military and naval expenditures rather than for redemption of the national debt, fear that the regular army would be used for law enforcement, suppression of the Republican opposition by means of the Alien and Sedition laws, war on the side of England perhaps, and "warping the public mind towards Monarchy."[6]

In February, 1798, Madison wrote that "public opinion alone can save us from our hot-headed Executive."[7] Letters commenting upon Adams in April, May, and June referred to his follies, violent passions, heretical policies, degrading language, and grotesque and tragicomic acting.[8] As President, it seemed to him, Adams was completely confirming Franklin's characterization of him as "always an honest man, often a wise one, but sometimes wholly out of his senses."[9] In its invidious hostility, a comparison of Adams with Washington was unique in Madison's lifetime correspondence:

There never was perhaps a greater contrast between two characters than between those of the present President & his predecessor, altho' it is the boast & prop of the present that he treads in the steps of his predecessor. The one cool considerate & cautious, the other headlong & kindled into flame by every spark that lights on his passions: the one ever scrutinizing into the public opinion, and ready to follow where he could not lead it; the other insulting it by the most adverse sentiments & pursuits. W. a hero in the field, yet overweighing every danger in the Cabinet—A. without a single pretension to the character of a soldier, a perfect Quixotte as a statesman: the former chief magistrate pursuing peace every where with sincerity, tho' mistaking the means; the latter taking as much pains to get into war, as the former to keep out of it. The contrast might be pursued into a variety of other particulars—the policy of the one in shunning connections with the arrangements of Europe, of the other in holding out the U.S. as a makeweight in the Balances of power; the avowed exultation of W. in the progress of liberty every where, & his eulogy on the Revolution & people of France posterior even to the bloody reign & fate of Robespierre—the open denunciations by Adams of the smallest disturbance of the ancient discipline order & tranquility of despotism, &x &c &c.[10]

The harsh terms that Madison used in 1798 to castigate Adams were applied to no other man during his entire career.

Madison and Jefferson expressed the hope that the extreme measures adopted by Congress in the summer of 1798 would provoke a public reaction against them.[11] Jefferson was more specific than Madison in suggesting that the new land taxes would be the main cause for a change of opinion. On September 26, 1798, he wrote to Archibald Hamilton Rowan: "The purse of the people is the real seat of sensibility. It is to be drawn upon largely, and they will then listen to truths which could not excite them through any other organ."[12] On November 26, 1798, he wrote to John Taylor: "Indeed, the Doctor is now on his way to cure it [XYZ delusion], in the guise of a tax gatherer ... this ["excessive taxation"] ... will carry reason & reflection to everyman's door, particularly in the hour of election."[13] To Archibald Stuart, he wrote on May 14, 1799: " ... as long as the presses can be protected, we may trust to them for light; still more perhaps to the taxgatherers."[14]

But there were days in 1797, 1798, and 1799, when Jefferson despaired of winning a national majority to his side. Disunion he ruled out in a long letter to John Taylor, June 1, 1798,[15] but he was not averse to lawful means by which state governments under the control of Republicans might be used to combat federal power. General statements about the necessity of relying on the state governments for protection and specific proposals which he sought to have brought before the Virginia Assembly began to appear in his correspondence during the first year of Adams' administration.[16] As early as August, 1797, asserting that an appeal to Congress would be futile, he turned to the Virginia House of Delegates for a protest against the charge made by a federal grand jury that Samuel J. Cabell and other Virginia congressmen circulated letters to their constituents which disseminated calumnies against the government of the United States.[17] In September, 1798, he drafted resolutions for a state legislature to declare the Alien and Sedition laws unconstitutional.[18] In early October he approved an arrangement by which these resolutions were to be introduced in the Kentucky legislature.[19] Also, in October, 1798, he proposed petitioning the Virginia legislature to enact legislation requiring election of jurors and providing compensation for Virginians who suffered penalities from the Sedition Act.[20] In November, 1798, he recommended to Madison, Wilson Cary Nicholas, and John Taylor that the Virginia legislature adopt resolutions similar to those introduced in the Kentucky legislature.[21]

As disturbed as he was by the trend of events, Madison, in his replies to Jefferson, avoided approving in general terms a strategy of seeking protection from state governments; he offered no objections to Jefferson's remarks on the subject, but he was noncommital in his responses. Furthermore, nothing in the record points to Madison as the originator of any of the procedures which Jefferson proposed in August, 1797 and October, 1798.

Nothing is known with certainty about his having a role in drafting the resolutions which John Breckinridge introduced in the Kentucky legislature on November 8, 1798. He may well have known nothing of them before he visited Jefferson at Monticello in October.[22] He probably saw a text of the resolutions for the first time when he received a letter of November 17, 1798, in which Jefferson stated:

I enclose you a copy of the draught of the Kentucky Resolutions. I think we should distinctly affirm all the important principles they contain, so as to hold to that ground in the future, and leave the matter in such a train as that we may not be committed absolutely to push the matter to extremities, and yet may be free to push as far as events will render prudent.[23]

Presumably Jefferson in this letter to Madison was offering advice about resolutions to be introduced in the Virginia legislature in December. It appears from this letter to Madison and from letters to John Taylor on November 26 and Wilson Cary Nicholas on November 29, that Jefferson desired the Virginia Resolutions to duplicate the resolutions which had been introduced in the Kentucky legislature on November 8.[24]

Resolutions similar to the Kentucky Resolutions were introduced in the Virginia legislature on December 10 by John Taylor. Thirty-two years later, when he was eighty years old, Madison recalled that he had penned "the draft of the resolutions offered in 1798 by the Virginia Assembly." Writing to James Robertson on March 27, 1831, he said that he had retained no copy of his own draft and he could not remember whether the resolutions as introduced by John Taylor were exactly the same as his. He was able to recall, he said, that he had described "the powers of the Federal Government as resulting from the compact to which the States *alone* are parties." He presumed but was not absolutely certain that his draft also contained the phrase "*not law, but null void and of no force and effect.*"[25]

A letter to Jefferson, December 29, 1798, indicates that Madison was satisfied when the Virginia legislature deleted from Taylor's resolutions the words "null" and "void." In this letter he pointed out that an ordinary legislature, as distinguished from a special state convention with constituent powers, was not "the legitimate organ" to make "ultimate" judgments about "infractions" of the Constitution. "This was a reason of great weight for using general expressions that would leave to other States a choice of all the modes possible of concurring in the substance, and would shield the Genl Assembly agst the charge of Usurpation in the very act of protesting agst the usurpations of Congress."[26]

The Kentucky and Virginia Resolutions of 1798 failed to aid the cause they were intended to promote. Indeed, they proved a political liability in every state in the Union.[27] Even in Virginia the Federalists found that they were a political asset, enabling them to put the Republicans on the defensive with the charge that their hidden and ultimate tendency was a disruption of the Union. They were approved by no other Southern state and condemned in resolutions adopted by the Northern legislatures.

Under these circumstances, Madison was persuaded to become a candidate for the legislature in March, 1799. Six Virginia congressmen, in urging him to become a candidate, had written in a letter of February 7, 1799: " . . . it is quite needless to point out *to you*, the powerful agency of *wise* and *firm* State measures in preserving the general government within the just Limits of the Constitution."[28] John Taylor had told him he would be needed in Richmond to reply to Patrick Henry, who was coming out of retirement to attack the Resolutions of 1798.[29]

Jefferson in the early months of 1799 showed a revived interest in the prospect of combating the Federalist measures of 1798 by a repudiation of them in the Congressional elections.[30] By the end of the summer, however, he was no longer expressing optimism about winning a national majority. He was anxious that the positions of Kentucky and Virginia be reaffirmed and, in a letter of August 23 to Madison, said that it might be necessary "to sever ourselves from that union we so much value, rather than give up the rights of self government which we have reserved, & in which alone we see liberty, safety & happiness."[31]

Madison conferred with Jefferson at Monticello about the contents of the letter of August 23. He apparently advised against any mention of disunion as an ultimate consequence of oppressive measures. In a letter to Wilson Cary Nicholas, September 5, 1799, Jefferson wrote: "Mr. M. who came, as had been proposed, does not concur in the *reservation* proposed above; and from this I recede readily, not only in deference to his judgment, but because, as we should never think of separation but for repeated and enormous violations, so these, when they occur, will be cause enough of themselves."[32]

Between August and November, 1799, circumstances changed so much that Jefferson became quite eager to follow the less provocative course advocated by Madison. By November, he was aware of a serious split in the Federalist party between the Hamilton and Adams wings, knew that the President had ordered the departure of a special mission to France, and perhaps most important of all, was encouraged by the October elections in Pennsylvania which brought the first major defeat for the Federalists since Adams was inaugurated. For the first time since 1796, Republican prospects for winning the national elections in 1800 were encouraging.

On November 22, 1799, Jefferson wrote to Madison: "Some late circumstances changing considerably the aspect of our situation, must affect the line of conduct to be observed."[33] It is in the context of Jefferson's assessment of "new circumstances" that a letter which he wrote to Madison on November 26, 1799, must be placed. All of the implications of what Jefferson presumably was saying to Madison in that letter may be indicated by placing them between brackets in the following quotation:

I mentioned that new circumstances would require consideration as to the line of conduct they would require from us. Our objects according to my ideas, should be 1. peace even with Great Britain. 2. a sincere cultivation of the Union. 3. the disbanding of the army on principles of economy and safety. 4. protestations against violations of the true principles of our constitution, merely to save them, and prevent precedent and acquiescence from being pleaded against them [as had been done in the Virginia Resolutions of 1798]; but nothing to be said or done which shall look or lead to force, and give any pretext for keeping up the army [as had been done in the Kentucky Resolutions of 1798 in those statements that referred to null and void]. If we find the monarchical party [the Federalist party] split into pure Monocrats [the High Federalists under the leadership of Hamilton] and the Anglo-monocrats [Federalists under the leadership of President Adams], we should leave them alone to manage all those points of difference [about negotiations with France, taxes, enforcement of the Alien and Sedition laws, presidential appointments, Adams' candidacy for re-election] which they may chuse to take between themselves, only arbitrating between them by our votes [in the elections of 1800], but doing nothing to hoop them together.[34]

When Madison went to Richmond as a member of the House of Delegates in December, 1799, his main task was to write and obtain approval (January 7, 1800) for a report that defended the Resolutions of 1798. Most important from the standpoint of "the line of conduct to be observed" in the light of "new circumstances" was the denial that the Resolutions of 1798 implied the use of force to nullify acts that states declared unconstitutional.[35]

The Virginia Resolutions of 1798 had been even more vague than the Kentucky Resolutions as to the ultimate sanctions to be invoked against unconstitutional acts of Congress. They had said that the states were obligated "to interpose for arresting the progress of the evil, and for maintaining within their respective limits, the authorities, rights and liberties appertaining to them." As explained by Madison in the report of January 7, 1800, interposition "for arresting the progress of the evil" meant simply that the states should express an "opinion, unaccompanied with any other effect than what they may produce on opinion by exciting reflection."[36] In other words, resolutions by state legislatures declaring a federal act unconstitutional were not different from other declarations of opinion, either by a legislative or by a non-governmental body.

Madison kept Vice President Jefferson informed about the progress of the report in the legislature.[37] He also told him about the difficulties he encountered in passing a bill of great interest to his presidential candidacy. An act designed to insure Jefferson all the electoral votes of Virginia by changing from voting by districts to voting for a statewide ticket of electors barely obtained the necessary majority.

Madison explained to Jefferson, January 18, 1800: "The plan of a Gen Ticket was so novel that a great number who wished it shrunk from the vote, and others, apprehending that their Constituents would be still more startled at it, voted against it, so that it passed by a majority of 5 votes only." Seventeen years later, James Pleasants of Virginia said in the Federal House of Representatives: "I do not believe that all the united force of its advocates could then have carried the measure through that body, but for the weight of character of James Madison."[38]

Elections held in the spring of 1799 indicated that Jefferson had a chance of losing in two or three districts in Virginia. If the presidential election of 1800 were to be as close as that of 1796, these votes might make the difference between victory and defeat. Hence the importance of this measure in the eyes of men who were working for Jefferson's election in 1800.

Jefferson prudently curtailed his letters to Madison between December, 1799 and November, 1800. In his letter of November 22—the same in which he said that the "line of conduct to be observed" must be affected by some "late circumstances"—he said that he would trust nothing to the post office during the ensuing twelve months. He knew that Madison would understand his reasons. Letters from Madison dated December 29, January 4, 9, 12, 18, and February 14 remained unacknowledged until March 4, "for reasons which were explained."[39]

Whatever Madison could do for Jefferson's candidacy in 1800 had to be done in Virginia. His most important contribution of course was in the legislature that approved the statewide-ticket bill and the report of January 7, 1800. He also was one of several prominent Virginians whose names appeared as presidential electors on the "Republican Ticket" in 1800.[40]

From the time he learned of the victory of the Republicans in New York state in May, 1800, until the House of Representatives began its ballotings on February 11, 1801, Madison was moderately confident that Jefferson would win the presidency. He foresaw the possibility that Republican electors might cast an equal number of votes for Jefferson and Burr, but probably assumed that the latter would withdraw his name rather than permit the House of Representatives to reject the former.[41] Even when some Republicans began to talk of a civil war if the Federalists attempted to select a President by an extra-legal procedure, he remained calm and presumably confident of victory.[42]

Jefferson, foreseeing "storms of a new character" for the month of February, urged Madison in a letter of December 19 to be in Washington before the beginning of the new administration: "I know that your appearance on the scene before the departure of Congress, would assuage the minority, and inspire in the majority confidence and joy unbounded, which they would spread far and wide on their journey home."[43] On February 18, the day after he was selected President by the House, Jefferson again asked Madison to come to Washington, this time suggesting that he arrive after March 4: "As you do not like to be here on that day, I wish you would come within a day or two after."[44]

On January 10 Madison explained why he could not come: "My health still suffers from several complaints, and I am much afraid that any changes that may take place are not likely for the better. The age and very declining state of my father are making also daily claims on my attention, and from appearances it may not be long before these claims may acquire their full force." In answer to Jefferson's second request, he regretted that he would have to postpone a decision because of his father's death on February 27.[45]

Not until May 1 did he arrive in Washington. The next day he was sworn in as Secretary of State. Four days later he wrote to Monroe: "I find myself in the midst of arrears of papers &c &c, which little accord with my unsettled health."[46]

The new Secretary found "the mass of business in the department, at all times considerable, swelled to an unusual size by sundry causes." During the next two months it became "absolutely necessary" for him to devote his full time to his public duties. The "feeble state of health" which he brought with him to Washington continued; by July 10, he was eager to get away for a visit to Virginia within the next two weeks. He wrote to William C. Nicholas that he was "admonished to hasten" his departure by a "slight attack of bile" to which his constitution was "peculiarly prone."[47]

CHAPTER X

Republican Secretary of State

MADISON WAS FIFTY YEARS OLD WHEN HE BECAME SECRETARY
of State. Although he was to have sixteen years of uninterrupted
public service before him, he was already beyond his physical
and mental prime. There was no faltering in his analytical and
dialectical powers, and his capacity to master factual details and
intricate reasoning remained unimpaired. But earlier sparks of
originality and explorative thought were gone. Still flexible in
tactical maneuvering, Madison as Secretary of State was largely
occupied with applying ideas of the 1790's to problems of the
next decade.

There were reasons other than ingrained habits and biological
processes for Madison's continuing to think as he had in the
1790's. First, of course, there was a widespread expectation
among Republicans that the purpose of winning power was to
put into effect what they had been championing in the opposition. The President and his Secretary of State clearly shared this
almost universal opinion among those who had fought the battle
against the Federalists for a decade. Secondly, the situation in
Europe after 1803 was sufficiently continuous with the past to
make the policies advocated by Madison while in the third and
fourth Congresses seem pertinent to the conduct of foreign
policy.

As Secretary of State, Madison was in Washington at the same
time that Jefferson was there. Occasions for the two men to write
letters to each other were few. Except for a period of about three
months in 1805, when Dolly was receiving medical treatment in
Philadelphia, what each man said to each other about foreign
policy and diplomatic negotiations was largely unrecorded.[1] At
several points, as in the 1790's, Madison may have encouraged
Jefferson to give second thoughts to his first impulses; but the
harmony of views that had prevailed in the 1790's survived un-
disturbed, despite occasional rumors to the contrary. Writing to
Jefferson on May 30, 1809, Madison said: "Nothing could exceed
the folly of supposing that the principles and opinions mani-

fested in our foreign relations were not, in the main at least, common to us."²

Negotiations to achieve the major foreign policies of the administration were carried out by the American ministers in Madrid, Paris, and London, all of whom, during Jefferson's first term, had been personally acquainted with Madison since the conventions of 1787 and 1788. These policies were formulated by the President in consultation with Madison, who in turn wrote instructions and carried out diplomatic correspondence connected with them. In Washington, Madison seldom carried out sustained negotiations comparable to those carried out in the foreign capitals. His most serious and prolonged negotiations were those undertaken in January, 1808, when he attempted to obtain redress for grievances arising from the attack of a British ship upon the *Chesapeake*.³

With only a few exceptions, the men with whom Madison negotiated in Washington were condescending or contemptuous toward the new republic to which they were assigned. Prejudiced in advance against American institutions and customs, repelled by what they considered the crass cupidity of Americans as money-makers, residing in a sprawling, half-built village which splashed mud on them in the winter and suffocated them with heat in the summer, subjected to what they considered deliberate indignities in their social and official relations, they thought of themselves at the same time as having to deal with a greedy government that was incessantly grasping for more land and more commerce while their own countries were engaged in a war for survival. It is doubtful that any Republican Secretary of State could have established rapport with the European diplomats in Washington at that time. Madison did not.

Anthony Merry, the British minister from 1803 to 1806, believed that the party of Jefferson exemplified all the worst features of American democracy. Like the French ministers in the 1790's, he was on friendly terms with the opposition leaders. He was also aghast at the new etiquette introduced by Jefferson and Madison, which the latter thought was only appropriate to "true Republican principles," but which impressed the Secretary of the British legation as demagogic posing for electioneering purposes. Whatever their motives, Merry was not forgiving of their conduct. When the President and Secretary of State failed to assign him and his wife the conventional place of honor among their dinner guests, he refused further invitations.

Madison informed Monroe in London that no affront was intended and was in turn assured that Merry's complaints were causing no real trouble in negotiations with the British ministry.[4]

The one diplomatic triumph of the Jefferson administration was the treaty with France providing for the cession of Louisiana. This treaty transferred to the United States far more territory that Madison had asked for in his instructions to the American negotiators in Paris. At one time it seemed that even the small amount of territory sought could not be obtained without the use of force and an alliance with Great Britain, but the President played for time, staved off Congressional impetuosity, and ultimately the vicissitudes of European war and diplomacy presented the kind of opportunity that Madison and Jefferson liked to exploit to American advantage. Napoleon, confronted with a costly rebellion in Haiti, decided that he could not afford a great empire in North America and war in Europe simultaneously. In April, 1803, he offered to sell to the United States the whole of Louisiana (all of the present-day states of Arkansas, Iowa, Missouri, and Nebraska; and parts of Louisiana, Minnesota, Oklahoma, Kansas, Colorado, Wyoming, Montana, North Dakota, and South Dakota).

The major disputes with Spain and Great Britain remained unresolved while Madison was Secretary of State. The Spanish government grudgingly acquiesced in the transfer of Louisiana to the United States but firmly rejected Jefferson's and Madison's definitions of its boundaries and refused to sell any of its territory along the Gulf Coast. In Britain, Rufus King was able to negotiate two conventions dealing with debts and boundaries and came very close to achieving an agreement about impressment, but interference with American shipping and seizures of American seamen increased, especially after 1805. In 1806 William Pinkney and James Monroe negotiated a treaty which obtained British concessions affecting trade with the West Indies, but it made no reference to impressment, failed to provide indemnifications for past spoliations and was less favorable than Jay's Treaty in its provisions for trade with the British East Indies. It fell considerably short of fulfilling Madison's instructions to the American negotiators.[5]

In 1807 hostility toward Britain was greater than at any time since 1794. By an Order in Council of January 7, 1807, neutral ships were to be seized if they attempted to trade between European ports from which British ships were excluded. On

March 3, the British minister in Washington showed Madison and Jefferson a copy of the treaty which Monroe and Pinkney had signed on December 31, 1806. Madison expressed "the greatest astonishment and disappointment" that it contained nothing on impressment and said he "thought it would be impossible to ratify without that."[6] President Jefferson declined to ask for a special session of the Senate to ratify the treaty. Monroe and Pinkney were instructed to resume negotiations, but in the ensuing months they were not able to obtain what they had failed to obtain in 1806. On June 22, 1807, the British ship *Leopard* attacked the American warship *Chesapeake*, killing three seamen, injuring eighteen, and impressing four others from the crew. Thereupon the President barred American ports to British warships, demanded reparations, alerted the state militias to be ready for war, and assigned gunboats for the defense of New York, Charleston, New Orleans, and Chesapeake Bay.

Jefferson thought the country more excited than at any time since the Battle of Lexington. Nevertheless, he decided to leave the "question of war, non-importation, and other measures, uncommitted" to Congress. On July 4, in consultation with the cabinet, he decided to summon Congress to meet on October 26, unless new occurrences should render an earlier call necessary.[7]

In a letter of July 17 to Monroe, Madison described the continuing "insolence and hostility" of the British squadron in American waters:

Merchant vessels arriving and departing have been challenged, fired at, examined and detained within our jurisdiction, with as little scruple as if they were at open sea. Even a Revenue Cutter conveying the Vice President and his sick daughter from Washington to New York and wearing her distinctive and well known colours did not escape insult. Not satisfied with these outrages, the British Commodore Douglass advanced into Hampton Roads with his whole squadron ... to Norfolk; and actually blockaded the town by forcibly obstructing all water communication with it. ... These enormities superadded to all that have gone before to say nothing of British violences against our vessels in foreign ports, as in Lisbon and Canton, form a mass of injuries and provocations which have justly excited the indignant feelings of the nation and severely tried the patience of the Government.[8]

On July 30, Jefferson issued a presidential proclamation calling Congress to meet on October 26 to consider "great and

weighty matters claiming the consideration of the Congress."
On December 18, he sent a short message to the House and
Senate proposing an embargo on American exports. Along with
his message he submitted the text of a recent Order in Council
which directed British warships to remove all British seamen
from neutral ships. By this time, he had also received English
newspapers that were forecasting further restrictions on neutral
trade with Europe, but he omitted references to them in the
final draft of his message.[9] Already, about five weeks before the
embargo message, the British ministry had in fact imposed new
restrictions. By an Order in Council of November 11, 1807,
neutral vessels desiring to trade with ports from which British
carriers were excluded, in order to avoid seizure by the Royal
Navy, were required to obtain licenses and pay imposts in British-controlled ports. When the embargo was enacted, Madison
wrote two months later, the "language of the British Gazettes
with other indications" left little doubt that Orders such as
those of November 11 were "meditated."[10]

Napoleon's reply to the British Orders in Council of November 11 made it impossible for American ships to comply with
them without subjecting themselves to seizure if they entered
continental ports under French control or if they happened to
encounter French privateers on the high seas. His Milan De-
cree of December 17, 1807 announced that all ships sailing
from British-controlled ports or submitting to the Orders in
Council would be dealt with as if they were British ships.

British and French seizures of American cargoes between
1805 and 1807 did not put a stop to the expansion of trade
which had occurred since 1793. The total dollar value of American exports in 1807 was the highest of any year prior to 1835
and was more than triple the value of 1793. Fifty-five per cent
of the total exports were of foreign origin, a measure of the
volume of the American carrying trade. Although foreign-pro-
duced exports exceeded domestic exports, the dollar value of
the latter was also greater than in any year prior to 1816.[11]

The effect of the British and French restrictions of 1807 on
the volume of American trade cannot be ascertained. In 1808
American trade was drastically reduced by enforcement of
prohibitions imposed by Congress. Under the terms of the Embargo Act of December 22, 1807, no ships could carry exports
from the United States; and under the terms of a Non-Importation Act which became effective on December 14, 1807, selected items of British manufacture could not be imported into

the United States. In 1808 the dollar value of exports dropped to 22,430,000. In 1807 the total value had been 108,343,000. In 1808 the total value of imports was 56,990,000; in 1807 the figure had been 138,500,000.[12]

The economic-reprisal measures supported by the Jefferson administration in 1807 were not a result of foreign blows to over-all national prosperity. They were a response to complaints by individuals who suffered losses of property or who incurred increased operating expenses because of higher insurance rates and inconveniences necessitated by compliance with British and French requirements; to complaints against the British practice of searching American ships for suspected deserters and impressing into the British navy seamen whose citizenship was disputed by the American government; to suspicions that the British were using the war as an instrument for monopolizing European commerce rather than using commerce as a weapon of war; and to fears that exclusion of American exports from the continent of Europe in a prolonged war would ultimately threaten national prosperity, or at least deprive the United States of specie necessary to pay for that portion of British imports which could not be paid for by specie earned from American exports in Britain.

There was an almost unanimous belief among Republicans that submission without some form of retaliation would be an abdication of national honor and independence, a reversion to the inferiority of a colonial status without its benefits. Few in Congress, even among the Federalists, would publicly admit that they favored submission. On December 13, 1808, the House of Representatives, by a vote of 118 to 2, approved the following resolution: "Resolved, that the United States cannot, without a sacrifice of their rights, honor, and independence, submit to the edicts of Great Britain and France."[13]

The embargo message of December 18, 1807, followed closely a text drafted by Madison,[14] but his role in the passage of the Non-Importation Act of 1806 and the Embargo Act of 1807 is obscure. His continuing belief in the efficacy of economic retaliation is known from a recorded conversation with John Quincy Adams and from letters addressed to Jefferson, Monroe, and William Pinkney, but evidence is scant as to the exact timing and form of retaliation that he preferred.[15] Nothing is known of his attempts to influence Congress to vote for these measures.

Many years later Madison was convinced that the embargo,

"if enforced would have been effectual, and could have been enforced, if instead of relying on a fidelity to the law, violations of it had been guarded against by arming Coasting Cruisers." If "faithfully executed," he wrote to Henry Wheaton, July 11, 1824, "it would have produced a crisis in the British West Indies that might have extorted justice without a resort·to war."[16]

Madison probably held this same view in 1809; at least nothing in the documentary record contradicts such an assumption. Nevertheless, President-elect Madison made no attempt to prevent Congress replacing the Embargo with the Non-Intercourse Act of March 1, 1809; or rather nothing in the records shows that he made such an attempt.

Generally, constitutional scruples inhibited Madison's taking the initiative in obtaining legislation that he favored. When the initiative came from Congress he responded to the extent of submitting reports and diplomatic correspondence, discussing legislation with individual members in private conversation, and occasionally helping committees in the preparation of reports and legislation. He also may have attempted to influence Congressional opinion on foreign policy by writing or suggesting editorials for the Washington *National Intelligencer* and by distributing copies of his *Examination of British* [trade] *Doctrine* to members of Congress.[17]

Madison also remained aloof from party politics while he was Secretary of State. For leaving a few Federalists in the State Department, he was criticized by some Republicans.[18] He took no part in the elections of 1802, 1804, and 1806, and played a passive role in the election of 1808. His nomination and election to the presidency in 1808 was managed by others, notably by Wilson Cary Nicholas and William B. Giles of Virginia.[19] Giles told John Quincy Adams that he had "never said a word" about the election to Madison, "for he should have thought it indelicate, and he believed the same of Colonel Nicholas." Charles J. Ingersoll wrote in 1836: "It has been stated on high authority, that while a candidate for the presidency, no one, however intimate, ever heard him open his lips or say one word on the subject."[20]

The men who worked for Madison's candidacy knew of course that the Secretary of State, by not objecting to what they were doing in his behalf and by not endorsing another man, was giving tacit consent to his own nomination and election. They also observed that Jefferson was giving no support to either George Clinton of New York or James Monroe of Virginia, the only prominent Republicans who contested Madison's succession to the presidency. Because all the party leaders knew of the long-standing and intimate friendship between Jefferson and Madison, only a declaration from one of these two men in favor of another candidate could have changed the prevailing belief that the President wanted his Secretary of State to succeed him and that the latter was quite ready to do so. Jefferson and Madison remained silent as to their preferences.

Madison was carried into the presidency by the momentum of public approval for Jefferson which had been built up prior to 1807 by national prosperity and the President's skill as a party leader. Counterforces generated by discontent with the embargo on foreign trade were already operating by the fall of 1808, but they had not accumulated sufficiently to constitute a serious threat to Republican supremacy. The Republicans retained a majority in both houses of Congress, and Madison received 70 per cent of the electoral vote. George Clinton of New York, who was elected Vice President by the Republicans, received the votes of six presidential electors from New York. Charles Cotesworth Pinckney, Federalist candidate for President, received 27 per cent of the electoral votes.

CHAPTER XI

President: Republican Diplomat

A GREAT DEAL ABOUT THE POLICIES AND METHODS OF PRESI-
dent Madison will be better understood if the continuing presence of Congressman Madison is kept in mind. As President, the
author of the Helvidius Letters and the critic of Jay's Treaty was
overscrupulous in avoiding any appearance of trying to dominate
Congress, of usurping the war power of Congress, or of denying
the right and duty of Congress to initiate foreign policies of its
own or to criticize those of the executive. The President who had
opposed armies and navies in 1794 was reluctant to ask Congress
to levy taxes for military preparations—even after November,
1811, when he was already convinced that war would probably
come within a few months. The author of the commercial resolutions of January, 1794 was reluctant to abandon completely his
faith in the efficacy of economic retaliation. And in dealing with
a Congress to which the President was ever ready to accord a
wide jurisdiction in matters of foreign policy, Madison was dealing with many Republicans who continued to share his own
aversion to armies, navies, taxes, public debts, and strong executive powers.

President Madison and his Congressional supporters also had
memories of recent experiences that sustained the judgment that
their own political beliefs were the most popular at election time.
They knew what an American today would find hard to grasp—
namely, that economy in government was the strongest appeal
that could be made to the electorate. They knew that taxes levied
during the Adams administration for the expanded army and
navy were largely responsible for Federalist losses in late 1799
and in 1800. And they knew that Jeffersonian economies were
partly responsible for the election victories of 1802, 1804, 1806,
and 1808.

In his inaugural address, Madison called attention to another
memory that was to have a powerful influence on attitudes toward foreign policy during his administration. He said: "The
present situation of the world is indeed without a parallel, and

that of our country full of difficulties. The pressure of these, too, is the more severely felt because they have fallen upon us at a moment when the national prosperity being at a height not before attained, the contrast resulting from the change has been rendered the more striking."[1]

The Federalists put the blame for the interruption of national prosperity upon prohibitions enacted by Republican Congresses but agreed with Madison that the post-1807 depression was harder to bear because of the great boom that preceded it. In June, 1812, Congressman Samuel Taggart of Connecticut said in a public statement released to the press: " ... never was the export trade of the United States in a train of more successful experiment, than when it was suddenly and unexpectedly arrested by that deadly incubus, the embargo. I have sometimes heard the Northern merchant denominated the spoiled child of commercial, and the Southern cotton planter called the spoiled child of agricultural prosperity."[2]

The predicament of foreign policy during Madison's first term was this: the President and a majority in Congress wanted unmolested trade in noncontraband exports to all unblockaded ports in Europe. This aim they sought to achieve without increasing taxes, without going into debt, without building up a navy, without building up an army, without suffering the deprivations which the embargo of 1807 had entailed, and without going to war.

Excluded from President Madison's choices was a settled policy of "trade-at-your-own-risk." He seems to have assumed that such a policy would not be tolerated by a large segment of the public and that if tried by Congress would in practice give rise to incidents which would lead to a clamor for war. His own reasons, however, were seldom presented to the public or in his private correspondence. His stated objections were that such a policy would (1) surrender complete control of European trade to the country that controlled the seas, (2) be unjust in that it would hurt some American shippers more than others, (3) and be tantamount to a surrender of national independence and honor. Leaving "commerce to shift for itself," he wrote to Jefferson on July 22, 1810, "would not have borne an honorable appearance; though the discredit would have been mitigated by examples of powerful nations, and still more by the peculiarities of the actual state of the world."[3]

By "leaving commerce to shift for itself," the Madison administration would have promoted a return to the national prosperity that ended with the embargo of 1807 but would have risked incidents provocative of war. On the other hand, by following a policy of legally required economic isolation, the Madison administration would have continued the economic depression, but would have obviated those occasions upon which British and French officers humiliated American sailors and merchants; dishonorable incidents could then have occurred only to American lawbreakers.

When Madison came into the presidency, the majority in Congress had no desire to make a choice between total avoidance of the British and French restrictions and total acceptance. The great majority wanted dollars and honor. The result was a series of compromises that permitted some trade and some retaliation.

The Non-Intercourse Act of March 1, 1809, which replaced the embargo of 1807, prohibited trade with Great Britain and France as long as they continued to defy American objections to their orders and decrees, but permitted trade with neutral countries. Macon's Bill Number Two, enacted on May 1, 1810, legalized trade with all countries but permitted severance of trade with the enemy of whichever belligerent was the first to accept American terms.

Privately, Madison expressed his dislike for the act of 1810. He preferred a continuation of some form of economic coercion without interruption and feared that war would result from such a policy before an opportunity would be presented for invoking the economic reprisals for which it provided. The American people, he thought, might not tolerate the losses, injuries, and indignities that would probably arise from permitting shippers to trade at their own risk pending the establishment of satisfactory relations with one of the belligerents.[4]

Besides "trade-at-your-own-risk," President Madison excluded two other possible courses. He would not consider a written alliance for a stipulated period, and he would not engage in a naval war such as had occurred during Adams' presidency. He never presented an argument for the rejection of these two possible courses.[5]

He was willing to move to the very brink of an alliance with either Britain or France, but he was never willing to promise that he would continue to boycott or wage war against either of these countries after it had removed its barriers to American commerce. He was willing to tolerate relationships which would function the same as an alliance on a day-to-day basis, but he never left any doubt in the minds of French and British diplomats that he would make a separate agreement whenever American terms were met. He encouraged the British and French to surmise that economic coercion and war might place the United States on the side of the country that met American terms for foreign trade, as it did in 1812; but Canning and Napoleon alike were aware that he would continue to seek a separate peace, as he did during the War of 1812. One reason Foreign Minister Canning rejected the agreement which David Erskine made with Madison in April, 1809, was the fact that it did not guarantee a continuation of non-intercourse with France.[6]

Madison's reasons for withholding such a guarantee were twofold. First, under the Constitution the Congress had the power to regulate foreign trade. Secondly, he wanted to have a free hand to continue negotiations with France.

According to Madison's calculations, if a satisfactory settlement could be reached with one side, the other might be expected to come to an agreement in order to forestall a *de facto* alliance between the United States and its enemy. His strategy necessitated devious and subtle tactics. With one power he would bargain for a settlement by dangling prospects of its gaining a differential advantage over its adversary. Once, however, the settlement was reached with the first belligerent, the opportunity to remove such a disadvantage would be presented as an incentive for the second power to come to an agreement.

If not tricky, it was certainly a tortuous and precarious course which President Madison pursued. Considering the policies and means which the President and Congress ruled out, it was about the only course available to him. That it almost succeeded is a tribute to his deft craftsmanship in the conduct of American diplomacy.

The only time that Madison was truly optimistic that he would succeed was in the first five months of his presidency; that is, prior to his learning that the British ministry in London had repudiated an agreement which he negotiated with David Erskine in April. After learning the grounds of rejection and after receiving insulting and provocative communications from Erskine's successor in Washington, he was pessimistic about success.

Some Republicans began to talk of war, but Madison continued to put his main reliance on economic coercion. After learning of the rejection of the Erskine Agreement, he issued a proclamation on August 9 which put a stop to the trade which had been allowed since June 10 on the assumption that the agreement would be accepted. Once more the Non-Intercourse Act of March 1, 1809 prohibited trade with both Great Britain and France. Macon's Bill Number Two, enacted by Congress on May 1, 1810, legalized trade with all countries, but six months later Madison was able to take advantage of its terms to threaten Britain with a severance of trade. He interpreted a flimsy promise of Napoleon to mean that his decrees had ceased to violate the neutral commerce of the United States and announced in a public proclamation of November 2 that the act of May 1, 1810, provided accordingly for a resumption of non-intercourse with Britain within three months unless that nation altered its edicts. On March 2, 1811, Congress enacted a new law which forbade the entry of British goods and ships into the United States.

When Madison issued his proclamation of November 2, 1810, he did not know for sure that the French had in fact repealed their decrees against American commerce. He only knew by means of a letter received from William Pinkney in London that the American minister to France, John Armstrong, had been informed in August by the French foreign minister, the Duc de Cadore, that they would cease to have effect after November 1 if the British revoked their Orders in Council and renounced "the new principles of blockade" or if the United States would "cause their rights to be respected by the English."[7] Since Napoleon continued after November to confiscate American cargoes and the British continued to defend their Orders in Council on the grounds that his decrees were in fact still in effect, Napoleon immediately gained the advantage of depriving Britain of American trade and increased the probabilities of embroiling his enemy in a war with the United States. Napoleon's gains seemed to be Madison's losses: the latter seemed to have been the dupe of the former.

Madison was of course disappointed that Napoleon failed to repeal his decrees in such a way that the British could not possibly claim that their Orders in Council were retaliatory. If Napoleon had carried out a policy of complete and unequivocal repeal of his decrees of 1806 and 1807, the invocation of non-intercourse against Great Britain would not have seemed discriminatory, Federalist charges that he was pro-French would have seemed less plausible, and the British claim that their

Orders in Council were retaliatory would have been discredited.

If the Orders in Council could have been shown to have some purpose other than retaliation, the presumption would have been all the greater that their real aim was to exclude Americans from markets which the British sought to monopolize for their own merchants and shippers. If the real aim of the Orders was to exclude a peaceful competitor from European markets rather than weaken the capacity of an enemy to wage war, they would have been doubly humiliating to national pride and could have inflicted chronic injury to American foreign trade: they would have been ample justification for either continuing economic coercion or going to war.

Privately, Madison expressed anger at Napoleon in 1811 and 1812, but it was not the anger of a person who felt outraged from having been duped.[8] What he saw was that Napoleon's interference with American shipping enabled domestic critics of his foreign policy to argue that Britain had some justification for continuing the Orders in Council and that the United States had little justification for retaliating against that country alone. Madison was exasperated that Napoleon was creating political obstacles for his maintaining commercial non-intercourse or going to war with Great Britain, either of which he thought should be perceived as more advantageous to France than the existing situation.

Although Napoleon's policy toward the United States in 1811 and 1812 seemed absurd to Madison, Cadore's communication to Armstrong had its uses for him. In the first place, it provided him with an excuse to revive economic coercion against Great Britain. In the second place, if the British should decide that revocation of the Orders was desirable because of loss of American trade, it could be cited by them as the reason for a change of policy and thus avoid the appearance of yielding to American coercion. Madison was aware that the British would not want to admit to yielding to American pressure and that they would probably accept any ostensible repeal of Napoleon's decrees as valid if they decided to rescind their restrictions on American commerce.[9] Indeed, when the British did at last decide to suspend their Orders affecting American commerce, they gave as their official reason the repeal of Napoleonic decrees as reported in a document which the Emperor had supposedly signed at St. Cloud in April, 1811, and which had no known existence prior to May, 1812. If the British had not been looking for a pretext for repealing their Orders they surely would have questioned the authenticity and validity of the St. Cloud document as much as they had questioned Cadore's announcement of August, 1810.

Madison's precipitous acceptance of the Cadore notification of August, 1810 as a satisfactory change of policy toward the United States, together with the hairsplitting arguments which he used in his diplomatic discussions to prove to the British that it was actually carried out insofar as a neutral shipper on the high seas could legally demand, were logical derivatives of his beliefs about the Orders in Council, namely, that : (1) they should not be tolerated without some form of retaliation; (2) they would almost certainly be retained if the United States failed to employ economic coercion and/or war against them; (3) their abandonment as a result of American coercion would be made easier for the British if they could give repeal of Napoleon's decrees as the reason; (4) if they were to be a justification for going to war against Britain, their purpose of eliminating the United States as a commercial competitor in European markets should be exposed.

After 1810, American legislation and British orders affecting commerce were the main subjects of negotiation in London and Washington. Except for a short time in March, 1811, when he seems to have had a slight hope for a change of policy if rumored changes in the Perceval ministry should prove to be correct, Madison continued to express a pessimistic outlook.[10] During the summer of 1811 he probably began to think about a deadline when war would have to supplant or supplement economic retaliation. On July 24, 1811, he called Congress to meet on November 4. When Congress met, men close to the administration were assuming that war would come before the end of the session, unless Britain changed its policy toward neutral commerce in the meantime.

Madison had no confidence that a change would occur. He wrote to John Quincy Adams on November 15, 1811:

The pretensions of G. Britain . . . shows a predetermination to make her Orders in Council co-durable with the war. . . . The question to be decided, therefore, by Congress, according to the present appearances, simply is, whether all the trade to which the orders are and shall be applied is to be abandoned, or the hostile operation of them to be hostilely resisted. The apparent disposition is certainly not in favor of the first alternative, though it is more than probable that if the second should be adopted, the execution of it will be put off till the close of the session approaches; with the exception, perhaps, of a licence to our Merchantmen to arm in self-defence, which can scarcely fail to bring on war in its full extent, unless such an evidence of the declaration of the United States to prefer war to submission should arrest the cause for it.

Dolly Madison wrote on December 20, 1811: "I believe there will be war. Mr. Madison sees no end to the perplexities without it and they seem to be going on with the preparations."[11]

Many observers of the President and the twelfth Congress, including the British and French ministers, remained in doubt until May, 1812, that war would come. In a letter to John Taylor, June 13, 1812, James Monroe, who had been Secretary of State since April, 1811, gave this explanation of the misunderstanding of the administration's policy:

But the misfortune is that we have been so long dealing in the small way of embargoes, non-intercourse, and non-importation, with menaces of war, that the British government has not believed us. Thus the argument of war, with its consequqnces, has not had its due weight with the government. We must actually go to war before the intention to make it is credited either here or abroad. The habitual opponents ... have unceasingly circulated the report that the Executive did not intend to make war, and thereby deceived the people, and deceived the British government, depriving our country of the effect which that argument might have had in the British cabinet.[12]

Vigorous, unambiguous, and publicized preparations for war to come within a stipulated period might have offered some advantages in negotiations with Britain in 1812. On the other hand, such an open threat, if it should fail in its diplomatic purposes, would have probably provoked speedier counter preparations for defense by the British, would have jeopardized the safe return of American ships to their ports, and would have diminished the element of suprise in timing the invasion of Canada. Doubting that a threat of war would affect the British, Madison preferred not to relinquish the military advantages of leaving the British uncertain about his plans.[13]

Madison's methods of leadership were partly responsible for the misjudgment of his policy during the first session of the twelfth Congress. He was deferential and indirect in presenting his views to Congress. His mild requests for moderate additions to the army, navy, and militia did not seem like the proposals of a President who expected war soon. He was unwilling to abandon economic coercion as a weapon of diplomacy. His language was conciliatory and moderate; he avoided inflammatory statements such as President Adams had issued in 1798; his stress was on peaceful ways of reaching agreement. At no time did he issue ultimatums. The fact that he avoided proclaiming an unequivocal deadline for a negotiated settlement produced an appearance of indecision, vacillation, or even insincerity. Madison's patience seemed inexhaustible; the promised show-down always' appeared postponable to some indefinite time in the future.

Madison's manner was so moderate, conciliatory, and patient that some Federalists believed that he was secretly opposed to war and only yielded to the demands of the War Hawks in his own party in order to obtain their support for re-election in 1812. In fact, the views of Madison and the War Hawks were alike in their assumption that war must come before the end of the session unless an agreement was reached with Great Britain. His differences with them were in manner, aggressiveness, and inspirational appeals to the public; in ways of financing and mobilizing the armed forces; in conceptions of the diplomatic purposes of an invasion of Canada and the continuation of economic coercion; and the role of the President in announcing a war policy.

If the War Hawks affected Madison in any way after November, 1811, it was probably in pressing him to submit special messages to Congress advocating a policy of war. The author of the Helvidius Letters apparently preferred that the Congress impose embargoes and declare war without official solicitation on the part of the executive. He may also have been persuaded that Congress would in fact support a war message and would assume its share of responsibility for the state of preparedness.[14]

Federalists who guessed that Madison was secretly opposed to war prior to May, 1812 were mistaken in thinking that he changed his mind because of the demands of the War Hawks. Nevertheless, it is quite possible that Madison's opinion that the United States should resort to war if a settlement could not be obtained during the first session of the twelfth Congress was influenced by the fact that a presidential election was forthcoming in 1812. The great majority of Republicans, including Madison himself, had been saying since 1807 that the United States could not submit indefinitely to the Orders in Council; that unless Britain changed its policy war must ultimately be the only alternative to a "trade-at-your-own-risk" policy. And a "trade-at-your-own-risk" policy had been rejected overwhelmingly. The Federalists would have been able to make powerful use of charges of pusillanimity, insincerity, and outright dishonesty in the election of 1812 if Madison had attempted to prolong negotiations. He might well have had a rebellion within his own party, too, if he had not discreetly made known his intention to support war by the end of the session. If the War Hawks had any decisive influence on Madison other than persuading him to ask Congress for war in a formal message, that influence was felt by the fall of 1811. For Madision to have decided against war in 1812 would have been to repudiate the position that he and a majority of Republicans had repeatedly claimed for their party.

By the close of March, 1812, Madison was acting upon the assumption that war with England would come within the next two months. Already he was selecting commanders for armies to invade Canada from New York state and Michigan Territory. On April 1 he sent to Congress a special message prososing a sixty-day embargo; in one sentence he said that such a measure was "expedient, under the circumstances." Privately he explained to Jefferson that the embargo was preliminary to war. On April 15, he called upon the governors to "hold in readiness to march at moment's warning, their respective proportions of the one-hundred thousand militia" provided for by Congress in a bill which he signed on April 10.[15]

Reports that arrived in Washington during the last week of May confirmed Madison's previous skepticism about reaching a settlement without war. From France there was no indication of a change in the practices which supported the British contention that Napoleon had never in fact carried out his alleged promise of August, 1810. From Britain there was no indication that the Orders in Council of 1807 would be revoked unless Napoleon permitted noncontraband merchandise purchased in the British Isles to be carried by all neutral shippers to all continental ports.[16]

On May 27 and May 28, the British minister in Washington, Augustus J. Foster, conversed with Monroe and Madison about the text of a dispatch from Foreign Minister Castlereagh, dated April 10, which contained a lengthy review of French policy which was said to justify and require continuation of the Orders in Council. For Madison, Castlereagh was offering no grounds for altering the plans for war which he had been making during the previous two months. In a letter to Henry Wheaton ten years after he left the presidency, Madison remembered the dispatch of April 10 as crucial in confirming his decision to propose war without further delay:

In none of the Comments on the Declaration of the last war, has the more immediate impulse been sufficiently brought into view. This was the letter of Castlereagh to Foster, which according to the authority given, the latter put into the hands of the Secretary of State, to be read by him, and by the President also. In that letter it was distinctly & emphatically stated that the orders in Council to which we had declared we would not submit, would not be repealed, without a repeal of internal measures of France, which not violating any neutral right of the U.S. they had no right to call on France to repeal, and which of course could give to G.B. no imaginable right agst. the U.S. (see the passages in the War Message and in the Committee Report of 1812 both founded on the letter without naming it). With this formal notice, no choice remained but between war and degradation, a degradation inviting fresh provocations, rendering war sooner or later inevitable.[17]

Edward Coles, the President's secretary, had a similar recollection of the importance of the dispatch of April 10:

Although the conduct of England had been such as to create fears to such an extent as to make him desirous of adding to our defences and preparing for the probability of our difficulties ending in war, he did not entirely despair of preserving peace, until the British Govt. made known the fact, that a repeal of the obnoxious decrees of the French Govt., as far as they concerned us, would not induce England to alter in a similar way her more annoying orders in council; but contended that France must not only repeal her decrees against us, but against all the world, before England would consent to repeal or modify her orders. On this being avowed it closed the door to peace, in Mr. Madison's opinion, and made war inevitable, and from that time he never doubted or hesitated for a moment, but his mind was made up and irrevocably fixed on war, as the only course left us by the conduct and position assumed by England.[18]

CHAPTER XII

President: Diplomatic Commander-in-Chief

IN HIS WAR MESSAGE OF JUNE 1, 1812, MADISON REVIEWED the conduct of Great Britain toward the United States since 1803. The main body of his account was devoted to the obstinate refusal of the British government to revoke its "pretended" blockade of 1806 and its Orders in Council of 1807. He pointed to British responses to various proposals of his government to show that British practices were not in accord with their own professed aims and principles. The real aim of the British, he argued, was to open the markets of her enemy to British products. American commerce with the continent was objectionable to Britain because it interfered with the monopoly which she coveted for her own commerce and navigation and not because it added to the military power of the Napoleonic empire. The purpose of Britain's war against "the lawful commerce of a friend" was to "better carry on a commerce with an enemy." By their "predatory measures," the British had cut off "the great staples" of the United States from their "legitimate markets," and had aimed "a destructive blow" at their agricultural and maritime interests.

The emphasis which Madison placed upon the Orders in Council reflected the preoccupation of his diplomacy with Great Britain since 1807. What he said was an accurate summary of the consistent position he had maintained toward them since he had been Secretary of State and President.

Two other sources of friction between the two countries were also introduced into his war message: (1) the impressment of "thousands of American citizens" into the British navy and (2) the recent renewal of warfare on the frontiers by "savages" in "constant intercourse with British traders and garrisons."

The issue of impressment, except for the single case of the *Chesapeake*, had been deliberately kept in abeyance since 1807 in order not to complicate the negotiations for repeal of the British Orders affecting trade. Privately, to the American minister in London, Madison expressed indignation at the continuance of impressment and implied that the issue would be brought forward again once the other maritime issues were settled. On January 16, 1812, in response to a House request, he submitted to Congress a report prepared by the Secretary of State which recorded a total of 6,257 cases of impressment since 1803. The authors of a House report of November 29, 1811, which reviewed "the just complaints of our merchants against the plunder of their ships and cargoes," stated that they could not "refrain from presenting to the justice and humanity of their country, the unhappy case of our impressed seamen." Foster, the British minister in Washington, was quite aware that impressment was a serious grievance though not a topic of formal negotiation.[1]

Yet, the fact remains that at no time before he composed his message of June 1, 1812, did Madison suggest that failure to obtain a satisfactory settlement of the impressment issue would result in war. From the standpoint of national honor and dignity, impressment was the most important justification of war. But the most important justification of war was clearly not the most important factor which influenced the President to decide for war in the spring of 1812.

The alleged agency of the British in Indian hostilities in Indiana Territory had played no part in Madison's negotiations with the British, nor had he made any complaints, public or private, before the message of June 1, 1812. In his message to Congress, November 5, 1811, he had said nothing about British complicity when he had reported "several murders and depredations committed by Indians" and "menacing preparations" on the Wabash "under the direction of a fanatic of the Shawanese tribe."[2] There is no evidence that the opinion which he had formed in 1811 about the probability of war in 1812 was influenced in any way by the Indians. Reports about British instigation of the Indians who fought Governor William Henry Harrison's army near Tippecanoe Creek on November 7, 1811, could have influenced his ultimate decision for war only by contributing to the Congressional support which he deemed necessary before submitting a war message.

Madison never believed that a war with Britain was necessary in order to eliminate the Indian menace in territories bordering Canada. Although he mentioned a link between hostile Indians and the British in his war message, an agreement on this subject was not necessary to prevent or terminate war in 1812.

Introduction of the impressment and Indian issues into his message had domestic political advantages inasmuch as they enlarged the range and enthusiasm of support for war, notably in the West and South. At the same time they complicated a settlement with Britain, as Madison had clearly understood prior to June, 1812. Just as a new pressure for concessions was to be applied on Britain in the form of an invasion of Canada, Britain was presented with additional reasons for opposing a settlement with the United States; in short, the advantage of an additional coercive force was negated to a degree by the added incentive for the British to resist.

In his war message Madison said nothing about annexing foreign territories. He was of course planning an invasion of Canada when he submitted the message, but nothing that he wrote or said before June, 1812, indicated that the goal of such an invasion was annexation of territory. He refrained from announcing the objectives of forthcoming military operations, but his stated terms for peace in 1812 and 1813 implied that they were strategic, that is, to hold conquered territory temporarily with the intention of surrendering it whenever the British agreed to a satisfactory settlement of the maritime disputes. To be sure, Secretary of State Monroe on at least two occasions drafted arguments that could be used to indicate to the British the wisdom of their relinquishing Canada, but annexation of territory was never a condition for peace, and Madison surely would have rejected territorial gains in return for acceptance of the British position on maritime disputes.

Madison's message of June 1, 1812, did not reflect all the motivations of all Americans who wanted war with Britain. Some believed that annexation of territory should be a primary aim of an invasion of Canada. Also, there can be no doubt that some, especially in Georgia and Tennessee, expected that American troops would move into Spanish territory to prevent smuggling, Indian raids, or the landing of British troops, and that military operations in that region would lead to its permanent occupation by the United States. That annexation of Canadian territory was not a personal motive for Madison is quite certain. Less certain is the effect of his desire for Spanish territory upon his war policy in 1812; the records which show that he had been trying to subvert Spanish rule in the region south of Mississippi Territory and Georgia fail to disclose whether he thought a war with Britain would be useful in achieving that purpose. However, even if one accepts the conjecture that he foresaw that a war with Britain might provide a pretext for sending troops into Spanish territory, the conclusion does not necessarily follow that such an anticipation had any decisive influence upon his advocacy of war in 1812. Basically his war policy in 1812 was shaped by the maritime disputes; if the United States had at that time been exercising undisputed sovereignty over all territory between the Mississippi River and the Atlantic coast of Florida, his policy toward Britain would have been the same as it was.[3]

In his message of June 1, 1812, Madison was candid in admitting that the French government "had authorized illegal captures by its privateers and public ships" and that "other outrages" had "been practiced on our vessels and our citizens within the jurisdiction of France." He abstained, however, from recommending "definitive measures" with respect to that nation "in the expectation that the result of unclosed discussions" in Paris would "speedily enable Congress to decide with greater advantage on the course due to the rights, the interests, and the honor of our country."

If Madison was still thinking as he had when he wrote to Jefferson on May 25, he had not ruled out the possibility of a triangular war. But he thought that such a war would present a "thousand difficulties" and only highly problematical advantages. Above all, he had written, war with France would shut all the ports of continental Europe to American cruisers, which could do little without their use.[4]

A large number of senators, however, were ready to decide immediately for war against France. On June 17, fourteen senators voted for immediate hostilities against both Great Britain and France; seventeen would have been a majority of those voting on this resolution.

In the meantime, the House had already approved war against Britain on June 4 by a vote of 79 to 49. After various amendments to start hostilities against France in one form or another had been defeated, the Senate on June 17 approved war against Britain alone by a vote of 19 to 13.

Opposition to war proved a great obstacle in waging it, since the large minority against the war when it began did not diminish subsequently. The militias of the New England states, except for Vermont in 1812 and 1814, never joined the federal forces along the Northern frontier. New York militiamen were balky about serving in Canada. Trade was carried on with the enemy. Moneyed men who subscribed to war loans in New

England were few. In many constituencies north of the Potomac and east of the Hudson and Delaware Rivers, congressmen and newspapers carried on an incessant criticism of the war.

Madison may have made a great mistake in proposing a war to which such a large segment of the country was opposed. Certainly the opposition was a serious liability, as he well understood. Yet, it is well to recall that he saw the second war against Great Britain from a perspective that included none of the wars since 1815. His basis of comparison was the first war against Britain, which had been fought successfully with an opposition within the country as large as that of 1812 and more actively enlisted on the side of the enemy. Furthermore, if there was a large element in the United States against war, so also was there a large element in Canada which had no desire to fight the Americans.

Opposition to war probably would have been silenced if Madison's strategy of quick conquests in Canada had been achieved. Madison had planned for rapid and simultaneous invasions of Canada at three points: across the St. Lawrence at Montreal and across the Niagara and Detroit Rivers. The first to get started—that which was to advance into the western sector of the peninsula north of Lake Erie—ended in a disastrous fiasco at Detroit on August 16, when General Hull surrendered his army to General Brock. In October about eleven hundred men crossed the Niagara, but, after about six hundred of this number fought vainly to hold Queenston Heights while militia on the American side refused to come to their rescue, they were either killed or captured. In late November a new commander on the Niagara front announced another invasion with bombastic fanfare, but when a small vanguard of several hundred men suffered heavy casualties and when he came to believe that the number of troops ready to cross the river was too small to insure victory, he abruptly called it off. No crossings of the St. Lawrence were made in 1812.

These failures were due to the absence of trained, disciplined, and spirited armies capable of quick and coordinated movements; to the dilatory and confused direction given by superannuated generals whose knowledge of warfare gained in the Revolutionary War was vitiated by a lack of will and vitality; to the skillful and imaginative defensive movements of General Brock on the Canadian side; to a common belief in New York and New England that militiamen had no obligation to fight on foreiggn soil; to the lack of naval support for the Ameri-

can armies operating around Lake Erie; and to defective communications between the President and the commanders of the
armies of invasion.

Most inexcusable on the part of the President was his failure
to provide speedy notification of the declaration of war to the
commanding generals. The commander of the army defending
the Canadian frontier at Malden learned that war had been
declared four days before the American commander who was
supposed to invade that area. The War Department letter that
notified General Hull that war had been declared on June 18
was received on July 2. It was transmitted by regular post in the
part of its journey east of Cleveland.[5]

Also, not uncharacteristically, Madison's intention to begin
the war with an invasion of Canada, which was recorded in his
private correspondence and which was reputedly the subject of
private conversations with the newly appointed generals who
visited Washington in the spring of 1812, was not affirmed in
official written orders. Hull thought that his first orders following the declaration of war were indefinite. On July 7 he wrote
to the Secretary of War: "In your letter of the 18th of June [the
day war was declared], you direct me to adopt measures for the
security of the country and wait for further orders;—I regret
that I have not a larger latitude." Madison himself reported to
Congress that an army which had been put into Michigan Territory for the purpose of carrying out operations in Canada
possessed orders to act offensively that were "discretionary."[6]

Grand strategy at the beginning of the war was affected by
deficiencies in political support and naval power. An attack on
the British base at Halifax, which might have disrupted communications between the British Isles and Canada, seems not to
have been seriously considered by Madison, presumably because the navy lacked the ships and the New England states
would not provide the troops essential for the success of such
an expedition. Also, although he appreciated the worth of naval
support for military operations around Lake Erie, neither he
nor Congress had taken steps to have it available when the war
started. The conquest of Montreal was very much desired by
Madison in order to cut off the flow of supplies to the British
armies and their Indian allies in western Canada, but the ineffectiveness of General Dearborn and the opposition to war in
areas that were to provide militia and volunteers for the army
in eastern New York necessitated his shifting the main offensive to the West. In the course of the summer, Madison was

forced by circumstances to put his main reliance upon the army under General Hull which was to move across the Detroit River. A frightened public opinion in Kentucky, Ohio, and Indiana Territory demanded protection from the Indians and public enthusiasm for war in those areas provided men who were willing to fight in an invading army; political pressures and immediate military feasibility shifted the main attack away from Montreal.[7]

Despite these several shortcomings in strategic planning and despite the bumbling and stumbling of the armies in New York state, Madison was probably right when he later argued that the whole course of the war would have been altered if General Hull had conducted a vigorous offensive campaign against General Brock, instead of retreating into the fort at Detroit and abjectly surrendering without a fight:

> What a contrast would the success so easy at the outset of the war have presented! A triumphant army would have seized on Upper Canada and hastened to join the armies at the points below; the important command of Lake Erie would have fallen to us of course; the Indians would have been neutral or submissive to our will; the general spirit of the country would have been kindled into enthusiasm; enlistments would have been accelerated; volunteers would have stepped forward with redoubled confidence & alacrity; and what is not of small moment, the intrigues of the disaffected would have been smothered in their embrio state.

Instead, Madison continued, the people of Canada

> not indisposed to favor us, were turned against us; the Indians were thrown into the service of the enemy; the expence & delay of a new armament were incurred; the western militia & volunteers were withheld from offensive cooperation with the troops elsewhere by the necessity of defending their own frontiers and families against incursions of the Savages; and a general damp spread over the face of our affairs.[8]

Madison has often been criticized for taking the country into a war that it was unprepared to fight. Although the army in June had fewer trained men and weapons than the President and a majority in Congress had earlier proposed, it was not in fact less prepared than the enemy it faced in 1812. Madison's fault was not that he asked an American army to invade territory defended by a much stronger army but that he expected the generals whom he had selected, without positive and unequivocal commands from the President, to wage the kind of war it had some chance of winning in 1812. As Madison said, a bold campaign by Hull might have changed the course of the war, but the President did nothing to insure boldness on the part of his generals, and there was nothing in the past of any one of them to cause one to presume that he would not require prodding from higher authority. General Hull was not an Andrew Jackson and Madison had no reason to think he was.

Concentration of historical criticism on the military failures of Madison's administration has obscured weaknesses in the strategy of seeking a settlement of maritime disputes by means of a war in Canada. This strategy rested upon the doubtful assumption that the British would consider losses of Canadian territory more harmful to their war against Napoleon and to their economy than surrender of impressment and the advantages derived from the Orders in Council. In 1795 Madison himself had argued that the British were more vulnerable in their commerce than in Canada. How much, if any, he had modified that belief by 1812 is not clear; but surely he had not completely reversed it. From the beginning of the war he intended to use privateers and navy vessels to prey upon enemy commerce with all countries. By mid-August he had probably made up his mind to continue legislation that deprived the British of American trade.[9]

Another doubtful assumption about the strategy of trading territorial conquests for a settlement of the maritime disputes was that the Americans themselves would be willing to surrender their "hostage." They might well come to think Canadian territory worth more than American seamen or the trade advantages to be obtained by repeal of the Orders in Council. Monroe, the Secretary of State, wanted the British to know that Canadian territory, if occupied by American troops for a prolonged period, might become difficult to surrender.[10]

Even if the campaigns of 1812 had been as successful as Madison had hoped for—even if they had been as successful as the Japanese campaigns of 1941 and 1942—they may have had less effect on Britain's maritime policy than continuation and enlargement of the attack on her commerce. Presumably, however, military victories would have brought more political support to the administration.

The initial failures of the armies of invasion were known when the presidential election occurred. They may have contributed somewhat to a reduction of Madison's electoral vote below the number he had received in 1808. Madison's 128 electoral votes, of which 95 were from states south and west of Pennsylvania, were 59 per cent of the total; in 1808 he had received 70 per cent. His losses were in New York, New Jersey, and Maryland. He would have been defeated by a margin of eleven votes if his opponent, DeWitt Clinton, Republican mayor of New York City, had been able to add Pennsylvania to the states he carried. Clinton was supported by a coalition of antiwar Republicans and Federalists.

Madison was aware that "success alone would put an end" to criticisms of his administration. To William Wirt, he wrote on September 30, 1813: "This is the test by which public opinion decides more or less in all cases, and most of all, perhaps, in that of military events."[11]

In 1813 and 1814, with one notable exception, American armies of invasion continued to be stalled or to falter, and, except for a small sector bordering the Detroit River and Lake Erie, no civil territory in Canada was brought under military occupation. There were, however, occasional victories on land and sea that prevented a complete collapse of morale, gained a slight amount of territory, shattered the war-making power of the Indians, and prevented capture of fortified places on American soil. In his messages to Congress Madison always had some good news to report: battles won by gallant seamen in single-ship engagements during the first six months of the war, damage inflicted on British commerce by privateers and navy cruisers, Commodore Oliver H. Perry's momentous naval victory on Lake Erie, General William Henry Harrison's triumphant Thames River campaign with its far-reaching effects upon Britain's Indian allies in the North, treaties of peace and alliance with Indian tribes, successful defenses against enemy forays into Ohio, New York, and Virginia, and Jackson's defeat of the Creeks in Mississippi Territory.

After April, 1813, the British blockaded ports south of Rhode Island, and their ships repeatedly launched marauding parties against farms and villages along the coasts and inlets of Chesapeake Bay. By May, 1814, the whole American coast, New England included, was covered by the blockade. On land, by July, 1814, enemy armies were preparing to invade the United States on three widely separated fronts.

The opposition thrived on the adversities of 1813 and 1814; yet it never increased in numbers as much as it did in virulence. In the elections for the fourteenth Congress held in 1814, Federalist gains in New England were not enough to give them a majority in either house of Congress.

Even if the critics of war were never able to persuade a majority of the voters to repudiate his administration, Madison believed that the British were encouraged to look forward to ultimate victory by their knowledge of the opposition to war in the United States.[12] Privately, Madison strongly condemned the opponents of war, but his public references to them were few and muted. While the opposition was merciless in attacking "Mr. Madison's War," the President himself did not attempt to place the main responsibility for his failures upon the aid which he believed his critics gave to the enemy.

Madison refused to use governmental power to restrain criticism of his administration. Nor did he give encouragement to vigilantes to harass or intimidate those whose patriotism he doubted. Only a few isolated cases of mob actions against newspaper editors occurred during the war. There were no committees of public safety, no tarring and feathering of the disloyal, and no confiscations of property for political reasons—as there had been during the Revolutionary War. There was no sedition law such as John Adams had signed during the quasi-war with France in 1798. There were no presidential suspensions of the writ of *habeas corpus*, no imprisonment of civilians by military tribunals, no suspension of newspapers by military edicts, and no meddling in elections by the military—as were to happen during the Civil War. Measures taken during the war years of 1917 and 1918 had no precedents in the War of 1812: there were no espionage laws, no barring of antiwar publications from the U.S. mails, and no network of semi-official spying upon citizens whose patriotism was questioned by their neighbors. There was no forced evacuation of citizens from their homes in order to remove all chances of secret aid to the enemy—as was to be done during the first year of the war against Japan. Of the wartime presidents of the United States, none had more provocations than Madison to condone the same infringements upon individual liberties that occurred during the presidencies of Lincoln, Wilson, and Franklin Roosevelt. Yet, no other wartime president has permitted more freedom to the opponents of war.

The President's policy toward disaffection may have had practical political benefits. Suppressive measures may well have aggravated discontent in coastal New England. His forbearance may have prevented the malcontents from becoming recruits for the British army or advocates of secession. Perhaps Madison deserves credit for not driving the opposition to desperate measures, the consequences of which might have been disastrous to the integrity of the American Union as it had been established in 1789.

Toward the British Madison was not so charitable. In his messages to Congress and other public statements he charged that there was no justification for the harm which they had inflicted upon American commerce and seamen before the war, for their refusal to make peace, for their seeking an alliance with savage Indian tribes, for treating captured British-born American soldiers as if they were criminals, for permitting a wanton destruction of property by their landing parties along the shores of Chesapeake Bay, and for encouraging slaves to seek their protective custody. He denounced the enemy many times and for many reasons, using a variety of epithets in their superlative form to express his indignation. But the line of his argument seemed more designed to convince the British that they were guilty of wrongdoing than to arouse an angry fighting spirit among Americans. Madison lacked the capacity to arouse patriotic fervor by appealing to either the base passions or the sublime ideals of mankind.

Throughout the war, the problem of maintaining political support for his administration presented Madison with a dilemma in making appointments. On the one hand, political support was to be gained by the military successes that only the most capable administrative and military leadership could produce. On the other hand, men who were mediocre or ineffective in performing the duties of their office sometimes commanded political support in areas where there was strong opposition to the war. When deciding whether to replace an incompetent man, Madison could never afford to ignore the political support which his administration would gain or lose by the change. Also, in order to be as inoffensive as possible to men of political influence, he had to consider carefully his manner of ordering transfers and dismissals.

There were often good political reasons for the particular appointees he selected and for his cautious manner in dismissing the men they replaced. General Dearborn, General Hull, and Secretary Eustis demonstrated their ineffectiveness during the first three months of the war, but for several reasons the President could not afford a peremptory or brash dismissal of the three men at the same time. All three had been important party leaders in Massachusetts, had been closely associated with Jefferson, and were from a state that was a notorious stronghold of antiwar sentiment. Hull of course was not treated tenderly and was the first to go. Eustis stayed at the head of the War Department until December 3, when he voluntarily resigned. Dearborn held his command until July, 1813, when Madison apologetically transferred him to a nominal post. In selecting William Henry Harrison to succeed Hull, Madison was influenced by the support he had among political leaders in the areas which provided most of the troops for that command, and in choosing John Armstrong to succeed Eustis he was giving representation in his cabinet to pro-war Republicans in New York state. In September, 1814, when Monroe replaced Armstrong, the latter had lost any trust that the President had ever had in him and was highly eligible to become a scapegoat for the burning of Washington; yet Madison eased him out of office instead of publicly calling for his resignation—seeking at the same time to fill the vacancy at the head of the State Department with Governor Tompkins, the most prominent pro-administration Republican in New York state. In July, 1814, in selecting the man to command the army defending Washington, he probably chose William Winder because he was the brother of the Governor of Maryland, whose state militia was desperately needed to combat an impending invasion by a seaborne army heading for Chesapeake Bay. The five men appointed in 1814 to negotiate for peace represented different factional and sectional interests and varying attitudes toward war.[13]

Madison did not of course make these appointments solely upon political grounds. Harrision, Armstrong, and Winder had previous military and administrative experience that qualified them for their appointments at the time they were made. So also, the five peace commissioners had experience and talents which rendered them qualified as individuals to carry out the diplomatic negotiations entrusted to them.

Madison's patience in the face of hostility and ineptitude stemmed perhaps as much from personal traits as from the creed of a statesman or tactics of a politician. Very much the same man that he had been throughout his career, he was as reluctant as ever to question the motives and intelligence of his fellow countrymen. He was sensitive to the feelings of others and always ready to see their merits as well as their weaknesses. He was aware that circumstances could produce both failures and successes for which an individual in office might undeservingly be blamed or praised. He was not inclined to attribute success or failure to personal qualities alone. He much preferred to win support for his opinions by gentle and quiet persuasion rather than a bold assertion of personal confidence or an arbitrary command deriving its force from the power of his office. He never acted as if the presidential office conferred upon its incumbent a special wisdom or sagacity. He continued to be as deferential toward Congress as he had been before the war; he permitted his department heads a wide latitude of opinion and authority; and only after careful deliberation did he overrule his Secretary of War or commanding generals in the field.

When Madison made his plans to invade Canada with the expectation of trading conquered territory for a settlement of the maritime disputes, he failed to reveal whether war was to be a substitute or a supplement for economic coercion. If the President's mind was expressed in a private letter by his Secretary of State to a friend, one would have to assume that Madison intended to abandon trade restrictions: on June 13, Monroe wrote to John Taylor that trade would soon be more flourishing than at any time since 1807—that the United States would "trade & fight, and fight and trade." Similar inferences could be drawn from a letter of June 10, 1812, in which his Secretary of Treasury requested Congress to repeal the non-importation act in order to increase revenue from import duties.[14]

Yet the President himself wrote nothing on the subject, either in his war message or in his private letters, and he gave no known support to those Republicans in Congress who strongly urged repeal of trade restrictions following the declaration of war. Apparently, Republicans who voted for war had no prior understanding as to what would happen to the ban on trade with Great Britain. John C. Calhoun proclaimed in a House speech that he would have never voted for war if he had thought it was going to be an appendage to non-importation, while Alexander McKim of Maryland said exactly the opposite.[15]

On June 24, 1812, the House voted 63 to 58 against repeal of non-importation. Whether Madison was pleased or displeased with this action is not known. If he thought then as he thought before and after the summer of 1812, he would of course have been pleased. Yet, one cannot be absolutely sure that his subsequent support of restrictions was an uninterrupted continuation of his long-standing advocacy of economic coercion, for information came to Washington in early August which could have caused a revived interest in non-intercourse by a person who had relinquished it in June.

Between August 6 and August 14 the State Department received authoritative reports that the Liverpool ministry, prior to the declaration of war, had decided to suspend the Orders in Council. This knowledge gave support to men like McKim who had voted for war but had argued that it would be less effective than economic measures in bringing the British to terms. Madison in a letter to Jefferson on August 17, 1812, attributed the change of British policy to a combination of non-importation and the threat of war. A diplomatic note to Jonathan Russell in London dated August 21 stated that non-importation "had become a measure of war, and the most efficient."[16]

In his message to Congress, November 4, 1812, Madison offered his first wartime recommendation on the subject of commercial legislation when he asked for further restrictions against trading with Great Britain. In a special message of February 2, 1813, he called for an embargo on all exports in foreign ships. In a special message of July 20, 1813, he asked for an embargo on all exports so long as U.S. ports were blockaded. In a special and secret message of December 9, 1813, he asked for an embargo and strict enforcement of non-importation. His recommended embargoes had military as well as economic purposes: they had the prewar aims of reducing imports into the British Isles and colonies, but they also sought to deprive British soldiers and sailors of provisions produced in the United States.

In December, 1813, Madison's proposed embargo was approved in the House by a vote of 85 to 57 and in the Senate by 20 to 14. Earlier in the year there had been a stalemate between the supporters and opponents of his recommendations. Repeal of non-importation was defeated in February, 1813, while an embargo bill was defeated in the Senate in June.

At the close of 1813, an effective embargo could do no more than block exports from the New England states, which were still exempted from the blockade, and stop the selling of American flour and beef to the British army and navy. Earlier, in Madison's first term, an embargo might have reduced shipments of wheat to Portugal and Spain which the British permitted to pass through their blockading squadrons while Wellington's army was fighting the Peninsular Campaign.[17]

An unwanted consequence of the embargo in early 1814 was to assist the British in blocking U.S. exports from going to areas which were then being opened up to trade by collapse of

Napoleonic rule. At the same time, curtailment of exports from New England had little effect on the British economy and aroused further antagonism in that region among men who were to vote in state elections to be held in April.[18] Under these circumstances, Madison abruptly decided to call for abandonment of the policy which he had supported continuously in some form since 1806. In a special message of March 31, 1814, which cryptically alluded to important advantages to be gained from adapting commercial legislation to "extensive changes" in Europe favorable to the United States, he asked Congress to permit all except enemy vessels to import and export property not owned by subjects of an enemy country.[19] A bill incorporating his proposal was approved in the two houses by votes of 115 to 37 and 26 to 14. After April 14 trade was unrestricted with neutral countries, except for a ban on their importing merchandise owned by British subjects. British products, if not owned and shipped by British subjects could be brought into the United States. Thenceforth Madison was dependent upon warfare unassisted by economic coercion to achieve the objects of his diplomacy.

Terms for an armistice and a peace settlement had been offered early in the war. "At the moment of the declaration of war," Monroe wrote on August 21, 1812, "the President, regretting the necessity which produced it looked to its termination and provided for it."[20] His terms were made known in a conversation with the British minister in Washington on June 23, in diplomatic instructions to the American chargé d'affaires in London dated June 26, July 27, and August 21, and in replies to British offers for an armistice received in August and October.[21] In his message of November 4, 1812, he summarized the position he had taken in these negotiations:

These terms required that the orders in council should be repealed as they affected the United States, without a revival of blockades violating acknowledged rules, and that there should be an immediate discharge of American seamen from British ships, and a stop to impressment from American ships, with an understanding that an exclusion of the seamen of each nation from the ships of the other should be stipulated, and that the armistice should be improved into a definitive and comprehensive adjustment of depending controversies.

At the beginning of the war, when he was still expecting the American armies to invade Canada, Madison assumed that any temporary cessation of hostilities would be a military advantage to the British. He was not interested in an armistice unless it was accompanied by an understanding that the peace settlement would be satisfactory to the United States. In August and October he rejected British offers for an armistice that were based upon the assumption that repeal of the Orders in Council were sufficient grounds for ending the war.[22] After his message of June 1, he was not willing to stop the war without some settlement of the impressment issue.

In 1813, Madison continued to seek negotiations with the British. When a proposal of the Russian Tsar to serve as mediator arrived in Washington on March 7, he quickly accepted the offer. Without knowing that the British foreign minister had already rejected mediation, he sent Albert Gallatin and Thomas F. Bayard to Saint Petersburg to serve with John Quincy Adams on a mission for peace negotiations.

Instructions drawn up for the American commissioners on April 15, 1813 contained an offer designed to obviate all the practical obstacles to British surrender of the practice of impressment. Under the terms of an administration-sponsored act which Madison had signed on March 3, the commissioners were authorized to state that if native American citizens were barred from British ships, no British-born seamen, unless naturalized after living continuously in the United States for five years, would be permitted after the war to serve on American ships. The President preferred an agreement based upon this act, but he indicated a willingness to revise the terms of naturalization so as to deny employment to all British-born seamen, alien or naturalized, except those who had already acquired citizenship.[23]

In its practical operations, the act of March 3 could have never permitted more than a few hundred British-born seamen to serve on American ships; and if one accepts the generally held assumption that the number of British-born seamen in American service exceeded the number of American-born seamen in British service, it should have conceded to the British all the practical benefits of impressment. The British government, however, showed no interest in an agreement based upon the approach suggested by the act of March 3. It also continued to reject Russian mediation and outwardly seemed completely uninterested in discussing any issue with the American government. Yet, while rejecting mediation, Foreign Minister Castlereagh was not averse to making informal contacts that signified his willingness to negotiate directly with the United

States. His first formal offer to negotiate came in a note dated November 4, 1813. Madison accepted the offer in a note of January 5, 1814 and shortly thereafter added Henry Clay and Jonathan Russell to the peace mission in Europe.

CHAPTER XIII

President: Peacemaker and Prophet

BOTH THE NECESSITY AND FEASIBILITY OF WAR IN 1812, AS
judged by Madison, as well as his first statement of terms for a
peace settlement, had been very much affected by his belief that
the policies and power of the European belligerents would remain basically unchanged for the foreseeable future. If he had
expected a revocation of the Orders in Council when he talked
to Foster on May 28 and June 23 he would not have asked for war
on June 1 and he probably would not have included settlement
of the impressment issue as a condition for stopping it. If he had
foreseen an early end to the European war, he would not have
proposed war, for peace in Europe would have terminated the
maritime disputes which he said required the United States to go
to war against Great Britain. Also, his decision for war and his
first statement of terms for ending it had been affected by the
assumption that the war in Europe would prevent the British
from sending large military and naval forces to North America.

Settlement of the impressment issue, which had not been
necessary to prevent war, became the essential purpose for continuing it. The irony of fighting an enemy which had conceded
what would have prevented war before it started was com-
pounded as the future unfolded in a way quite different from
what Madison had envisaged on June 1, 1812. Repeated attempts
to invade Canada ended in retreats; the few victories north of
Lake Erie and Lake Ontario brought no losses of Canadian territory capable of persuading the British to change their position on
impressment. In Europe, Napoleon's decline, of which there
were no signs when Madison proposed war, began with his disastrous retreat from Moscow in October, 1812.

Abdication of Napoleon on April 5, 1814, brought the European war to its close and meant the end of occasions for impressment and the other maritime disputes which Madison had said
were the causes of the war. And just at the time when the original
issues of the war became obsolete, so then did the obstacles of
waging war increase, for peace in Europe also made possible

massive reinforcements of the British armies in North America by veterans of the European campaigns.

Madison was receiving unfavorable reports from Europe throughout the early months of 1814. By January 27 he knew that Napoleon's army was in "serious danger" and by March 10 that it had suffered "a catastrophe." In the months of May and June he was eagerly awaiting intelligence pertaining to British terms for peace and the number of troops and vessels being transferred from Europe to North America.[1]

Under the influence of adverse reports from Europe, the administration modified previous instructions to the peace commissioners. On June 24 the cabinet agreed to a peace treaty which would refer impressment and commercial issues to postwar negotiations. Two days later a letter arrived in Washington which had been sent from London by Bayard and Gallatin on May 6. Its prognosis of the policies of Great Britain and the European powers was decisive in causing a complete abandonment of "the principal remaining object of the war": on June 27 the commissioners were authorized to accept a peace that made no reference to impressment. The decisions of June 24 and June 27 were responsible for new instructions received by the American commissioners in the city of Ghent on August 8, the very day negotiations began with the British delegation.[2]

While retreating on the diplomatic front, the administration was at the same time adjusting military plans to conform to the new situation presented by peace in Europe. Throughout 1812 and 1813, the British and Canadians had followed a strategy of defense. The few incursions into American territory which they had made into western New York, northwestern Ohio, and the coastal fringes of Virginia and Maryland had had the limited objectives of raiding parties. After April, 1814, Madison had to assume that any future advances into American territory would be major campaigns of invasion; the strategy of the United States would necessarily have to change after British troops arrived from Europe in large numbers.

In the early summer, however, there still seemed to be time enough for another campaign of invasion. In a cabinet meeting of June 7, a decision was made to instruct Major-General Brown to capture Burlington Heights and the city of York. To forestall reinforcements for the area under attack, plans were made for diversionary movements along the St. Lawrence River between Kingston and Montreal.[3] This campaign began on July 3. After an inspiring victory won near Chippewa Creek, Brown proceeded as far as Queenston; but learning that the naval flotilla on Lake Ontario had not arrived off Fort George with supplies and guns and threatened by an enemy force that would soon be much larger than his own, he decided to retreat toward Niagara Falls. At Lundy's Lane on July 25 his army fought one of the most fiercely contested battles of the war. Audacious leadership, magnificent courage, and superb marksmanship did not prevent this honorable campaign from ending in another and final retreat by an American army of invasion. After Lundy's Lane, Brown's army moved farther southward on the Canadian side of the Niagara to Fort Erie, which was held until evacuated on November 5.

During the summer of 1814, Madison had more confidence in the generals in the field than in his Secretary of War. Looking into Armstrong's correspondence with Generals Brown, Izard, Jackson, and Harrison, he became convinced that the Secretary of War was withholding information from him and not seeking authorization for orders that should have the President's approval.[4] In a long letter to Armstrong dated August 13, Madison defined the jurisdiction and responsibilities of the Secretary of War;[5] the letter was in effect a sharp rebuke. Armstrong, however, did not resign and he offered no argumentative defense for himself. During the next two weeks his acts day by day signified his intention to comply literally with Madison's specifications of the Secretary's duties. Except when requested to do so by the President, he made no major decisions and took no initiatives that departed from prescribed procedures.

Even before August 13, in planning for the defense of Washington, the Secretary of War had already assumed a posture of passivity. Armstrong was sure that the enemy would never attack Washington, a city which had no military or economic value. Madison disagreed. He thought that "the eclat that would attend a successful inroad upon the capital, beyond the intrinsic magnitude of the achievement," would be worth the small skirmishes that could be expected with the few American troops then in the environs of the District. There would be a real danger of attack, if the enemy learned that there were no strong defenses to block his way.[6]

The issue of defending Washington was not mentioned in the letter of August 13, but it had in fact been a point of irritation between the President and Secretary of War throughout the summer. In June, Madison's apprehension about the defense of

Washington was known to individual members of the cabinet, but Armstrong remained unconcerned.[7] At last, on July 1, in a formal meeting with the heads of departments at the President's mansion, Madison himself brought forward a plan for the defense of the capital. There was little discussion of his proposals, and no dissent was expressed.[8] The next day General William Winder was placed in charge of a newly organized military district to carry out the plan.[9]

During the next six weeks, reports of recent failures and forecasts of future troubles accumulated in Washington. Brown's campaign ended in retreat. A waterborne expedition of about seven hundred men on Lake Huron failed to take Fort Michilimacinac. A large army of European veterans was being assembled near Montreal for an invasion of northeastern New York state, and a naval squadron was ready to assist this invasion by operating on Lake Champlain. A small British army occupied Eastport and Moose Island on the Maine frontier. The latest letters from the peace commissioners were still reporting that negotiations had not begun. Newspapers from London had been denouncing Madison as a tyrant who should suffer the same fate as Napoleon.[10] The President knew that the war could not much longer be financed without new loans and taxes.

On August 8 Madison issued a proclamation calling Congress to meet on September 19. His purpose for calling the next session to begin at this early date was stated in ominously vague language: "great and weighty matters" formed "an extraordinary occasion for convening" the House and Senate "to consult and determine on such measures as in their wisdom may be deemed meet for the welfare of the United States."[11] In his message of September 20 Madison awkwardly specified his reasons for calling Congress to meet before October 31:

Notwithstanding the early day which had been fixed for your session of the present year, I was induced to call you together still sooner, as well that any inadequacy in the existing provisions for the wants of the Treasury might be supplied as that no delay might happen in providing for the result of the negotiations on foot with Great Britain, whether it should require arrangements adapted to a return to peace or further and more effective provisions for prosecuting the war.[12]

On August 19, an army of forty-five hundred British veterans under General Ross landed at Benedict, Maryland, a village on the Patuxent River about twenty-five miles from Chesapeake

Bay and about forty miles from Washington. The defensive troops and fortifications then prepared to engage the invader were only a small fraction of what Madison had proposed six and a half weeks before. Only within the next five days was General Winder able to gather together a motley aggregation of some seven thousand men, most of whom were raw militiamen from Maryland and the District of Columbia.

Neither Madison nor Armstrong tried to improvise a strategy for meeting the British army that marched inland from Benedict, and neither offered much advice to General Winder.[13] Armstrong's reticence was noted by Treasury Secretary George W. Campbell, who suggested that the Secretary of War ought to be encouraged to assist Winder.[14] On the morning of August 24 Madison told Armstrong that his letter of August 13 should not be interpreted as a restraint upon giving advice to Winder. At Bladensburg later that day, just before the battle began, Armstrong conferred with Winder, but he recommended no changes in the deployment of troops already made. They were as satisfactory as circumstances permitted, he told Madison only a few minutes after talking to Winder.[15]

Madison twice visited Winder at his headquarters while Ross's army was on its way from Benedict to Bladensburg. On the evening of August 22 and the morning of August 23 he visited him at Old Fields about eight miles east of the District boundary; and on the morning of August 24, together with the heads of departments, he conferred with him near the Navy Yard. Nothing in the written records indicates that he saw any special disadvantages in the locations of these sites for command headquarters or any serious defects in Winder's disposition of troops.[16] To Dolly he wrote that the men who paraded before him at Old Fields were "in high spirits & made a good appearance."[17]

By the time he visited Old Fields he assumed that the crisis would be over before additional help could reach Winder.[18] He did, however, make at least two minor changes in the assignment of troops. Previous orders to the commander of militia in Fairfax County, Virginia, were changed so as to bring his entire regiment to Washington as speedily as possible, and Commodore Joshua Barney was permitted to move about five hundred sailors and marines from the Navy Yard bridge to join the forces astride the route between Bladensburg and Washington.[19]

Madison did not exert himself personally to arouse a fighting spirit among the troops under Winder's command. He made no exhortative speeches and issued no proclamations calling for an heroic defense of the national capital. His presence at Old Fields, at the Navy Yard, and at Bladensburg was primarily for convenience of communication, not to boost morale.

Calm as always, he disguised the feelings of despair and anguish which we must presume he felt at this time of impending doom. There was nothing in his deportment to incite panic. But, likewise, there was nothing to inspire a rallying of the collective will to resist conquest no matter what the costs. Neither the precipitous withdrawal of Maryland militiamen from Bladensburg nor the dauntless stand by Barney's men near the District boundary can be ascribed to the personal influence of the President.

From the afternoon of August 24 until the morning of August 28, 1814, Madison was chief magistrate for a government that ceased to function. As the British army under Ross made its way from Bladensburg to Washington, the President, several heads of departments, and General Winder fled in different directions. Already government records and civil servants had been evacuated to the countryside surrounding the District. By the morning of August 25 much of the capital was in charred ruins, General Ross having ordered the burning of the President's mansion, the halls of Congress, all the buildings housing the executive departments (except the patent and post offices), the rope walks, the equipment of the pro-administration newspaper *The National Intelligencer*, and several houses from which snipers had fired upon British soldiers. The Navy Yard was also burned, but by order of Secretary of the Navy Jones, in order to prevent its equipment from being put to use by the enemy.[20]

Madison had come back to Washington several hours before the British troops arrived. At about 6 P.M. he had easily escaped across the river to Virginia, where he spent two nights and a day.[21] Attorney General Rush was with him all this time; Secretary of the Navy Jones joined him during the day. Although never farther from the Potomac than Falls Church, the President was out of touch with the Secretaries of State, War, and Treasury, while the two department heads with him were out of touch with their subordinates. During the day of August 26, the President was in Maryland, going from a ferry above the Great Falls to Montgomery Court House and Brookeville without catching up with Winder's army en route to Baltimore. The next day, Saturday, August 27, Monroe notified him that Ross's troops were returning to their ships. He then decided to call upon the department heads to meet him at the capital. Accompanied by Rush and Monroe he rode from Brookeville to Washington, finishing his journey at about five in the afternoon.[22]

Since the evening of August 22, when he first went to Old Fields, he had spent only one night in Washington, and for many hours he had been on the jogging saddle of a horse. Even without the thoughts of disaster that must have haunted him night and day during the week that Washington burned, he underwent a trying ordeal for a man of his age and physical condition. He was then in his sixty-third year; it had been just one year since he was convalescing from a long illness which at one point brought him to the brink of death.

His only comfort as he moved furtively from place to place in Virginia and Maryland was the sympathy of friends with whom he lodged and reunion with his wife for part of a day and night at Wiley's Tavern on Difficult Run near Great Falls. Dolly Madison had left her home in Washington while the President was returning from Bladensburg, had gone to Virginia via Georgetown, had spent the night of August 24 only one mile from her husband, and had gone the next day to Wiley's Tavern. She remained in Virginia until she received a note from Brookeville asking her to come back to Washington.[23]

The next two weeks were as fraught with peril as the two that had just gone by. The day after Madison returned to Washington two officers from the District militia called upon him and announced that their brigade had unanimously resolved not to serve under a War Department headed by Secretary Armstrong, whom they denounced as the willing cause of the destruction of the city of Washington.[24] The city of Alexandria the same day capitulated to a squadron that had come up the Potomac, and it seemed that nearby Washington and Georgetown might soon be impelled to do the same. Ross's army, which had embarked at Benedict on August 30, landed again on September 12 at the mouth of the Petapsco River and the next day marched to within a mile and a half of Baltimore. Between August 31 and September 6 General Prevost moved an army of eleven thousand men to Plattsburgh, where he faced an American army markedly inferior in size and experience. On August 29 the commander of a landing party which occupied Fort Barancas near Pensacola issued a proclamation calling for the liberation of Louisiana. On September 1, General John C.

Sherbrooke began to land two thousand troops in Maine, and, after encountering resistance during the next eight days that was less than feeble, proclaimed the annexation of the coast between the Penobscot River and New Brunswick. Along the Niagara, British and Canadian troops held Fort Niagara on the New York side near Lake Ontario and held positions on the Canadian side from which they could renew assaults upon Brown's army in Fort Erie. All this time, the banks of Philadelphia, New York, and other cities outside New England were failing to make payments in specie. And no news came from Ghent as to the fate of the peace negotiations.

September 11 marked the beginning of a change for the better. On that day an American squadron commanded by Captain McDonough defeated the British squadron on Lake Champlain, and General Prevost began to withdraw his army from Plattsburgh. On September 14 the British fleet and army abandoned the siege of Baltimore. On September 15 a British squadron failed to take the fort guarding the entrance of Mobile Bay. On September 17 Brown launched a sortie from Fort Erie which induced his besiegers to withdraw northward to Chippewa Creek.

News from Lake Champlain arrived in Washington on the morning of September 19. In his message to Congress the next day, Madison was able to include the triumphs at Plattsburgh and Baltimore in his review of military and naval operations for 1814. In the victories before and after September 11 the President saw "a series of achievements" which had given "new lustre to the American arms." In addition to praising the gallant and spirited defenders of Plattsburgh and Baltimore, he told of "the splendid victories gained on the Canadian side of the Niagara," the "bold and skillful operations of Major-General Jackson" against the Creeks in Mississippi Territory, and the capture of "rich prizes" by privateers. His most extravagant eulogy was for the captain and crew of a ship that had surrendered to the enemy: David Porter and his "brave comrades" had "hidden" their loss of the *Essex* in a "blaze of heroism" that "merited all the effusions of gratitude which their country" was "ever ready to bestow on the champions of its rights and of its safety." Upon the defenders of Washington the President bestowed no laurels and no reprimands; only the invaders were mentioned:

In the events of the present campaign the enemy, with all his augmented means and wanton use of them, has little ground for exultation, unless he can feel it in the success of his recent enterprises against this metropolis and the neighboring town of Alexandria, from both of which his retreats were as precipitate as his attempts were bold and fortunate.[25]

Republicans in Congress were less ready than the President to forget the Washington debacle, but they had no desire to make it a subject of debate with the opposition. On September 23 they voted for a motion to appoint a committee of investigation. The chairman and majority of members appointed to the committee had been supporters of the administration. Written testimonials and records were quietly obtained from some twenty-six civil and military officers. The approach of the committee indicated that Madison was not likely to lose Congressional support from the most humiliating episode of the war and the one in which he was most directly involved. In its final report, submitted on November 29, there was no suggestion that the President should be censured or even admonished. It concluded that "the means authorized for the security of the 10th military district, by the President of the United States, in a cabinet council of the 1st of July, were ample and sufficient as to the extent of the force, and seasonable as to the time when the measures were authorized." The report was not debated. On February 4, 1815, "the order of the day on the report of the committee appointed on the 23rd September" was "postponed indefinitely."[26]

The British failures at Baltimore and Plattsburgh, welcome as they were when Madison composed his message of September 20, did not change fundamentally the situation which had prompted the President to call Congress into session at this time. The Treasury was exhausted. No authoritative declaration of British policy had come to Washington since the negotiations had begun at Ghent on August 8, but the scale of warfare in September implied a determination to continue the war and for purposes other than the mere frustration of American aims. The "principles and manner in which the war is now avowedly carried on," Madison told Congress, compelled them to infer that the British government was aiming "with undivided force a deadly blow at out growing prosperity, perhaps at our national existence."[27]

The general aims of British policy inferred from recent military operations were confirmed and itemized by dispatches from Ghent received in Washington on Saturday, October 8. In reports dated August 12 and August 19, the American commissioners had disclosed that the British delegates were asking for cession of a part of Maine, military and naval control of the Great Lakes, formation of an Indian buffer state north of the Ohio from which Americans would be excluded, a boundary line west of Lake Superior that would connect with the Mississippi River, the right of British subjects to navigate the full length of the Mississippi, and an equivalent for continuing the fishing rights granted to the United States in the treaty of 1783.[28]

Madison submitted the Ghent dispatches to Congress on Monday, October 10. Four days later, in order to contrast the aims of the two governments, he submitted instructions sent to the American mission since April 15, 1813, including of course those of June 27, 1814. The House on October 10 authorized the printing of ten thousand copies of the Ghent dispatches in order "to convince the people that an honest and fair effort had been made to obtain peace and it had been denied upon terms mutually honorable."[29]

Revulsion against the British terms brought support from some men previously associated with the opposition. Alexander Hanson and Thomas Oakely, hitherto severe critics of the war, spoke in the House for uncompromising resistance to such terms.[30] In a letter of October 19, Monroe told the American commissioners that their dispatches were producing the best effect in uniting all parties in a determined resistance to the extravagant pretensions of the enemy. He also said that printed copies of the dispatches should have a favorable influence on the continental powers. Charles J. Ingersoll said that Madison's use of the Ghent dispatches was "a master stroke of bold American policy."[31]

The American commissioners had expected negotiations to terminate because they believed on the basis of the extreme demands presented before August 19 that the British would never accept a peace based upon their instructions; and they neither expected nor desired a further retreat from the position approved by the cabinet on June 27. Despite the growing strength of British forces in North America, Madison's response was identical with the commissioners. He gave no thought to acceding to the British demands in order to keep the negotiations going. Monroe told the commissioners in his reply of October 19 that the President entirely approved their rejection of the British terms.[32]

The firm stand of the Americans at Ghent and the support they received from Madison were important factors in the ultimate outcome of the negotiations, for the British ministry knew that only the continuation of a costly war could hope to force the Americans to give in to their terms. In the showdown, Prime Minister Liverpool and Foreign Secretary Castlereagh were not willing to continue the high war taxes or add to England's mammoth public debt in order to finance an offensive war for terms, which, if ever accepted by the Americans, would become permanent grievances that would probably lead to another war within a few years. Also, they were uneasy about having their disposable forces across the Atlantic while striving to establish a satisfactory peace settlement in Europe.[33]

Exposure of the British terms brought additional verbal support for the war from congressmen and newspapers in the Middle States, but it had little effect in Massachusetts, Connecticut, and Rhode Island. The legislatures of these three southern New England states approved a convention to meet in Hartford, Connecticut, on December 15 to deliberate upon the constitutional disadvantages and military dangers besetting the "eastern section of the union." Also, from the President's point of view, Congress was derelict in failing to approve measures deemed essential for waging a war for national survival against a powerful and determined foe. Administration proposals were either rejected outright, amended to the point of unacceptability, or not approved until late in the session. Madison's disappointments were expressed in a private letter to Wilson Cary Nicholas. He wrote on November 26, 1814:

You are not mistaken in viewing the conduct of the Eastern States as the source of our greatest difficulties in carrying on the war, as it certainly is the greatest, if not the sole, inducement with the enemy to persevere in it. The greater part of the people in that quarter have been brought by their leaders, added by their priests, under a delusion scarcely exceeded by that recorded in the period of witchcraft; and the leaders are becoming daily more desperate in the use they make of it. Their object is power. If they could obtain it by menaces, their efforts would stop there. These failing, they are ready to go every length for which they can train their followers. Without foreign co-operation, revolts & separation will be hardly risked; and what the effect of so profligate an experiment may be, first on deluded partizans, and next on those remaining faithful to the nation who are respectable in their consistency, and even for their numbers, is for conjecture only. The best may be hoped, but the worst ought to be kept in view. In the meantime the course to be taken by the Govt is full of delicacy and perplexity; and the more so under the pinch which exists in our fiscal affairs, and the lamentable tardiness of the Legislature in applying some relief.[34]

When the Ghent commissioners had composed the reports that went before Congress on October 10, they had said that there was then no "hope of peace." In time, the original British demands were to be given up, haltingly, and one by one; but the next report, dated October 25, and submitted to Congress by Madison on December 1, was also drafted upon an occasion when there seemed no possibility of an agreement. Between October 8, 1814 and February 14, 1815, there was no time when Madison looked forward to a successful outcome of the negotiations; his expectation was that the next report from Ghent would announce the departure of the American mission.

In late December, 1814, as the President looked to the year ahead, what he saw was an indefinite continuation of the war, for which Congress was then making slow and inadequate preparations. What he saw immediately before the country were rumored threats of secession in the states sponsoring the Hartford Convention and credible evidence that the British were planning a seaborne invasion of Louisiana.

The threats of secession and invasion alike had to be met by men and resources then available to the executive. The task of defending New Orleans, the probable objective of a landing in Louisiana, was mainly in the hands of General Jackson. Monroe, serving as Secretary of War since September, eagerly cooperated with Jackson by providing estimates of the composition and probable destination of the British army being assembled at Jamaica and by providing promptly for authorizations to raise troops and supplies.

With utmost caution and discretion, Monroe and Madison also considered plans for dealing with an uprising in New England. Throughout the war Madison had been bothered by the disaffection in New England because of its effect upon the war and diplomatic negotiations. He had doubted, however, that it would lead to secession, from which few economic benefits would accrue in comparison with membership in the Union.[35] In December, 1814, he was still rather inclined to believe that the Hartford delegates would cling to the Union because of its long-term economic value, but, in case his hypothetical reasoning should prove wrong in its surmise, he cautiously outlined tentative plans for meeting overt resistance to the federal government. To crush any armed revolt that might occur, he in-

tended to employ troops in New York under the command of
Daniel D. Tompkins and loyal volunteers from the New England states. From letters sent to Secretary Monroe by Colonel
Thomas Jesup, assigned to Hartford as a recruiting officer, he
derived assessments of the secret proceedings of the convention based upon the observations of local people.[36]

All the threats facing the country, immediate and long-term,
were removed several weeks before the President ceased to
think of them as grave dangers. The negotiations at Ghent terminated on December 24, the Hartford Convention adjourned
on January 5, and the battle for the defense of New Orleans
ended on January 8. News of the adjournment of the Hartford
Convention was the first to arrive in Washington; its official
report, in failing to call immediately for forceful resistance to
the federal government, diminished anxieties even if it produced no rejoicing. News of the great victory at New Orleans
was known in Washington by February 5; it brought both signs
of relief and the happiest rejoicing since the capital moved to
the Potomac in 1800. Festive victory celebrations were still
fresh memories, when, on February 15, the *National Intelligencer* reported that a treaty of peace had come to the State
Department.[37]

Just one fact produced another outburst of rejoicing: the war
was over. That the treaty said nothing about the original aims
of the war was easily overlooked by all except the most intransi-
gent critics of the administration. Madison submitted the treaty
to the Senate on February 15. The next day it was ratified
unanimously.

The timing of the news of the defeat of the British at New
Orleans and their surrender at Ghent of the onerous demands
that had been publicized in October immediately created an
illusion in many minds that the United States had won the war.
This popular illusion was to be a lasting one in American history. But the President, whom the celebrants of 1815 praised
for his contribution to ending the war, was to receive little
commendation from posterity. Indeed, not only did Madison
fail to win lasting esteem from the Treaty of Ghent, he came to
be thought of as the worst of the wartime presidents between
John Adams and Harry Truman. That he took the country into
a war that it was unprepared to fight and mismanaged it from
the time it began came to be the simple and prevailing view.

Practical politicians who observed Madison personally when
he was President were less derogatory than the historians who

came after them.[38] Indeed, their appraisals, while not always laudatory, were not unfavorable. Perhaps men like Clay, Adams, Paulding, and Ingersoll were biased in his favor by having been associated with his party and his administration. Perhaps they, as well as his political opponent Daniel Webster, could not bring themselves to pronounce harsh judgments upon a man of such benign personal qualities. Perhaps all who presented a favorable view of his presidential leadership were simply magnanimous to an elder statesman out of appreciation for his earlier services in the founding of the republic.

Perhaps, too, as practical politicians, their judgments differed from the historians because they knew more intimately the political intricacies of his administration and unduly sympathized with a fellow practitioner of their own vocation. Perhaps they knew that the unfit man for a position, when selected by the President, had yet to prove his unfitness or was better than other men who would consent to service or could obtain approval from the Senate; perhaps they knew that the politically feasible alternative to a faulty course actually pursued might well have been a worse one; and perhaps they gave less weight to his maladroitness in administration, propaganda, and public finance than they did to his astuteness in the politics of personalities and the tactics of diplomacy. Perhaps, too, these practical politicians of the early days of the republic innocently believed that the maintenance of civil liberties in time of war was worth some sacrifice of efficiency.

The treaty of Ghent marked the end of an era for the nation. For twenty-two years American diplomacy, public finance, and economic prosperity had been indissolubly linked to the French Revolutionary and Napoleonic wars. Until 1808 exports and shipping had expanded greatly in response to war-making in Europe, but thereafter had been depressed by domestic legislation that failed in its ultimate aim of an even larger share for the United States of the booming wartime markets. Absence of war in Europe and North America provided the setting for the new era that began during the last two years of Madison's presidency.

Commercial and agricultural prosperity quickly returned, as export and shipping were resumed. Diplomatic negotiations, such as resulted in a commercial treaty with Great Britain in July, 1815, could now be conducted without nasty disputes about neutral and belligerent rights. Discussions about boundaries, fortifications, and Indians on the Canadian frontier could be conducted without considering their crucial impingement upon the outcome of a great war in Europe. On the Southern frontier, the United States, undistracted by the problems of a Europe at war, faced a Spain that was encountering rebellion in all of its continental colonies and which could turn to no war-time ally for diplomatic assistance as it attempted to hold its possessions east of the Mississippi. That Spain could long hold the Floridas, contiguous to a growing power that was determined to have them, while losing all of its colonies between the Rio Grande and Cape Horn, seemed highly improbable. On both the Northern and Southern frontiers, the Indian tribes that had suffered crushing defeats while Britain was fighting on their side surely could not expect, without a European ally, to win a war against the advancing white Americans. On the North African coast, the Algerine or Barbary pirates would be preying upon American merchant vessels which could now receive some protection from fighting ships previously employed against the British.

Characteristically, Madison entered the new era without proclaiming that the old was being left behind. In his messages to Congress in 1815 and 1816 he said little about the past.[39] Reverence for the federal republic was expressed, but its survival was attributed to the virtues of the American people and the inherent strength of their institutions, not to the policies or leadership of the Republican party. All the great issues that had dominated party politics for a quarter of a century were passed over in silence; the policies of his opponents were not disparaged and his own were not extolled. Without any announcement that he was doing so, he took a nonpartisan and forward-looking position. Neither Washington had been able to leave the presidency nor Jefferson enter it without some reference to the party strife of the preceding years.

Several of the measures recommended to the fourteenth Congress raised constitutional issues, each of which Madison dealt with in a different way. He made no mention of constitutional objections to protective tariffs, because he had not anticipated that any would be made. He intimated that a constitutional amendment would be necessary for federal roads and canals, when he first proposed them in his message of December 15, 1815; later, in a veto message of March 3, 1817, he argued that Congress could tax and legislate for the general welfare and common defense only by employing the delegated powers or powers properly implied from them, and that the power to build roads and canals was neither included among the delegated powers nor necessary to carry any one of them into effect. In recommending a national bank he deferred to the conclusion without adopting the reasoning of those with whom he had disagreed in 1791. When, on January 30, 1815, he vetoed a bank bill which failed to provide certain financial services to the public and to the government which he thought imperative, he waived

The question of the constitutional authority of the Legislature to establish an incorporated bank as being precluded in my judgment by repeated recognitions under varied circumstances of the validity of such an institution in acts of the legislative, executive, and judicial branches of the Government, accompanied by indications, in different modes, of a concurrence of the general will of the nation.

Not since his service in the Virginia legislature in the mid-1780's had Madison's thoughts been so strongly centered upon long-term policies affecting the economic growth and unity of the nation. Never in his career had he been so serenely confident about the future stability and well-being of the United States. His messages to the fourteenth Congress revealed no worry about the eighty million dollars that had been added to the prewar debt of thirty-nine millions. There were no pleas for a drastic curb of government expenditures in order to pay off the public debt in the shortest possible time, no hesitation in proposing measures that called for the greatest peacetime expenditures in the history of the republic. Debts and taxes were no longer viewed as necessary evils that should be kept to an absolute minimum; now they were seen as relative to the national wealth. Taken for granted was the prospect of a growing and prosperous economy that could easily provide the taxes to redeem the national debt and pay for increased annual expenditures.

Madison's messages of February 18, 1815, December 5, 1815, and December 3, 1816 forecast the measures that were to be championed by the leading national statesmen of the next decade. The elements of Henry Clay's "American System" were among his recommendations: protective tariffs, federal construction of roads and canals, and a national bank similar to the first Bank of the United States. Like John Quincy Adams, whose presidential messages were to call for more federal participation in economic and educational development than any before the twentieth century, he asked Congress to prescribe national standards for weights and measures and to establish a national university in the District of Columbia. His military and naval policy, also to prevail in the 1820's, represented a basic reversal of the position he had supported when in Congress in the 1790's. Asking for a standing army, a navy, fortifications, military academies, and a reorganization of the militia, he now proposed that the United States be partially prepared for war at all times. There was not even a warning that vigilance was required to prevent a standing army from becoming a threat to republican liberties. Concealment of his views on naval policy no longer characterized his writings: his defense of naval power that began during the war was continued in his peacetime messages. The manning of merchant ships exclusively by American citizens, which had been proposed during the war as an inducement for Britain to abandon impressment, was also advocated in time of peace in order to assure American vessels the services of seamen whom no foreign power could claim under any circumstances. Discriminatory navigation laws were advocated for the same reasons that they had been advocated in the first three Congresses.

Madison's rationale for the new policies was also much the same as that used during the next decade by Monroe, Clay, John Quincy Adams, and Calhoun. They were intended to promote national security, national independence, economic links between the parts of the Union, national economic growth, and enlightened progress generally. A self-contained, isolated economy was not their goal. Duties were to be levied to protect industries that would provide a source of supply for military needs and "primary wants of individuals" that could not be cut off by a foreign power. Expansion of the domestic market was to be selective and was to supplement not replace foreign markets. The future prosperity of the country, so optimistically anticipated, assumed a continually expanding foreign trade.

No longer was Madison meditating upon what had seemed to him the most fundamental problems of government in the 1780's and 1790's. Missing from his private letters and public addresses were any expressions of fearful anxiety about majorities in Congress or state legislatures abusing the interests of minorities, about either the federal or state governments encroaching upon the jurisdiction of the other or upon the property and civil rights of private citizens. Missing also was any discussion of the problem of resolving conflicts of economic interests so as to produce justice for individuals or to promote nationwide support for the Union. Government as an instrument for promoting the total wealth and power of the nation was now of much greater interest to him than government as an arbitrator of the internal disputes within society. He had become a Hamiltonian in a way that he had never been in the 1780's.

CHAPTER XIV

Nineteen Years at Montpellier

AFTER LEAVING THE PRESIDENCY, MADISON THOUGHT OF himself as permanently withdrawn from the "public theatre."[1] He resolved to have nothing to do with party politics, and as far as personalities and electioneering were concerned he succeeded. In the presidential elections of 1824, 1828, and 1832, he refused to indicate, even to his most confidential friends, any preferences. When nominated as an Adams elector in 1828, he announced that he could not permit his name to be used. When he wrote on constitutional questions or issues of public policy, he often requested that his views not be publicized, and he always attempted to phrase his arguments so as not to appear to be taking sides between rival candidates and parties. He deviated no more than three or four times from an avowal to recommend no one for appointive offices.

Neutral toward the politics of office-seeking, he was never indifferent toward public affairs, and he kept himself well informed about issues and leaders. Also, he was not averse to offering advice on public policies to men in high office. His letters to President Monroe and to Richard Rush when the latter served as minister to England, especially on questions of foreign policy, were as fully advisory as his letters had been when Jefferson occupied executive offices.

Withdrawal from the "public theatre" did not quite mean an absolute refusal to accept all positions of public service. In 1829 he was a delegate to the convention that revised the constitution of Virginia. Between 1817 and 1826, he assisted Jefferson in founding the University of Virginia and succeeded him as chairman of its Board of Visitors. He was president of the Albemarle Agricultural Society for several years. He accepted the presidency of the American Colonization Society in 1833, although, because of his physical condition at the time, he was well aware that the office was largely honorific.[2]

When Madison retired to his Montpellier estate in April, 1817, he seemed to have before him the opportunity to enjoy the management of his farms and have a leisurely life of social conviviality or seclusion according to his own personal preferences. On the eve of his departure from Washington, to which he was never again to return, he wrote: "I am in the midst of preparations to get to my farm, where I shall make myself a fixture, and where I anticipate many enjoyments, which, if not fully realized, will be a welcome exchange for the labors and anxieties of public life."[3]

John Adams thought Madison might be unhappy in his retirement because he had no children or grandchildren. His friend Jefferson thought differently: "I do not entertain your apprehensions for the happiness of our brother Madison in a state of retirement. Such a mind as his, fraught with information and with matter for reflection, can never know *ennui*. Besides, there will always be work enough cut out for him to continue his active usefulness to his country. For example, he and Monroe (the President) are now here on the work of a collegiate institution to be established in our neighborhood, of which they and myself are three of six Visitors. This, if it succeeds, will raise up children for Mr. Madison to employ his attention through life." Already, three weeks before making this prediction, Jefferson had held out to Madison the prospects of a "release from incessant labors, corroding anxieties, active enemies and interested friends," and a return to the "tranquility" and "independence" of his books and farm. A day of what was in store for him would be worth "ages" of what he was leaving.[4]

Released from the "anxieties" of public office, Madison for about ten years busied himself with the management of his farm and agricultural studies, read widely on a variety of subjects, and enjoyed visiting and being visited. But the amount of his time for leisure, privacy, and indulgence of his own predilections was much less than he had hoped for. To Robert Walsh, Jr., he wrote on December 22, 1827:

It is an error very naturally prevailing that the retirement from public service, of which my case is an example, is a leisure for whatever pursuit might be most inviting. The truth, however, is that I have rarely, during the period of my public life, found my time less at my disposal than since I took my leave of it, nor have I the consolation of finding, that as my powers of application necessarily decline, the demands on them proportionally decrease.[5]

In retirement Madison was still that same intriguing combination of shyness, modesty, assertiveness, sociability, and intellectuality that made him one of the rarest personalities in the history of political leadership. Something more than conventional etiquette and a sense of duty prompted him to devote much of his time to answering the many letters which came to him as a former President who had had a "prolonged & diversified career in the public service." His letters could have been shorter, and the number of politely perfunctory notes could have been much greater than they were. His mind, however, was much too active and the sociability of his intellect too strongly ingrained to permit routine replies to those who brought him something to think about. His lifelong interests in many subjects continued unabated; he was curious to be introduced to matters that had escaped his attention before; and he still had thoughts which he could not keep to himself. Qualities which he was inherently incapable of mentioning were responsible for part of the "extensive and often laborious correspondence" which he commented upon in his autobiographical memoir.[6]

His correspondents forced upon him letters and a "crowd of printed things"[7] upon topics as varied as schools, universities, and libraries; codification and simplification of the laws, penal reform, abolition of capital punishment, and the application of Benthamite utilitarianism to lawmaking; Malthusian and other theories of population and poverty; explanations of the variations of geological formations and biological species; methods of cultivation, agricultural chemistry, and rural economics; mechanical inventions; philology; phrenology; the harms of alcohol and tobacco; betterment of the condition of the Indian tribes; abolition of slavery; and communal living that sought to base society upon the principle of cooperation rather than competition.

The many ideas for changing the institutions of society to which he was exposed were fascinating. He enjoyed "the happiness of passing through a period glorious for our country, and, more than any preceding one, likely to improve the social condition of man."[8] Nothing "more truly glorious" could "animate the breast of man," he wrote to La Fayette, "than elevating and meliorating the condition of his race."[9] Even the perfectionists, such as Robert Dale Owen and Francis Wright, were heard with sympathetic understanding; he was skeptical about the success of their projects, but he gave specific and undogmatic reasons for his doubts and wished that something of value might be learned from them.[10] In a letter commenting upon Owen's "panacea" for eliminating the "distress" and "vicissitudes" of laboring people, he concluded: "With the knowledge of the impossibility of banishing evil altogether from human society, we must console ourselves with the belief that it is overbalanced by the good mixed with it, and direct our efforts to an increase of the good proportion of the mixture."[11]

Of the evils yet to be eliminated from American society, Madison told one of his correspondents, none was such a "dreadful calamity" and "filled so many with despair" as the institution of slavery.[12] His belief that the condition of the slaves in Virginia was much better than in colonial times[13] did not assuage his conscience. "The magnitude of this evil among us is so deeply felt, and so universally acknowledged," he wrote to Francis Wright, "that no merit could be greater than devising a satisfactory remedy for it."[14]

His remedy, voiced to several correspondents and visitors to Montpellier, called for voluntary, gradual, non-confiscatory emancipation, and for colonization of the freed Negroes in Africa. The greatest obstacle to general emancipation or manumissions by individual masters was the fate of the Negroes in freedom. He believed that the white society of the United States would not accept the blacks on a basis of equality, and freedom without equality would be worse for the blacks than slavery. Since the whole nation had shared in the responsibility for slavery, had gained some profit from it, and would benefit by the removal of an institution inconsistent with the basic principles upon which the republic was founded, he thought the whole nation should bear part of the costs. He suggested a constitutional amendment to authorize the federal government to use some of the proceeds from sale of the public lands for the purpose of assisting emancipation and colonization. Even with compensated emancipation, he knew that colonization might be opposed by some of the Negroes and by masters fearful of losing a needed labor supply. The objections of the latter could perhaps be overcome by the gradualness of resettlement and by a growing source of labor provided by European immigration.[15]

Madison was confident that his plan for eliminating slavery was just and practicable. When he expected such a plan to be carried out, however, remained indefinite. He was an active supporter of the American Colonization Society which transported about three thousand Negroes to Liberia between 1820 and 1834, but he declined to follow the example of his friend Edward Coles in manumitting his own slaves, and he never agitated publicly for general emancipation. His own slaves, he told Harriet Martineau, had a "horror of going to Liberia."[16]

According to Charles J. Ingersoll, he believed that the militant antislavery societies founded in the 1830's were harmful to the cause of abolition. His views of the abolitionists, however, as his views on abolition, were privately expressed. Despite the magnitude of the evil of slavery, he clearly had no desire to engage in public controversy about it.[17]

"Next to the case of the black race within our bosom, that of the red man on our borders is the problem most baffling to the policy of our country."[18] Such was Madison's estimation of the treatment of the Indians as another great evil remaining in the United States. On this subject, however, he wrote little. Perhaps the best summary of his views can be found in a letter to William Wirt, October 1, 1830, the conclusion of which stated an idea common to his thinking about the two subordinate races: "It is evident that they can never be tranquil or happy within the bounds of a State, either in a separate or subject character, that a removal to another home, if a good one can be found, may well be the wish of their best friends. But the removal ought to be made voluntary by adequate inducements, present and prospective; and no means ought to be grudged which such a measure may require."[19]

In retirement Madison was often solicited for his views on public policy and constitutional issues. He continued to adhere essentially to the same positions that he had taken during the last two years of his presidency, and since his views were generally accepted by Congress, the Presidents, and the Supreme Court in the 1820's, the first decade of his retirement was a period when he was quite satisfied with the course of national affairs. To be sure, advocates of federal roads and canals were divided on the necessity of a constitutional amendment, his successor Monroe adopting his own position and John Quincy Adams another, but this disagreement among the advocates of federal aid for national economic development was not especially disturbing to him. To Jefferson he wrote on February 17, 1825: "I consider the question as to canals, &c., as decided ... because sanctioned by the nation under the permanent influence of benefit to the major part of it; and if not carried into practice, will owe its failure to other than Constitutional obstacles."[20]

The dominant opinion in Congress and the Supreme Court during Monroe's presidency met with increasing resistance in his state and Madison sometimes found his views subjected to attacks from his fellow Virginians. He was at first surprised and puzzled that the constitutionality of protective tariffs was questioned. "Virginia appears to be the only State that now denies, or ever did deny, the power," he wrote on March 22, 1827.[21] Faced, however, with serious and widespread arguments that import duties could be levied for the sole purpose of raising revenue, he wrote several letters, one of which was published in a newspaper, in which he demonstrated that tonnage and import duties, beginning with the first Congress, had repeatedly been levied for the purpose of protecting shippers and manufacturers with no constitutional objections being raised.[22]

On the constitutional issues raised by the admission of Missouri into the Union, Madison was more nearly aligned to the side of his Virginia critics than the national majority. He was positive that Congress had no power to prevent the importation of slaves when coming from another state, he doubted that Congress could refuse to admit a state into the Union because its constitution permitted slavery, and he was unconvinced by the precedent of excluding slavery from the Northwest Territory that Congress had the constitutional authority to prohibit slavery in United States territories.[23]

The federal Supreme Court was a subject of increasing criticism in Virginia during Monroe's presidency because of a broad interpretation of its own powers. Madison thought the Court in several cases had offered opinions not essential for the decisions rendered but argued that state courts could not be the final arbiter when there were conflicts between federal and state jurisdiction. He cited his thirty-ninth *Federalist* as authority for a belief at the time of ratification that the Supreme Court was intended to exercise this power. He also used his thirty-ninth *Federalist* as the core for his argument that ratification of the Constitution established a compound system of government which divided sovereign powers between the state and federal governments. The system of government approved in 1787 and 1788 was *sui generis*; it could not be categorized according to the definitions of earlier ages.[24]

Madison thought that the power of the Supreme Court was exaggerated by its critics. Usurpation of state powers by the federal government was much more likely to follow from acts of Congress demanded by its constituents. He still believed, as he had since 1792, that the prevailing interpretation of the Constitution would be that which a national majority wanted. The proper distribution of federal and state powers in the long run could best be maintained by a national majority upholding such a distribution; not by minorities using state governments to resist the federal government.[25]

During Jackson's presidency, when South Carolina threatened to nullify the tariff laws of 1828 and 1832, he condemned the doctrine that state governments could lawfully use force against abuses or usurpations of power by the federal government. Alarmed by a crisis for the Union, fearful that a new generation of leaders was forgetting the advantages of the Union while becoming obsessed with minor and transient disadvantages, incensed that the spokesmen for the doctrine of state sovereignty and state nullification were citing the Virginia Resolutions of 1798 as justification for their theories, and nettled by the charge that he himself had changed his views on the Constitution, he cogently expounded the theory of divided sovereignty which he had already presented when replying to critics of the Supreme Court. At the same time, by elucidating and expanding upon the report which he had prepared for the legislature in 1799, he emphatically denied that Virginia had either declared or implied that a state could nullify an act of Congress. Several of the many letters he wrote on the Federal Union and the Virginia Resolutions of 1798 were comprehensive discourses upon these themes; one was published in the *North American Review* of October, 1830.[26]

More "painful" to him than he could express in "words" was the thought that the Union "should be broken up and scattered to the winds" because of the grievances proclaimed by the nullifiers.[27] As a cause of their "sufferings," he wrote, the protective tariff had been "vastly overrated."[28] Land prices, market prices, and the costs of production were the sources of their economic troubles, not the costs added to consumer goods resulting from taxes on imports. Farms in the seaboard states were having to compete with farms in the West that had the advantages of cheaper and more fertile lands; Virginia growers of wheat and tobacco had the added difficulties of holding their markets in Europe. Lowering the tariff would effect little improvement so long as these basic factors remained unchanged. The future for a prosperous Virginia he saw in improved methods of cultivation, a diversification of crops, and the introduction of manufactures.[29]

This detached diagnosis of the economic situation in Virginia was not the product of a man who enjoyed financial security himself. On February 24, 1826, he wrote to Jefferson: "Since my return to private life (and the case was worse during my absence in Public) such have been the unkind seasons, & the ravages of insects, that I have made but one tolerable crop of Tobacco, and but one of Wheat; the proceeds of both of which were greatly curtailed by mishaps in the sale of them. And having no resources but in the earth I cultivate, I have been living very much throughout on borrowed means."[30] During the next decade there were years when he harvested better crops than those described to Jefferson but their profitability was not sufficient to prevent his continuing indebtedness. His financial troubles were made all the worse by his undertaking to pay the bills of his wastrel stepson John Payne Todd in order to keep him out of debtor's prisons. In order to maintain his solvency, the owner of the Montpellier estate had to sell some of his other lands, and, after finding a buyer whose character he trusted, to sell some of his slaves.[31]

Before 1827 Madison made only a few references to his age. In 1821 he wrote that his age was daily disinclining him to use his pen. In 1823 he said that it was right for a man of his age in every situation "to look to the event which awaits us all" and in the same year said that he was "holding life itself by a short thread." The next year he wrote that he was "becoming sensible" of the "wear and tear of life" and that his life was contracting much faster than the demands upon it could be discharged. In 1825 and 1826 he began to think that his "decreasing remnant of time" required him "to narrow, instead of widening, the scope of" his "researches."[32] On September 17, 1825, he wrote: "I am compelled by other demands on my time, among them other reading tasks in which I am in arrears, to abridge very much the portion alloted for works on husbandry." On March 11, 1826, he wrote that "time" was "fast stealing" from him "the activity necessary for agricultural pursuits."[33]

The older Madison became the more his own past thrust upon him the same political and constitutional subjects that had preoccupied his time when he had held public office. He was known to be a careful custodian of documents recording the events in which he had participated. As the men who made the Revolution and the Constitution died off, he was called upon to search his papers or his memory for information that could not be found in the records already published. Resolved not to permit others to use his letters and not to publish his memoirs during his own lifetime, he was faced with the necessity of total silence or of revealing something of what he knew to inquiring correspondents and visitors. If he had said nothing, he would have permitted many errors to become embedded in printed histories and biographies and would have strengthened an interpretation of national history inimical to public policies which he thought best for the United States and subversive of the Federal Union which he had so prominently helped to found and maintain. Although he initiated no historical arguments and earnestly sought to continue his lifelong practice of letting calumnies die a natural death, he departed many times from the rule of restraint which he struggled to impose upon himself. A polite readiness to supply information and judgments deemed inoffensive to his contemporaries, a compulsion to justify his own motives and consistency in public service, and a reluctance to permit questionable history to serve unworthy public purposes induced him to divulge historical facts and expound interpretations of events which he had witnessed. Writing about the past, especially as applied to the nullification controversy, increasingly pre-empted the time and energy which he had devoted to non-political interests during the first decade of his retirement.

Whatever the mixture of motives that moved him to take part in the historic debate on nullification, their intensity may be gauged by the difficulties he surmounted in order to do so. These were years when writing for him was always awkward and often painful, when his crippled fingers had difficulty in handling the papers he searched, when his vision was fading and his reading had to be broken by intervals of rest, when everything he did was "tedious" and "laborious." And while suffering from these disabilities, he could never quite rid himself of the notion that active participation in public controversies by a retired statesman of his age was unbecoming and ineffective. A man of his age, he thought, "should distrust himself, whether distrusted by his friends or not, and should never forget that his arguments, whatever they may be, will be answered by allusions to the date of his birth."[34] To the historian Jared Sparks he wrote on June 1, 1831: "Having outlived so many of my cotemporaries, I ought not to forget that I may be thought to have outlived myself."[35]

During the years when he had been president of the agricultural society and helping Jefferson found the university, that is, between 1817 and 1826, his health had been generally good. He had continued to have occasional attacks of "bilious fever," but his illnesses during these years seem to have been less frequent than when he had been in public office. In 1827, however, his letters began to refer to rheumatism in his fingers. After 1831, there were many months when he was confined to his bed, sometimes suffering simultaneously from chronic rheumatism, fevers such as had afflicted him intermittently throughout his life, and from the debilitation of old age. By the last year of his life, he could do little reading because of failing eyesight, and his hands were so crippled that some of his letters had to be dictated to his wife or her brother John C. Payne. His mind, however, remained unimpaired to the very end, enabling him to match wits with Calhoun, Webster, and other great debaters of the Jackson era.

So unaffected was his mind by his physical deterioration that he was able at times to look upon his pain-ridden and emaciated body with almost comical detachment. To Monroe he wrote on April 21, 1831: "In explanation of my microscopic writing, I must remark that the older I grow the more my stiffening fingers make smaller letters, as my feet take shorter steps; the progress in both cases being at the same time, more fatiguing as well as more slow." Acknowledging his "heartfelt" appreciation for gloves and a warm hat sent to him by a friend, he wrote on November 20, 1832: "But there is another article of covering, which I need most of all & which my best friends cannot supply. My bones have lost a sad portion of the flesh which clothed & protected them, and the digestive and nutritive organs which alone can replace it, are too slothful in their operations."[36]

Despite his physical infirmities, his financial difficulties, and his mental agony during the nullification controversy, he never lost confidence in the future of the federal republic. To the very end he never lost his capacity to enjoy the company of intelligent and friendly visitors. His wife Dolly, city-bred and gregarious, in her sixties in the 1830's, stayed with him constantly in his rural retreat, caring for him tenderly, protectively, and with devotion; and extending her charming hospitality to neighbors and to guests who came from afar to visit him.

From the written accounts of several visitors we get our only look at "Montpellier"—a name which Madison regularly put on the date line but omitted as a topic of information or observation in the body of his letters. Charles J. Ingersoll described the grounds and the house as he approached them in May, 1836: "Nearer Mr. Madison's the country is more improved, and the mountain scenery is very agreeable. You enter his outer gate from the woods, and at once get into something like a park, with his well-looking house about half a mile off; the whole cleared and improved, with trees in clumps, and other signs of ornamental agriculture." Harriet Martineau, who visited Madison in February, 1835, wrote: "The dwelling stands on a gentle eminence, and is neat and even handsome in its exterior, with a flight of steps leading up to the portico. A lawn and wood, which must be pleasant in summer, stretch behind; and from the front there is a noble object in the horizon, the mountain-chain which traverses the state, and makes it eminent for its scenery. The shifting lights from the blue mountains were a delightful refreshment to the eye."[37] Margaret Bayard Smith, who had been there in August, 1828, wrote: "A large and commodious mansion, designed more for comfort and hospitality than ornament and display, rises at the foot of a high wooded hill, which, while it affords shelter from the north-west winds, adds much to the picturesque beauty of the scene. The grounds around the house owe their ornaments more to nature than art, as, with the exception of a fine garden behind, and a wide spread lawn before the house, for miles around the ever varying and undulating surface of the ground is covered with forest trees." The cultivated lands, naturally fertile and improved by judicious care, she noted, were a comparatively small part of the estate.[38]

The interior of the house was also described by Ingersoll: "The rooms are good; furnished with French carpets, large windows, a good many paintings and some statuary—altogether without any fashionable or very elegant equipment, yet in a gentlemanlike style of rural propriety." Miss Martineau had remarked that the "busts and prints" gave "an English air to the dwelling," which was otherwise "wholly Virginian." The drawing room, with its profusion of paintings, portraits, and busts, placed wherever they could be fixed, had appeared as a charming museum to Mrs. Smith.[39]

Except for decayed wings and colonnades in need of repair, the two-story brick mansion and its grounds were probably much the same as described when Madison died June 28, 1836.

"The excision of life is a painful operation, and the more quickly it is performed the better."[40] Madison had written these words many years before he had experienced the pain that can accompany the prolongation of life. At last, however, when the end did come, it was as he had wished. Shortly before he died he was still in command of his faculties; he was "as serene, philosophical, and calm in the last moments of existence, as he had been in all the trying occasions of life." He died "while sitting in his chair, without a pain or a groan."[41]

His place of burial was in a family plot on his own grounds. At the funeral were unlettered people who could not record their thoughts for posterity. James Barbour recalled their presence to friends and neighbors when he delivered his eulogy on this "good and great man"—

Many of you were at his funeral. You must have seen his slaves decently attired in attendance, and their orderly deportment; the profound silence was now and then broken by sobs—they attended the procession to the grave ... [Hearing] the fearful sentence "dust to dust" ... it was not only the body servant, who was standing directly by me, that by his sighs and sobs, showed how severely he felt his breavement, but the hundred slaves gave vent to their lamentations in one violent outburst that rent the air.

Barbour saw the irrepressible grief of his slaves as their testimonial that "in his private as in his public life, all was well".[42]

Madison left the historian and biographer many manuscripts recording the events in which he had participated. Few men have bequeathed more. And few who have left so much have revealed so little of his inner view of himself. Even the brief autobiographical memoir which he compiled in his eighties reads like the first draft of a biography for an encyclopedia. Typically, one of the few statements revealing his subjective feelings about his career was laconic, incidental, and not about himself alone; it was in a letter of February 24, 1826, written in reply to one from Jefferson which had touchingly characterized their lifelong friendship. In this letter we get a glimpse of his expectation that he would be remembered as a devoted public servant. He wrote:

You cannot look back to the long period of our private friendship & political harmony, with more affecting reflections than I do. If they are a source of pleasure to you, what ought they not be to me? We cannot be deprived of the happy consciousness of the pure devotion to the public good with which we discharged the trusts committed to us. And I indulge a confidence that sufficient evidence will find its way to another generation, to ensure, after we are gone, whatever of justice may be withheld whilst we are here.[43]

Notes and References

CHAPTER I

1. John Quincy Adams, *The Lives of James Madison and James Monroe, Fourth and Fifth Presidents of the United States, with Historical Notes of their Administrations* (Boston, 1850); James Barbour, "Eulogium upon the Life and Character of James Madison," *Niles Weekly Register*, November 12, 1836, pp. 170–75; Charles Jared Ingersoll, "James Madison," in *The National Portrait Gallery of Distinguished Americans*, edited by James B. Longacre and James Herring (4 vols., Philadelphia, 1834–39), vol. 3

2. Charles Francis Adams, ed., *Memoirs of John Quincy Adams, comprising Portions of his Diary from 1795 to 1848* (12 vols., Philadelphia, 1874–77), vol. 9, p. 305.

3. Charles Jared Ingersoll, *Historical Sketch of the Second War between the United States of America and Great Britain, Declared by Act of Congress, the 18th June, 1812, and Concluded by Peace the 15th February*, 1815 (4 vols., Philadelphia, 1845–52), vol. 1, p. 265.

4. George Tichnor Curtis, *Life of Daniel Webster* (2 vols., New York, 1870), vol. 1, p. 224.

5. Gaillard Hunt, ed., *The First Forth Years of Washington Society Portrayed by the Family Letters of Mrs. Samuel Harrison* [Margaret Bayard] *Smith* (New York, 1906), p. 300.

6. *Ibid.*

7. J. Q. Adams, *Madison*, p. 67; entry of July 29, 1836, in *J. Q. Adams Diary*, vol. 9, p. 306; William W. Story, ed., *The Life and Letters of Joseph Story* (2 vols., Boston, 1851); vol. 2, p. 420.

8. Ralph W. Ketcham, ed., "An Unpublished Sketch of James Madison by James K. Paulding," *Virginia Magazine of History and Biography*, vol. 53, no. 4, October 1945, p. 437.

9. Jefferson's autobiography in Albert Ellery Berg, ed., *The Writings of Thomas Jefferson* (20 vols., Washington, D. C., 1905–7), vol. 1, pp. 61–62.

10. *Annals of Congress*, 3rd Cong., 1st sess., p. 261; *Congressional Globe*, 24th Cong., 1st sess., pp. 599, 601.

11. *Niles Register*, November 12, 1836, p. 172.

12. *Register of Debates in Congress*, 24th Cong., 2nd sess. (Washington, 1837), p. 193.

13. *Ibid.*, 25th Cong., 1st sess., p. 491.

14. Max Farrand, ed., *The Records of the Federal Convention* (4 vols., New Haven, 1937), vol. 3, p. 94; Seth Ames, ed., *Works of Fisher Ames with a Selection from his Speeches and Correspondence* (2 vols., Boston, 1854), vol. 1, p. 36; Zephaniah Swift to David Daggett, December 13, 1794, in *Proceedings of the American Antiquarian Society*, new series, vol. 4, April 1887, p. 374.

15. Stanislaus M. Hamilton, ed., *The Writings of James Monroe* (New York, 7 vols., 1898–1903), vol. 4, p. 486; Henry Adams, *John Randolph* (Boston, 1894, pp. 202–3; James Parton, *Famous Americans of Recent Times* (Boston, 1867), p. 237; *Annals of Congress*, 9th Cong., 1st sess., pp. 597–600, 14th Cong., 1st sess., p. 804.

16. Chevalier de la Luzerne, Liste de Membres du Congress depuis l'années 1779 jusqu' en 1794, Transcripts, France. Affaires Etrangeres Memoires et Documents. Etats Unis, vol. 1, p. 278, copy of manuscript in Library of Congress; *American Historical Association, Annual Report for 1896* (2 vols., Washington, D.C., 1897), vol. 1, p. 595; Harold C. Syrett and Jacob E. Cooke, eds., *The Papers of Alexander Hamilton* (13 vols., New York, 1961–67), vol. 5, p. 488; J. P. Brissot de Warville, *New Travels in the United States of America. Performed in 1788* (London, 1792), p. 163.

17. *National Portrait Gallery*, vol. 3, p. 2; Farrand, ed., *Records*, vol. 3, p. 237.

18. May 5, 1839, letter in Pierpont Morgan Library, New York City, quoted by permission.

19. Ames, ed., *Works*, vol. 1, p. 49; *American Antiquarian*, vol. 4, p. 374.

20. *National Portrait Gallery*, vol. 3, p. 2; Bergh, ed., *Jefferson Writings*, vol. 1, p. 61.

21. *Niles Register*, November 12, 1836, p. 174; J. Q. Adams, *Madison*, p. 28.

22. Hunt, ed., *Forty Years of Washington*, pp. 6, 107.

23. *National Portrait Gallery*, vol. 3, p. 10.

24. Edward Coles to Hugh B. Grigsby, December 23, 1854, in Library of Congress.

25. Ames, ed., *Works*, vol. 1, p. 35; *Hamilton Papers*, vol. 5, p. 488; *American Antiquarian*, October, 1923, p. 299; Everett Somerville Brown, ed., *William Plumer's Memorandum of Proceedings in the United States Senate, 1803–1807* (New York, 1923), pp. 455, 478; John Beckley to James Monroe, July 13, 1806, manuscript in New York Historical Society; Robert L. Meriwether, ed., *The Papers of John C. Calhoun* (Columbia, S. C., 1959), vol. 1, p. 100.

26. Julian P. Boyd, ed., *The Papers of Thomas Jefferson* (Princeton, N. J., 1953), vol. 7, p. 97.

27. Luzerne, Liste de Membres; Farrand, ed., *Records*, vol. 3, p. 94; Ames, ed., *Works*, vol. 1, p. 42; Bergh, ed., *Jefferson Writings*, vol. 1, p. 61; J. Q. Adams, *Madison*, p. 48; Marshall quoted in William C. Rives, *History of ohe Life and Times of James Madison* (3 vol., Boston, 1859–68), vol. 2, p. 612 and William Wirt Henry, *Patrick Henry, Life, Correspondence and Speeches* (3 vols., Boston, 1891), vol. 2, p. 376.

28. *Historical Sketch* (1845), vol. 1, pp. 260–61; J. Q. Adams, *Madison*, p. 58.

29. *Niles Register*, November 12, 1836, p. 173; Ames, ed., *Works*, vol. 1, p. 35; *American Antiquarian*, April, 1887, p. 374. Madison wrote in a letter of August 5, 1833: "I do not possess a manuscript copy of a single speech, having never written one beforehand, nor corrected the reporter's notes of one beyond making it faithful in substance, and to be reported as such in the third, not in the first person." [William C. Rives, Philip R. Fendall, and James C. McGuire, eds.] *Letters and Other Writings of James Madison, Fourth President of the United States, Published by Order of Congress* (4 vols., Philadelphia, 1865), vol. 4, p. 305.

30. *Ibid.*; Jonathan Elliot, ed., *The Debates in the Several State Conventions, on the Adoption of the Federal Convention at Philadelphia in 1787* . . . (5 vols., Philadelphia, 1881), vol. 3, pp. 66, 305, 356, 395, 415, 439, 473, 538; Allen Clark, *Life and Letters of Dolly Madison* (Washington, D. C., 1914), p. 049; J. Q. Adams, *Diary*, vol. 1, p. 544; Gaillard Hunt, ed., *The Writings of James Madison* (9 vols., New York, 1900–10), vol. 9, p. 291.

31. Ames, ed., *Works*, vol. 1, p. 42; *American Antiquarian*, April, 1887, p. 374.

32. Brown, ed., *Memorandum*, pp. 388–89; *Annals of Congress*, 9th Cong., 1st sess., pp. 599–600.

33. Ames, ed., *Works*, vol. 1, p. 35; Bergh, ed., *Jefferson Writings*, vol. 1, p. 61.

34. *Annals of Congress*, 11th Cong., 2nd sess., p. 544.

35. Baron de Montlezun, *Voyage de New-Yorck, a la Nouvelle Orleans et de L'Orenoque ou Mississippi* (Paris, 1818), vol. 1, pp. 56–57; Richard Beale Davis, ed., *Jeffersonian America, Notes on the United States of America Collected in the Years 1805–6–7 and 11–12 by Sir Augustus John Foster, Bart.* (San Marino, Cal., 1954), p. 155; Richard Rush to his father, August 8, 1812, manuscript in Historical Society of Pennsylvania; George S. Hillard, ed., *Life, Letters and Journals of George Tichnor* (2 vols., Boston, 1876), vol. 2, p. 30; Minnie Claire Yarborough, ed., *The Reminiscences of William C. Preston* (Chapel Hill, N. C., 1933), p. 7; Edward Coles to Hugh B. Grigsby, December 23, 1854, in Library of Congress; *Historical Sketch* (1845), vol. 1, p. 264.

36. John P. Kennedy, *Memoirs of the Life of William Wirt, Attorney-General of the United States* (2 vols., New York, 1866), vol. 1, p. 339.

37. [Rives, ed.], *Letters of Madison*, vol. 2, pp. 588–91.

38. *Historical Sketch* (1845), p. 259.

39. Hillard, ed., *Tichnor*, vol. 1, p. 30.

40. William Meade, *Old Churches, Ministers and Families of Virginia* (2 vols., Philadelphia, 1857), vol. 2, pp. 99–100.

41. Gaillard Hunt, ed., *The Writings of James Madison* (9 vols., New York, 1900–1910), vol. 5, pp. 179, 211, 237, 435; vol. 6, pp. 342, 415, 419, 435; vol. 8, pp. 5–6, 18–19; vol. 9, p. 291; Charles R. King, ed., *The Life and Correspondence of Rufus King* (6 vols., New York, 1894–1900), vol. 1, pp. 331–32; Douglas Adair, ed., "James Madison's Autobiography," *William and Mary Quarterly*, third series, vol. 2, no. 2, April, 1945, pp. 191–209.

42. Henry Adams, *The Life of Albert Gallatin* (New York, 1943), pp. 487–88.

43. [Rives, ed.], *Madison Letters*, vol. 2, p. 572.

44. Boyd, ed., *Jefferson Papers*, vol. 8, p. 115.

45. Hunt, ed., *Madison Writings*, vol. 6, p. 51; Bergh, ed., *Jefferson Writings*, vol. 8, p. 207.

46. Dolly Madison, letter of May 15, 1839, in Pierpont Morgan Library, quoted by permission; Clark, *Dolly Madison*, p. 142.

47. Edward Coles to Hugh B. Grigsby, December 23, 1854, Library of Congress; Hugh Blair Grigsby, *The Virginia Convention of 1776...* (Richmond, Va., 1855), p. 85.

48. Martha Dangerfield (Mrs. Theoderick) Bland to Frances Bland Tucker, March 30, 1781, in *Virginia Magazine of Biography and History*, vol. 43, January, 1935, p. 43; Ames, ed., *Works*, vol. 1, p. 42.

49. Clark, *Dolly Madison*, pp. 136, 142, 158; *Story*, vol. 1, p. 196; Montlezun, *Voyage*, vol. 1, p. 53; Ingersoll, *Historical Sketch* (1845), vol. 1, p. 259; Edward Coles to Hugh B. Grigsby, December 23, 1854, Library of Congress.

50. Beale, ed., *Foster*, p. 140; Beckles Willson, *Friendly Relations, A Narrative of Britain's Ministers and Ambassadors to America 1791–1930* (Boston, 1934), p. 68.

51. Ames, ed., *Works*, vol. 1, p. 35; *Story*, vol. 1, p. 152; Davis, ed., *Foster*, p. 155; *Tichnor*, vol. 1, p. 34; Coles quoted in Henry S. Randall, *The Life of Thomas Jefferson* (3 vols., New York, 1858), vol. 3, p. 312; Edward Coles to Hugh B. Grigsby, December 23, 1854, in Rives Papers, Library of Congress.

52. Edward Coles to Hugh B. Grigsby, December 23, 1854, Rives Papers, Library of Congress.

53. Hunt, ed., *Forty Years of Washington*, p. 236; *Virginia Magazine of History and Biography*, October, 1959, p. 435; Davis, ed., *Foster*, p. 155; Pierre Irving, *The Life and Letters of Washington Irving* (4 vols., New York, 1862), vol. 1, p.

263.

54. [Mrs. Margaret Bayard Smith], "Mrs. Madison," in *National Portrait Gallery*; Hunt, ed., *Forty Years of Washington*, p. 351; Clark, *Dolly Madison*; Kathrine Anthony, *Dolly Madison: Her Life and Times* (New York, 1950); Dumas Malone, "Dolly Payne Madison," in *Dictionary of American Biography*, vol. 12, pp. 181–82; Lucia Beverly Cutts, ed., *Memoirs and Letters of Dolly Madison, Wife of James Madison, President of the United States* (Boston, 1887).

55. Clark, *Dolly Madison*. p. 93.

56. *Ibid*., p. 22.

57. Bergh, ed., *Jefferson Writings*. vol. 13, p. 190; Boyd, ed., *Jefferson Papers*. vol. 6, p. 380.

58. Edward Coles to Hugh B. Grigsby, December 23, 1854, Library of Congress.

59. Davis, ed., *Foster*, p. 140; Ames, ed., *Works*, vol. 1, p. 42; Syrett and Cooke, eds., *Hamilton Papers*, vol. 5, p. 488; Ingersoll, *Historical Sketch*, vol. 1, pp. 262, 265; *Congressional Globe*, 24th Cong., 1st sess., p. 599; *Niles Register*, November 12, 1836, p. 170.

CHAPTER II

1. Rives, *Madison*, vol. 1, pp. 22–23; Irving Brant, *James Madison. The Virginia Revolutionist* (Indianapolis, 1941), pp. 97–98.

2. Adams, *Madison*, p. 17; *Niles Register*, November 12, 1836, p. 171; *National Portrait Gallery*.

3. "Autobiography," *William and Mary Quarterly*, April, 1945, pp. 196–97; William T. Hutchinson and William M. E. Rachal, eds., *The Papers of James Madison* (Chicago, 1962), vol. 1, pp. 4–7; Douglass Adair, chapter on Madison in *The Lives of Eighteen from Princeton*, edited by Willard Thorpe (Princeton, N. J., 1946); Grigsby, *Virginia Convention of 1776*, p. 84; [Rives, ed.], *Letters*, vol. 4, p. 1.

4. Jacob N. Bean, *American Whig Society* (Princeton, N. J., 1933), pp. 54–57; *Madison Papers*, vol. 1, pp. 61–67.

5. Adams, *Madison*, p. 17.

6. *Madison Papers*, vol. 1, pp. 71–161.

7. *Ibid*., pp. 75, 84, 94.

8. *Ibid*., p. 80.

9. *William and Mary Quarterly*, April, 1945, p. 198.

10. Grigsby, *Virginia Convention of 1776*, p. 84. Madison's autobiography states: "He was restrained from entering into the military service by the unsettled state of his health and the discouraging feebleness of his constitution of which he was fully admonished by his experience during the exercises and movements of a minute Company which he joined."—*William and Mary Quarterly*, April, 1945, p. 199.

11. *Madison Papers*, vol. 1, pp. 114, 116, 153, 163.

12. Madison wrote to William Bradford, November 9, 1772: "I . . . have little spirit and alacrity to set about any thing that is difficult in acquiring and useless in possessing after one has exchanged Time for Eternity."—*Madison Paper*, vol. 1, p. 75.

13. *Ibid*., p. 96.

14. *Ibid*., pp. 101, 105, 106, 109, 111, 112.

15. *Ibid*., p. 96.

16. *Ibid*., p. 74, 75, 89.

17. *Ibid.*, p. 105.
18. *Ibid.*
19. *Ibid.*, p. 97.
20. *Ibid.*, p. 106.
21. Hunt, ed., *Madison Writings*, vol. 9, pp. 297–98.
22. *Madison Papers*, vol. 1, pp. 74, 96, 100; *William and Mary Quarterly*, April, 1945, p. 198.
23. *Madison Papers*, vol. 1, p. 101.
24. Rives, *Madison*, vol. 1, pp. 3–4, 8, 73; Brant, *Revolutionist*, pp. 24–27, 43, 49–51, 154–56, 307; *Madison Papers*, vol. 1, pp. 123–24, 147, 164, 184, 193, 223, 298, 316.
25. Patricia P. Clark, ed., "Madison Family Records," *Virginia Magazine of History and Biography*, vol. 66, no. 1, January, 1958, pp. 80–83; *Madison Papers*, vol. 1, pp. 212–13; Meade, *Old Churches*, vol. 2, pp. 96–98. James was born at Port Conway, Virginia, at the home of his mother's parents.
26. Brant, *Revolutionist*, p. 57.

CHAPTER III

1. Grigsby, *Virginia Convention of 1776*, pp. 83–86, 202; Rives, *Madison*, vol. 1, p. 122; "Autobiography," *William and Mary Quarterly*, April, 1945, p. 199; Hunt, ed., *Writings*, vol. 9, p. 293.
2. [Edmund] "Randolph's Essay on the Revolutionary History of Virginia, 1774–1782," *Virginia Magazine of History and Biography*, vol. 43, no. 4, October, 1935, pp. 307–8.
3. *William and Mary Quarterly*, April, 1945, p. 199.
4. Hutchinson and Rachel, eds., *Papers of Madison*, vol. 1, pp. 171–75, 179; *William and Mary Quarterly*, April, 1945, p. 199; Anson Phelps Stokes, *Church and State in the United States* (3 vols., New York, 1950), vol. 1, p. 380.
5. *Madison Papers*, vol. 1, p. 174.
6. Rives, *Madison*, vol. 1, pp. 173–74; Hugh Blair Grigsby, *The History of the Federal Convention of 1788* . . . (2 vols., 1890–91), vol. 2, pp. 99–100; Stokes, vol. 1, pp. 381–83.
7. *Ibid.*
8. *Madison Papers*, vol. 1, p. 193.
9. *William and Mary Quarterly*, April, 1945, p. 200; Rives, *Madison*, vol. 1, pp. 180–81; Herbert B. Adams, *The Life and Writing of Jared Sparks* (2 vols., 1893), vol. 2, p. 36; Elizabeth Fleet, ed., "Madison's Detached Memoranda," *William and Mary Quarterly*, third series, vol. 3, no. 4, October, 1946, p. 562. In his eulogy of 1836, James Barbour said: "Tradition ascribes it [Madison's defeat] to a successful effort to divide and array against each other the poor and the rich."
10. *William and Mary Quarterly*, April, 1945, p. 243; *Madison Papers*, vol. 1, p. 243.
11. *Madison Papers*, vol. 1, p. 242; Rives, *Madison*, vol. 1, p. 183; also Coles to Grigsby, December 23, 1854, in Library of Congress.
12. *Madison Papers*, vol. 1, p. 215; Rives, *Madison*, vol. 1, p. 183; Brant, *Revolutionist*, p. 315.
13. *Madison Papers*, vol. 1, pp. 214–15; Brant, p. 340.
14. Boyd, ed., *Jefferson Papers*, vol. 8, p. 35.
15. *Madison Papers*, vol. 1, pp. 214–52; Rives, *Madison*, vol. 1, pp. 184–208; Coles to Grigsby, December 23, 1854.
16. Hunt, ed., *Madison Writings*, vol. 9, pp. 404–5.
17. Rives, *Madison*, vol. 1, pp. 208, 215–16; Irving Brant, *James Madison*,

Nationalist, 1780–1787 (Indianapolis, Ind., 1948), p. 13; *Biographical Directory of the American Congress, 1774–1949* (Washington, D. C., 1950) lists delegates from states and includes short biographies of members of Congress.

18. Edmund C. Burnett, ed., *Letters of Members of the Continental Congress* (8 vols., Washington, 1921–38), vol. 5, p. 563.

19. *Madison Papers*, vol. 2, pp. 127–35, 195–97, 224, 231, 238, 241–42, 257–58, 302–3; vol. 3, pp. 148–154, 168–70, 188–90, 202–6; vol. 4, pp. 4–17, 168–169; Hunt, ed., *Madison Writings*, vol. 1, pp. 292–94, 301–2, 464–68; vol. 2, p. 4; Burnett, ed., *Letters*, vol. 6, pp. 451–52, 499.

20. *Madison Papers*, vol. 2, pp. 37–39, 61–62, 81, 89, 93, 103, 109, 125, 145, 157, 173–76; vol. 3, pp. 153, 266–67, 273, 281; vol. 4, pp. 192–93, 219, 288, 303–4, 314, 326–30, 403, 437; note especially vol. 2, pp. 145, 157; Hunt, ed., *Madison Writings*, vol. 1, pp. 226, 228, 292–93, 296, 409, 417, 418; Burnett, ed., *Letters*, vol. 6, pp. 420, 434–38, 451–52; vol. 7, p. 89.

21. Hunt, ed., *Madison Writings*, vol. 1, pp. 403–10, 418–23; Burnett, ed., *Letters*, vol. 7, pp. 89–90; quoted words in Hunt, vol. 1, p. 405.

22. *Madison Papers*, vol. 3, pp. 224–26, 275, 281–308; vol. 2, pp. 53–54, 72–90, 113–23, 136–38, 176–78, 191, 195, 202–5, 300–301; vol. 4, pp. 32, 38–40, 55–57, 132–35, 143, 154–59, 165, 178–80, 190, 196–99, 218–21, 241, 387; Hunt, ed., *Madison Writings*, vol. 1, pp. 225, 251, 261, 276–81, 292–300, 385, 461, 466, 476–77, 482; vol. 2, pp. 13, 19, 24–27; Burnett, ed., *Letters*, vol. 7, pp. 133, 187, 301, 332–33; Boyd, ed., *Jefferson Writings*, vol. 6, pp. 361, 364; note especially *Papers*, vol. 4, pp. 200–203 and Hunt, vol. 1, pp. 389–92.

23. *Papers*, vol. 2, pp. 303–4; vol. 3, pp. 129, 141–42, 348–49; vol. 4, pp. 387, 431; Hunt, ed., *Madison Writings*, vol. 1, pp. 175, 263, 288–98, 314, 330, 334–44, 353–54, 370, 382, 390, 393, 432; Burnett, ed., *Letters*, vol. 6, pp. 21, 549, 569–70; vol. 7, pp. 6, 7, 21, 25, 69, 120. For Madison's proposal to count slaves three-fifths of freemen in apportioning sums to be contributed by states, see Hunt, vol. 1, pp. 435 and 443.

24. Hunt, ed., *Madison Writings*, vol. 1, pp. 389, 397–403, 421, 442–43, 453–60, 472; Burnett, ed., *Letters*, vol. 7, pp. 169–70, 269; Boyd, ed., *Jefferson Papers*, pp. 263, 271.

25. *Madison Papers*, vol. 3, pp. 17–19, 318, 352, 369–70; Hunt, ed., *Madison Writings*, vol. 1, pp. 306, 314.

26. *Madison Papers*, vol. 3, pp. 18, 72.

27. *Ibid.*, p. 175; vol. 4, pp. 20–21.

28. *Ibid.*, vol. 4, p. 23.

29. Adams, *Sparks*, vol. 2, p. 34.

30. *Madison Papers*, vol. 3, pp. 131, 183; vol. 4, pp. 64, 127, 256, 448; Hunt, ed., *Madison Writings*, vol. 1, pp. 228, 241–43.

31. Boyd, ed., *Jefferson Papers*, vol. 6, p. 262.

32. *Ibid.*

33. *Ibid.*, p. 333.

34. *Ibid.*, vol. 2, p. 286; vol. 6, p. 335.

35. *Ibid.*, pp. 335–36.

36. Hunt, ed., *Madison Writings*, vol. 2, pp. 13–14, 22.

37. Boyd, ed., *Jefferson Papers*, vol. 6, p. 337; Hunt, ed., *Madison Writings*, vol. 2, p. 20.

38. Hunt, ed., *Madison Writings*, vol. 2, pp. 5, 20, 27; Boyd, ed., *Jefferson Papers*, vol. 6, pp. 337, 361, 377; Burnett, ed., *Letters*, vol. 7, p. lxxvii.

CHAPTER IV

1. Boyd, ed., *Jefferson Papers*, vol. 6, pp. 377, 537; Hunt, ed., *Madison Writings*, vol. 2, pp. 30–31; *William and Mary Quarterly*, April, 1945, p. 200.

2. Boyd, ed., *Jefferson Papers*, vol. 8, pp. 462–64.

3. Hunt, ed., *Madison Writings*, vol. 2, pp. 369–90.

4. *Ibid.*, p. 77; Boyd, ed., *Jefferson Papers*, vol. 7, pp. 421, 439–40, 444–45.

5. Boyd, ed., *Jefferson Papers*, vol. 7, pp. 7, 416, 446; vol. 8, pp. 416, 579.

6. *Ibid.*, vol. 7, p. 559; vol. 8, p. 41.

7. *Ibid.*, vol. 8, pp. 115, 416.

8. Hunt, ed., *Madison Writings*, vol. 2, p. 166.

9. Boyd, ed., *Jefferson Papers*, vol. 6, p. 550; vol. 7, p. 39.

10. Hunt, ed., *Madison Writings*, vol. 2, p. 154.

11. *Ibid.*, pp. 46, 154.

12. *Ibid.*, pp. 154–55.

13. *Ibid.*, p. 232; Boyd, ed., *Jefferson Papers*, vol. 10, p. 235.

14. Boyd, ed., *Jefferson Papers*, vol. 10, pp. 234–36, 457.

15. *Ibid.*, p. 605; Hunt, ed., *Madison Writings*, vol. 6, p. 214; Irving Brant, *James Madison, The Nationalist, 1780–1787* (Indianapolis, Ind., 1948), pp. 341–42; Abbot Emerson Smith, *James Madison: Builder, a New Estimate of a Memorable Career* (New York, 1937), p. 67.

16. Boyd, ed., *Jefferson Papers*, vol. 6, p. 550.

17. *Ibid.*, vol. 7, pp. 257, 260.

18. *Ibid.*, vol. 2, pp. 545–51; vol. 7, pp. 594–95; vol. 9, pp. 195–96; Hunt, ed., *Madison Writings*, vol. 2, pp. 99, 131–32, 142–46; Hamilton James Eckenrode, *Separation of Church and State in Virginia* (Richmond, Va., 1910), pp. 87, 102–11.

19. Boyd, ed., *Jefferson Papers*, vol. 8, p. 415; Hunt, ed., *Madison Writings*, vol. 2, pp. 88–89, 154, 183–91; vol. 9, pp. 249–50; Eckenrode, pp. 105–6.

20. Eckenrode, p. 113; Grigsby, *Virginia Convention of 1788*, vol. 2, p. 127.

21. Boyd, ed., *Jefferson Papers*, vol. 9, p. 196.

22. *Ibid.*, pp. 195–96; vol. 2, pp. 545–51.

23. Grigsby, *Virginia Convention of 1788*, vol. 2, pp. 135–36; Rives, *Madison*, vol. 1, p. 553; vol. 2, pp. 75–76, 155; Jefferson's statement in Bergh, ed., *Jefferson Writings*, vol. 1, p. 66; Edmund Pendleton told Madison that "nothing but" his "persevering assiduity would have ever accomplished that work at all, much less in so short a time."—quoted in Rives, *Madison*, vol. 2, p. 161.

24. Boyd, ed., *Jefferson Papers*, vol. 7, pp. 588–89, 598; vol. 9, p. 197; vol. 10, p. 576; vol. 11, pp. 152–53; Hunt, ed., *Madison Writings*, vol. 2, pp. 99, 203–7, 211; Grigsby, *Convention of 1788*, pp. 99, 122.

25. Boyd, ed., *Jefferson Papers*, vol. 7, pp. 123, 360, 401–2, 414–15, 589–92; vol. 9, pp. 197–201; vol. 10, p. 576; Hunt, ed., *Madison Writings*, vol. 2, pp. 100–101, 148, 199, 222, 243, 398; Grigsby, *Convention of 1788*, vol. 2, pp. 89, 149–50; Rives, *Madison*, vol. 1, pp. 543–53, 623–27; vol. 2, pp. 70–71.

26. Rives, *Madison*, vol. 1, pp. 567–70, 596–99; vol. 2, p. 161; Grigsby, *Convention of 1788*, vol. 2, pp. 84, 118–19, 316; Hunt, ed., *Madison Writings*, vol. 2, pp. 55–56, 206, 210–11; Boyd, ed., *Jefferson Papers*, vol. 7, pp. 595–96; vol. 9, p. 199.

27. Hunt, ed., *Madison Writings*, vol. 2, pp. 396–97; Boyd, ed., *Jefferson Papers*, vol. 9, pp. 201, 334; vol. 10, p. 576.

28. Boyd, ed., *Jefferson Papers*, vol. 7, p. 597; vol. 8, pp. 413, 579–80; vol. 9, p. 198; Hunt, ed., *Madison Writings*, vol. 2, pp. 156–60, 194–98, 201, 235; Grigsby, *Convention of 1788*, vol. 1, pp. 52, 56; vol. 2, pp. 140–47; Rives, *Madison*, vol.

2, pp. 13–18, 48–49.

29. Hunt, ed., *Madison Writings*, vol. 2, pp. 99–100, 402.

30. *Ibid.*, pp. 54, 160–77; Boyd, ed., *Jefferson Papers*, vol. 7, pp. 360, 401.

31. Hunt, ed., *Madison Writings*, vol. 2, pp. 193, 198, 201, 223, 233, 396–97; vol. 9, pp. 246, 289–90; Boyd, ed., *Jefferson Papers*, vol. 9, pp. 197–99, 204–8.

32. Hunt, ed., *Madison Writings*, vol. 2, pp. 235, 243, 245, 256; Boyd, ed., *Jefferson Papers*, vol. 9, pp. 334–35, 519, 660.

33. Boyd, ed., *Jefferson Papers*, vol. 10, p. 233.

34. Burnett, ed., *Letters*, vol. 8, p. 460.

CHAPTER V

1. Boyd, ed., *Jefferson Papers*, vol. 10, p. 231; Hunt, ed., *Madison Writings*, vol. 2, pp. 272–82, 400–401; vol. 9, pp. 544–45.

2. Hunt, ed., *Madison Writings*, vol. 2, pp. 283–84, 296–97, 301, 400; Boyd, ed., *Jefferson Papers*, vol. 10, p. 574.

3. Hunt, ed., *Madison Writings*, vol. 2, p. 296, quotation, p. 275; Boyd, ed., *Jefferson Papers*, vol. 10, p. 575; *William and Mary Quarterly*, April, 1945, p. 202.

4. Rives, *Madison*, vol. 2, p. 145; Hunt, ed., *Madison Writings*, vol. 2, pp. 277, 282; Boyd, ed., *Jefferson Papers*, vol. 10, p. 575.

5. Hunt, ed., *Madison Writings*, vol. 2, pp. 307, 315–19, 322, 336; Boyd, ed., *Jefferson Papers*, vol. 11, pp. 219–23.

6. Hunt, ed., *Madison Writings*, vol. 2, pp. 319, 404–7; vol. 9, pp. 72–73.

7. *Ibid.*, pp. 315–20, 406–7.

8. *Ibid.*, vol. 3, pp. 102, 215; vol. 5, p. 27.

9. *Ibid.*, vol. 2, p. 347.

10. *Ibid.*, pp. 361–69. He described the "multiplicity, mutability, and injustice" of the laws of the states.

11. *Ibid.*, pp. 324–33, 336–40, 344–52.

12. Boyd, ed., *Jefferson Papers*, p. 320.

13. Hunt, ed., *Madison Writings*, vol. 2, pp. 409; vol. 9, pp. 502–3; [Rives, ed.], *Letters*, vol. 4, pp. 312–13.

14. Hunt, ed., *Madison Writings*, vol. 2, pp. 409–10; quotation ("some leading propositions") from *Ibid.*, p. 237; vol. 7, p. 166; vol. 9, pp. 502, 531, 555; Rives, *Madison*, vol. 2, pp. 182, 272–73; [Rives, ed.,], *Letters*, vol. 3, p. 521; Farrand, ed., *Records*, vol. 3, pp. 20, 22–24.

15. Max Farrand, *The Framing of the Constitution of the United States* (New Haven, Conn., 1913), p. 61.

16. Forrest McDonald, *We the People, the Economic Origins of the Constitution* (Chicago, 1963), pp. 72–73, 86–92.

17. *William and Mary Quarterly*, April, 1945, p. 204.

18. Hunt, ed., *Madison Writings*, vol. 2, p. 411.

19. *Ibid.*, pp. 335, 354, quotation, p. 410; Boyd, ed., *Jefferson Papers*, vol. 11, pp. 219, 309; biographical sketches of Virginia delegates (Washington, Randolph, Mason, George Wythe, John Blair, and James McClurg) in the *Dictionary of American Biography*, edited by Allen Johnson, Dumas Malone, and Harris E. Starr (22 vols., New York, 1946).

20. Hunt, ed., *Madison Writings*, vol. 2, p. 409; similar statements in *ibid.*, vol. 9, pp. 502, 531.

21. Boyd, ed., *Jefferson Papers*, vol. 9, p. 401; Farrand, ed., *Records*, vol. 1, p. 17.

22. Adams, *Sparks*, vol. 1, p. 561.

23. Text in Farrand, ed., *Records*, vol. 1, pp. 20–23; Hunt, ed., *Madison Writings*, vol. 3, pp. 17–21; Charles C. Tansill, ed., *Documents Illustrative of the Formation of the Union of the American States* (Washington, D. C., 1927), pp. 116–19.

24. Since the records of the proceedings and debates of the convention are available in several different editions, dates of speeches rather than page numbers are given for citations. This paragraph is based upon remarks and speeches made by Madison on May 30, 31, June 1, 2, 5, 6, 7, 8, 12, 13.

25. May 31, June 6.

26. *Federalist* Number 37.

27. June 1, 8, 12.

28. June 6, 7, 8.

29. *Ibid*.

30. Hunt, ed., *Madison Writings*, vol. 3, pp. 443–44; Farrand, ed., *Records*, vol. 2, pp. 19–20; Tansill, *Documents*, p. 387.

31. Adams, *Sparks*, vol. 2, pp. 227–29.

32. August 23, 24.

33. July 17.

34. July 19.

35. July 19, 25.

36. August 15.

37. July 17.

38. June 8.

39. August 28; Boyd, ed., *Jefferson Papers*, vol. 12, p. 276.

40. August 28.

41. August 28.

42. August 17, 18, 20, 21, 22, 23.

43. August 16, 21, 25, 29.

44. *Ibid*.

45. August 21, 24.

46. August 22.

47. August 25.

48. September 4, 5.

49. September 6.

50. September 8.

51. Boyd, ed., *Jefferson Papers*, vol. 12, p. 103.

52. Hunt, ed., *Madison Writings*, vol. 2, pp. 410–11.

53. *Ibid*.

54. *Ibid*., vol. 9, p. 533.

55. Wilson proposed popular election of presidential electors on June 2.

56. Randolph and Mason refused to sign. Randolph (September 15) called for a second convention but did not exclude the possibility of his supporting ratification. Mason said (September 15) that he would neither sign nor support ratification unless a second convention was proposed by the Philadelphia delegates. In early October, Mason issued a statement expounding his objections to the Constitution in which he called for additional checks on a government which had become less trustworthy when Virginia's share in electing the Senate and President fell short of what he had at one time expected. Mason's statements of objections are in Farrand, ed., *Records*, vol. 2, pp. 637–40. Madison commented upon the refusal of Randolph and Mason to sign in letters to Washington, October 18, and to Jefferson, October 24.

CHAPTER VI

1. Jacob E. Cooke, ed., *The Federalist* (Middletown, Conn., 1961), pp. ix–xxx, 56, 422, 599–606.

2. Hunt, ed., *Madison Writings*, vol. 5; [Rives, ed.], *Letters*, vol. 1, pp. 337–493; Elliot, ed., *Debates*, vol. 3; *Annals of Congress*, 1st Cong., 1st sess.; David McCarrell, "The Formation of the Republican Party in Virginia" (doctoral dissertation, Duke University, 1937), pp. 19–34; King, ed., *King*, vol. 1, pp. 330–37, 358–59; Moncure D. Conway, *Omitted Chapters of History Disclosed in the Life and Papers of Edmund Randolph* (New York, 1888), pp. 95–129; Robert Allen Rutland, *The Ordeal of the Constitution, the Antifederalists and the Ratification Struggle of 1787–1788* (Norman, Oklahoma, 1965).

3. Hunt, ed., *Madison Writings*, vol. 5, p. 246.

4. *Ibid.*, pp. 123–234; Elliot, ed., *Debates*, vol. 3; Grigsby, *Convention of 1788;* Jackson Turner Main, *The Antifederalists, Critics of the Constitution, 1781–1788* (Chapel Hill, N.C., 1961), pp. 223–33.

5. Hunt, ed., *Madison Writings*, vol. 5, pp. 179, 271.

6. For estimates made by Madison between October 14, 1787, and April 22, 1788: *ibid.*, pp. 1, 3, 7, 14, 41, 54, 64–66, 75, 103, 108.

7. *Ibid.*, pp. 3l, 176, 231, 271–74, 375–76, 382–85.

8. *Ibid.*, pp. 319–20, 370–88; Irving Brant, "Madison: On the Separation of Church and State," *William and Mary Quarterly*, third series, vol. 8, no. 1, January, 1951, pp. 13–14; Robert Allen Rutland, *The Birth of the Bill of Rights, 1776–1791* (Chapel Hill, N.C., 1955), pp. 195–96; McCarrell, "Republican Party in Virginia," pp. 49–55.

9. Hunt, ed., *Madison Writings*, vol. 5, p. 378; *Annals of Congress*, 1st Cong., 1st sess., pp. 435, 442–43; Edward Dumbauld, *The Bill of Rights and What It Means Today* (Norman, Oklahoma, 1957), pp. 41, 208.

10. Dumbauld, pp. 36, 161–62.

11. *Ibid.*, pp. 32–38; Hunt, ed., *Madison Writings*, vol. 5, pp. 370–89; *Annals of Congress*, 1st Cong., 1st sess., pp. 433, 706, 722, 723, 729, 761, 770.

12. Hunt, ed., *Madison Writings*, vol. 5, pp. 339–61, 412; vol. 9, p. 532; Rives, ed., *Letters*, vol. 4, pp. 220–22; *William and Mary Quarterly*, April, 1945, p. 203. He also spoke frequently on locating the national capital.

13. *Annals of Congress*, 1st Cong., 1st sess., p. 437.

14. Hunt, ed., *Madison Writings*, vol. 5, pp. 361–65, 390–412; *Annals of Congress*, 1st Cong., 1st sess., pp. 461–65, 495–501, 546–47, 576–79, 581.

15. Hunt, ed., *Madison Writings*, vol. 5, pp. 403–4; *Annals of Congress*, 1st Cong., 1st sess., pp. 500, 812–813; Charles Warren, "History of the Federal Judiciary Act of 1789," *Harvard Law Review*, vol. 7, no. 1, November, 1923, p. 124; [Rives, ed.], *Letters*, vol. 4, pp. 220–21.

16. Hunt, ed., *Madison Writings*, vol. 5, p. 342; *Annals of Congress*, 1st Cong., 1st sess., p. 112.

17. Hunt, ed., *Madison Writings*, vol. 5, pp. 342–46, 359; [Rives, ed.], *Letters* vol. 4, p. 487; *Annals of Congress*, 1st Cong., 1st sess., pp. 109–15, 181–90, 201–2, 236–40, 245–46, 331–32.

18. *American Historical Association, Annual Report of 1896* (2 vols., Washington, D. C., 1897), vol. 1, p. 595; Syrett and Cooke, eds., *Hamilton Papers*, vol. 5, p. 488.

19. Hunt, ed., *Madison Writings*, vol. 5, p. 421; [Rives, ed.], *Letters*, vol. 1, p. 485.

20. [Rives, ed.], *Letters*, vol. 1, p. 475.

21. John C. Fitzpatrick, ed., *The Writings of George Washington* (39 vols., Washington, D. C., 1931–1944), vol. 30, pp. 310, 323, 369–70, 374–75, 393–94, 414–15; Hunt, ed., *Madison Writings*, vol. 5, pp. 355, 371, 425; *The Journal of William Maclay, United States Senator from Pennsylvania, 1789–1791* (New York, 1927), pp. 94–95, 119; Douglas Southall Freeman, *George Washington, a Biography*, vol. 6 [*Patriot and President* (New York, 1954)], p. 188; *Annals of Congress*, 1st Cong., 1st sess., pp. 247–48.

22. Fitzpatrick, ed., *Washington Writings*, vol. 30, p. 415.

23. Syrett and Cooke, eds., *Hamilton Papers*, vol. 5, pp. 439, 525–27.

CHAPTER VII

1. Hunt, ed., *Madison Writings*, vol. 5, pp. 363, 395; *Annals of Congress*, 1st Cong., 1st sess., pp. 378, 496.

2. *William and Mary Quarterly*, April, 1945, pp. 204–5.

3. Hunt, ed., *Madison Writings*, vol. 5, pp. 458–61; vol. 6, pp. 5–43; *Annals of Congress*, 1st Cong., 2nd sess., pp. 1340–41, 1534–43; *William and Mary Quarterly*, October, 1946, p. 542.

4. *Ibid.*, vol. 6, p. 19; Noble Cunningham, *The Jeffersonian Republicans, the Formation of Party Organization, 1789–1801* (Chapel Hill, N.C., 1957), p. 5; Dumas Malone, *Jefferson and his Time* [*Jefferson and the Rights of Man* (Boston, 1951)], vol. 2, pp. 300–301. Madison was present at a meeting in which Hamilton and Jefferson talked about the assumption and district bills, but he did not change his vote.

5. Henry Cabot Lodge, ed., *The Works of Alexander Hamilton* (12 vols., New York, 1904), vol. 9, pp. 514–15.

6. *Ibid.*, pp. 516, 521, 524, 529.

7. Hunt, ed., *Madison Writings*, vol. 6, pp. 106, 110–16; John C. Fitzpatrick, ed., *Washington Writings*, vol. 31, p. 395; vol. 32, pp. 45–48.

8. Fitzpatrick, ed., *Washington Writings*, vol. 33, pp. 122–24; Freeman, *Washington, a Biography* [*Patriot and President* (New York, 1954)], vol. 6, pp. 345–47; John Alexander Carroll and Mary Wells Ashworth, *George Washington, a Biography* [*First in Peace*], vol. 7 of the biography unfinished by Freeman (New York, 1957), pp. 132–34; Hunt, ed., *Madison Writings*, vol. 6, pp. 199–203.

9. Hunt, ed., *Madison Writings*, vol. 6, p. 107.

10. Bergh, ed., *Jefferson Writings*, vol. 9, p. 120.

11. *Ibid.*, vol. 8, pp. 204–6; Hunt, ed., *Madison Writings*, vol. 6, p. 53; quotation from Hunt, vol. 9, p. 404.

12. Hunt, ed., *Madison Writings*, vol. 6, p. 51; vol. 9, p. 405.

13. George Dangerfield, *Chancellor Robert R. Livingston of New York. 1746–1813* (New York, 1960), p. 255; Philip M. Marsh, "The Jefferson-Madison Vacation," *Pennsylvania Magazine of History and Biography*, vol. 71, no. 1, January, 1947; quotation in Samuel Flagg Bemis, *Jay's Treaty, A Study in Commerce and Diplomacy* (New York, 1924), p. 84.

14. Hunt, ed., *Madison Writings*, vol. 6, pp. 46–47; [Rives, ed.], *Letters*, vol. 4, p. 306; Bergh, ed., *Jefferson Writings*, vol. 8, p. 133; Cunningham, *Republicans. 1789–1801*, pp. 13–16; Lewis Leary, *That Rascal Freneau* (New Brunswick, N.J., 1941), pp. 186–92.

15. Hunt, ed., *Madison Writings*, vol. 6, p. 117.

16. *Ibid.*, vol. 6, pp. 62, 69; Cunningham, *Republicans, 1789–1801*, pp. 15–18.

17. Fitzpatrick, ed., *Washintgton Writings*, vol. 31, p. 395; Freeman, *Washing-*

ton, vol. 6, pp. 331, 346.

18. Cunningham, *Republicans, 1789–1801*, pp. 22–23; O. G. Libby, "Political Factions in Washington's Administrations," *The Quarterly Journal of the University of North Dakota*, vol. 3, no. 4, July, 1913, p. 304.

19. Lodge, ed., *Hamilton Works*, vol. 9, pp. 521, 517.

20. *Ibid.*, pp. 515–16, 523; *Annals of Congress*, 2nd Cong., 1st sess., p. 437.

21. These essays are in Hunt, ed., *Madison Writings*, vol. 6, pp. 70–120.

22. [Rives, ed.], *Letters*, vol. 1, p. 561; Cunningham, *Republicans, 1789–1801*, pp. 20–22, 29, 45–48.

23. Lodge, ed., *Hamilton Works*, vol. 7, pp. 229–303; quotation from p. 241.

24. Hunt, ed., *Madison Writings*, vol. 6, p. 117; Philip Marsh, ed., *Monroe's Defense of Jefferson and Freneau Against Hamilton* (Oxford, Ohio, 1948); Philip Marsh, "Madison's Defense of Freneau," *William and Mary Quarterly*, third series, vol. 3, no. 2, April, 1946, pp. 269–80; Philip Marsh, "The Vindication of Mr. Jefferson," *The South Atlantic Quarterly*, vol. 45, no. 1, January, 1945, p. 66.

25. John Beckley to Madison, September 2, 1792, manuscript in New York Public Library.

26. Marsh, *Monroe's Defense*, pp. 9–10, 37–41; *William and Mary Quarterly*, April, 1946, pp. 272–73; *South Atlantic Quarterly*, January, 1945, pp. 62–66.

27. Bergh, ed., *Jefferson Writings*, vol. 8, p. 443.

28. Cunningham, *Republicans, 1789–1801*, p. 50.

29. *Annals of Congress*, 2nd Cong., 2nd sess., pp. 760, 898, 851, 639, 1162–71.

30. Ames, ed., *Works*, vol. 1, p. 127.

31. *Annals of Congress*, 2nd Cong., 2nd sess., pp. 955–63.

32. *Annals of Congress*, 2nd Cong., 2nd sess., pp. 754, 761, 835, 955, 958–59, 963, 1174–1286; Dice Robins Anderson, *William Branch Giles, a Study in the Politics of Virginia and the Nation from 1790 to 1830* (Gloucester, Mass., 1965), pp. 20–21.

33. Quotation in Hunt, ed., *Madison Writings*, vol. 6, pp. 124–25. In his speech of March 1, 1793, Madison referred to the "honorable and independent motives of Giles in proposing the resolutions."—*Annals of Congress*, 1st Cong., 2nd sess., p. 934. In his narratives given to Jared Sparks in 1827 and in his "Detached Memoranda," Madison said nothing about himself when discussing the authorship and presentation of the Giles resolutions.—Adams, *Sparks*, vol. 2, p. 33; *William and Mary Quarterly*, October, 1946, pp. 545–48.

34. *Annals of Congress*, 2nd Cong., 2nd sess., pp. 934–45. Although Madison refrained from charging in his speech that the nation had suffered material losses from Hamilton's transactions, he voted for Giles's seventh resolution which declared that "the Secretary of the Treasury did not consult the public interest, in negotiating a loan with the Bank of the United States, and drawing therefrom four hundred thousand dollars, at five per cent per annum, when a greater sum of public money was deposited in various banks, at the respective periods of making the respective drafts."—*Ibid.*, p. 959.

35. *Ibid.*, p. 963.

36. *Ibid.*, p. 962; [Rives, ed.], *Letters*, vol. 1, p. 576.

37. In the course of replying to critics of the investigations who charged that they had been initiated too late to permit sufficient time for the Secretary to prepare his reports and for the Congress to debate them adequately, Madison gave an explanation of the inquiries that assigned their origins to proceedings connected with a bill that was debated between December 24 and 26. The necessity of the inquiries, Madison asserted, had not been perceived until the bill paying $2,000,000 to the bank brought out "the darkness in which the House had

remained" about certain matters.—*Annals of Congress*, 2nd Cong., 2nd sess., p. 934.

CHAPTER VIII

1. *Annals of Congress*, 3rd Cong., 1st sess., p. 375.
2. Hunt, ed., *Madison Writings*, vol. 6, p. 124.
3. Letter in Library of Congress.
4. Hunt, ed., *Madison Writings*, vol. 6, pp. 125–32; Bergh, ed., *Jefferson Writings*, vol. 9, pp. 10–12, 30, 33–39, 56–57, 70–71, 75–78, 88, 96–97, 108–9.
5. [Rives, ed.], *Letters*, vol. 1, p. 584.
6. Hunt, ed., *Madison Writings*, vol. 6, p. 138.
7. Text of Helvidius Letters in *ibid*., pp. 138–88; quotations in *ibid*., pp. 135, 137, 139.
8. *Ibid*., pp. 138–41; *William and Mary Quarterly*, October, 1946, p. 567.
9. *Ibid*., p. 174.
10. *Ibid*., pp. 127, 135, 139, 179, 188–94, 197.
11. Bergh, ed., *Jefferson Writings*, vol. 9, pp. 34, 88–89, 121, 148.
12. Letters of May 27 and June 13 in Hunt, ed., *Madison Writings*, vol. 6, pp. 130–33; letter of September 1 in *ibid*., pp. 189–90.
13. *Ibid*., p. 129; Bergh, ed., *Jefferson Writings*, vol. 9, pp. 17–120.
14. *Annals of Congress*, 3rd Cong., 1st sess., pp. 155–58.
15. Hunt, ed., *Madison Writings*, vol. 6, p. 198.
16. [Rives, ed.], *Madison Letters*, vol. 2, p. 6.
17. *Ibid*., vol. 4, p. 488; *Annals of Congress*, 3rd Cong., 1st sess., pp. 375–78, 433, 437, 438; Alexander DeConde, *Entangling Alliance: Politics and Diplomacy under George Washington* (Durham, N.C., 1958), pp. 92–93.
18. [Rives, ed.], *Letters*, vol. 4, pp. 488–92, 500; *Annals of Congress*, 3rd Cong., 1st sess., pp. 155–58, 210–11, 215–16, 379–82.
19. [Rives, ed.], *Letters*, vol. 4, p. 498.
20. *Ibid*., p. 492.
21. *Ibid*., pp. 491–93; Hunt, ed., *Madison Writings*, vol. 6, p. 209; *Annals of Congress*, 3rd Cong., 1st sess., pp. 221, 274.
22. [Rives, ed.], *Letters*, vol. 4, pp. 491, 496.
23. *Ibid*., vol. 2, pp. 5, 8; *Annals of Congress*, 3rd Cong., 1st sess., pp. 201–2, 207, 507–8.
24. *Ibid*., pp. 90, 605; Hunt, ed., *Madison Writings*, vol. 6, p. 215.
25. [Rives, ed.], *Letters*, vol. 2, pp. 23, 32; vol. 4, pp. 497–501.
26. Hunt, ed., *Madison Writings*, vol. 6, p. 216.
27. *Ibid*., p. 217; [Rives, ed.], *Letters*, vol. 2, p. 14; vol. 4, p. 505; *Annals of Congress*, 3rd Cong., 1st sess., pp. 622, 630, 730.
28. *Annals of Congress*, 3rd Cong., 1st sess., pp. 434, 438, 531, 597, 1307–11; Hunt, ed., *Madison Writings*, vol. 6, pp. 216–18; [Rives, ed.], *Letters*, vol. 2, pp. 9–10, 14.
29. *Annals of Congress*, 3rd Cong., 1st sess., pp. 548, 463–64, 466, 713–14; Lodge, ed., *Hamilton Works*, vol. 7, p. 374.
30. *Annals of Congress*, 3rd Cong., 1st sess., pp. 120, 127, 129, 130, 729, 739, 747, 754, 758; Hunt, ed., *Madison Writings*, vol. 6, p. 218.
31. Hunt, ed., *Madison Writings*, vol. 6, p. 217; [Rives, ed.], *Letters*, vol. 4, p. 495.
32. Hunt, ed., *Madison Writings*, vol. 6, pp. 220–21.
33. [Rives, ed.], *Madison Letters*, vol. 2, p. 22.

34. Eugene Perry Link, *Democratic-Republican Societies, 1790–1800* (New York, 1965), p. 131.

35. Hunt, ed., *Madison Writings*, vol. 6, p. 222–23.

36. *Ibid.*, p. 223.

37. *Annals of Congress*, 3rd Cong., 2nd sess., p. 947; Hunt, ed., *Madison Writings*, vol. 6, p. 221.

38. Hunt, ed., *Madison Writings*, vol. 6, p. 222; [Rives, ed.], *Letters*, vol. 2, p. 21; *Annals of Congress*, 3rd Cong., 2nd sess., p. 692.

39. *Annals of Congress*, 3rd Cong., 2nd sess., pp. 934–35; [Rives, ed.], *Letters*, vol. 2, pp. 22, 25.

40. *Annals of Congress*, 3rd Cong., 2nd sess., p. 947; [Rives, ed.], *Letters*, vol. 2, p. 22.

41. [Rives, ed.], *Letters*, vol. 2, pp. 19, 24.

42. *Annals of Congress*, 3rd Cong., 2nd sess., pp. 1221, 1222.

43. [Rives, ed.], *Letters*, vol. 2, p. 35.

44. *Annals of Congress*, 3rd Cong., 2nd sess., pp. 1116–18; Hunt, ed., *Madison Writings*, vol. 6, p. 232; [Rives, ed.], *Letters*, vol. 2, p. 36.

45. Hunt, ed., *Madison Writings*, vol. 9, pp. 144, 281; [Rives, ed.], *Letters*, vol. 3, p. 595; the text of his *Political Observations*, dated April 20, 1795, in [Rives, ed.], *Letters*, vol. 4, pp. 485–505.

46. Hunt, ed., *Madison Writings*, vol. 9, p. 281.

47. John Alexander Carroll and Mary Wells Ashworth, *George Washington, a Biography*, vol. 7 [*First in Peace*, completing the biography by Douglas Southall Freeman], pp. 260–61, 291; Conway, *Randolph*, p. 267; Hunt, ed., *Madison Writings*, vol. 6, pp. 257–59.

48. Hunt, ed., *Madison Writings*, vol. 6, pp. 237–38.

49. Bergh, ed., *Jefferson Writings*, vol. 9, pp. 309–10.

50. Hunt, ed., *Madison Writings*, vol. 6, pp. 234–35, 238–57, 279–95.

51. *Ibid.*, pp. 237, 258–61, 265, 300; [Rives, ed.], *Letters*, vol. 2, pp. 43, 63, 69, 75, 95, 97–99.

52. Hunt, ed., *Madison Writings*, vol. 6, pp. 263–79; *Annals of Congress*, 4th Cong., 1st sess., pp. 771–83.

53. *Annals of Congress*, 4th Cong., 1st sess., pp. 969–75, 1291; [Rives, ed.], *Letters*, vol. 2, pp. 95, 98–99.

54. [Rives, ed.], *Letters*, vol. 2, pp. 100–101.

55. [Rives, ed.], *Letters*, vol. 2, p. 104.

56. In Stanislaus M. Hamilton, ed., *The Writings of James Monroe*, vol. 2, pp. 65, 138, 208, 216, 267, 353, 354, 403–4, 443.

57. [Rives, ed.], *Letters*, vol. 2, pp. 24, 37, 41, 65–67, 73, 82–83, 93, 96–97, 101–3.

58. *Ibid.*, p. 107.

59. *Ibid.*, p. 37.

60. *Ibid.*, vol. 4, pp. 491, 496–97.

61. *Ibid.*, vol. 2, p. 83; Hamilton, ed., *Monroe Writings*, vol. 3, pp. 23–25.

62. Madison to James Monroe, September 29, 1796, letter in Library of Congress.

63. Bergh, ed., *Jefferson Writings*, vol. 9, pp. 296, 301–2, 351.

64. [Rives, ed.], *Letters*, vol. 2, p. 38.

65. *Ibid.*, pp. 83, 103; Cunningham, *Republicans, 1789–1801*, pp. 102–6; Noble E. Cunningham, "John Beckley: An Early American Party Manager," *William and Mary Quarterly*, third series, vol. 13, no. 1, January, 1956, pp. 47–49.

66. Hunt, ed., *Madison Writings*, vol. 6, pp. 298, 302–4; Bergh, ed., *Jefferson*

Writings, vol. 9, pp. 355–59.

67. *Annals of Congress*, 4th Cong., 2nd sess., pp. 1598, 1611, 1613, 1615–17, 1622, 1635, 1636, 1667.

68. Hunt, ed., *Madison Writings*, vol. 6, pp. 302, 305, 307.

69. *William and Mary Quarterly*, April, 1945, p. 203.

CHAPTER IX

1. Hunt, ed., *Madison Writings*, vol. 6, pp. 307–8.

2. *Ibid.*, p. 319.

3. Bergh, ed., *Jefferson Writings*, vol. 10, p. 23.

4. *Ibid.*, p. 319.

5. Adams, however, was not distrustful of Madison. To Jefferson, in March, 1797, he proposed that Madison represent his administration in France [George Tucker, *The Life of Thomas Jefferson* (2 vols., London, 1837), vol. 2, p. 7]. Quotation from [Rives, ed.], *Letters*, vol. 2, p. 122.

6. [Rives, ed.], *Letters*, vol. 2, pp. 121–50; quotation, p. 122.

7. Hunt, ed., *Madison Writings*, vol. 6, p. 309.

8. *Ibid.*, pp. 311, 315, 321, 323–24.

9. *Ibid.*, p. 325.

10. *Ibid.*, p. 310.

11. *Ibid.*, pp. 320, 322, 324.

12. Bergh, ed., *Jefferson Writings*, vol. 10, p. 60.

13. *Ibid.*, p. 64.

14. Paul Leicester Ford, ed., *The Writings of Thomas Jefferson* (10 vols., New York, 1892–99), vol. 9, pp. 66–68.

15. Bergh, ed., *Jefferson Writings*, vol. 10, pp. 44–47.

16. *Ibid.*, vol. 9, pp. 419, 424; vol. 10, p. 3.

17. Adrienne Koch and Harry Ammon, "The Virginia and Kentucky Resolutions: An Episode in Jefferson's and Madison's Defense of Civil Liberties," *William and Mary Quarterly*, third series, vol. 5, no. 2, April, 1948, pp. 152–53.

18. Nathan Schachner, *Thomas Jefferson, a Biography* (2 vols., New York, 1957), vol. 2, p. 610; Dumas Malone, *Jefferson and his Time [Jefferson and the Ordeal of Liberty* (Boston, 1962)], vol. 3, pp. 400–401.

19. Schachner, *Jefferson*, vol. 2, pp. 613–14; Malone, p. 401.

20. Koch and Ammon, pp. 153–54; Ford, ed., *Jefferson Writings*, vol. 8, pp. 456, 451–55; Harry Ammon, "The Republican Party in Virginia, 1789 to 1824," (doctoral dissertation, University of Virginia, 1948), pp. 174–77; Schachner, p. 614; Malone, p. 398.

21. Letters to Madison and Taylor in Bergh, ed., *Jefferson Writings*, vol. 10, pp. 63–65, to Nicholas, in Ford, ed., *Writings*, vol. 8, p. 483.

22. Schachner, *Jefferson*, p. 617; Ford, ed., *Writings*, vol. 8, p. 449.

23. Bergh, ed., *Jefferson Writings*, vol. 10, p. 62.

24. Same as footnote 21.

25. Hunt, ed., *Madison Writings*, vol. 10, pp. 444–47.

26. *Ibid.*, vol. 6, pp. 328–29.

27. Manning J. Dauer, *The Adams Federalists* (Baltimore, 1953), pp. 30–31; Stephen G. Kurtz, *The Presidency of John Adams, the Collapse of Federalism, 1795–1800* (Philadelphia, 1957), pp. 359–62; Harry Ammon, "The Republican Party in Virginia," p. 201; David McCarrell, "The Formation of the Jeffersonian Party in Virginia" (doctoral dissertation, Duke University, 1937), pp. 239–40.

28. Hunt, ed., *Madison Writings*, vol. 6, p. 341.

29. Koch and Ammon, p. 163.

30. Bergh, ed., *Jefferson Writings*, vol. 10, pp. 67, 72, 83, 87–88, 91–96, 103–5, 115, 119, 122–24; Ford, ed., *Writings*, vol. 9, pp. 5–6, 15, 39, 65, 67, 70.

31. Koch and Ammon, p. 165.

32. Bergh, ed., *Jefferson Writings*, vol. 10, p. 131.

33. *Ibid.*, p. 133.

34. Manuscript letter, Library of Congress.

35. Text of report in Hunt, ed., *Madison Writings*, vol. 6, pp. 341–406.

36. Text of the resolutions of December 21, 1798, in *ibid.*, pp. 326–31; quotation from report of January 7, 1800, in *ibid.*, p. 402.

37. *Ibid.*, pp. 342–47.

38. *Ibid.*, p. 347; statement of January 30, 1817, in *Annals of Congress*, 14th Cong., 2nd sess., p. 800.

39. Bergh, ed., *Jefferson Writings*, vol. 10, p. 154.

40. Cunningham, *Republicans, 1789–1801*, pp. 152, 196; *William and Mary Quarterly*, April, 1945, p. 206. In a letter of March 3, 1834, Madison said that the part he "had borne in promoting" Jefferson's "election to the Chief Magistracy" explained his becoming a member of his cabinet. —Hunt, ed., *Madison Writings*, vol. 9, p. 533.

41. [Rives, ed.], *Letters*, vol. 2, pp. 160, 162–70.

42. Hunt, ed., *Madison Writings.*, vol. 6, pp. 412, 418.

43. Bergh, ed., *Jefferson Writings*, vol. 10, p. 185.

44. *Ibid.*, p. 203.

45. Hunt, ed., *Madison Writings*, vol. 6, pp. 415–17.

46. *Ibid.*, p. 420.

47. *Ibid.*, pp. 425–26.

CHAPTER X

1. Letters from Jefferson to Madison in 1805 are in Bergh, ed., *Jefferson Writings*, vol. 11, and/or Ford, ed., *Jefferson Writings*, vol. 8. Letters from Madison to Jefferson, dated August 2, 7, 20, September 14, 30, October 5, 16, 20, 1805, are in the Library of Congress. None for 1805 are in either the Hunt or Rives editions of Madison's published writings.

2. Irving Brant, *James Madison, Secretary of State, 1800–1809* (Indianapolis, Ind., 1953), pp. 118, 162, 198–99, 278–79, 287, 303–04; J. Q. Adams, *Diary*, vol. 9, p. 306; quotation, Hunt, ed., *Madison Writings*, vol. 8, p. 60.

3. Letters and official instructions addressed to King, Pinckney, and Livingston are in Hunt, ed., *Madison Writings*, vol. 6; [Rives, ed.], *Letters*, vol. 2; *American State Papers, Foreign Relations*, vol. 2. Madison's memorandum on the negotiations of early 1808 are in Hunt, ed., *Madison Writings*, vol. 8, pp. 1–17.

4. Hunt, ed., *Madison Writings*, vol. 7, p. 76; [Rives, ed.], *Letters*, vol. 2, p. 196; Hamilton, ed., *Monroe Writings*, vol. 4, pp. 150, 208, 221; Willson, *Friendly Relations*, p. 43.

5. Charles E. Hill, "James Madison," in *The American Secretaries of State and their Diplomacy*, edited by Samuel Flagg Bemis (10 vols., New York, 1927–29), vol. 3, pp. 112–20; Bradford Perkins, *Prologue to War, England and the United States, 1805–1812* (Berkeley and Los Angeles, 1963), pp. 134–36; Hunt, ed., *Madison Writings*, vol. 7, pp. 418–40.

6. Beckles Willson, *America's Ambassadors to England (1785–1928), a Narrative of Anglo-American Diplomatic Relations* (London, 1928), p. 91; Willson, *Friendly Relations*, p. 56.

7. Bergh, ed., *Jefferson Writings*, vol. 1, pp. 470–78; James D. Richardson, ed., *A Compilation of the Messages and Papers of the Presidents, 1789–1897* (10 vols. Washington, D.C., 1896–99), vol. 1, pp. 422–28; quotation in Bergh, ed., *Jefferson Writings*, vol. 11, p. 269.

8. Hunt, ed., *Madison Writings*, vol. 7, p. 463.

9. *Annals of Congress*, 10th Cong., 1st sess., pp. 2327–30; Hunt, ed., *Madison Writings*, vol. 9, pp. 192–96; Bergh, ed., *Jefferson Writings*, vol. 16, pp. 69–70; Henry Adams, *History of the United States of America during the Administration of Thomas Jefferson* (2 vols., New York, 1930), vol. 2, book 4, pp. 166–71.

10. Quotation in Hunt, ed., *Madison Writings*, vol. 8, p. 17; vol. 9, pp. 193–94; [Rives, ed.], *Letters*, vol. 4, pp. 359–60.

11. U. S. Bureau of the Census, *Historical Statistics of the United States, Colonial Times to 1957* (Washington, D. C., 1960), p. 538.

12. Emory R. Johnson, T. W. Van Metre, G. G. Huebner and D. S. Hanchett, *History of Domestic and Foreign Commerce of the United States* (2 vols., Washington, D. C., 1915), vol. 2, p. 20.

13. *Annals of Congress*, 10th Cong., 2nd sess., p. 853.

14. Bergh, ed., *Jefferson Writings*, vol. 16, pp. 69–70; Henry Adams, *History of the United States of America during the Administration of Thomas Jefferson* (2 vols., New York, 1930), vol. 2, book 4, p. 169.

15. Adams, *Diary*, vol. 1, p. 408; Hunt, ed., *Madison Writings*, vol. 6, p. 414; vol. 8, p. 45; Henry Adams, ed., *The Writings of Albert Gallatin* (3 vols., Philadelphia, 1879), vol. 1, p. 367; Madison to Jefferson, September 14, 1805, letter in Library of Congress.

16. Hunt, ed., *Madison Writings*, vol. 9, p. 194. In his *Life of Thomas Jefferson*, George Tucker said that Madison had told him "more than once" that "the administration had indisputable evidence of the fact" that "repeal of the embargo was a mistake." —Vol. 2, p. 345. For effects of embargo on expornd imports of the British Isles and West Indies, see Bradford Perkins, *Prologue to War*, pp. 166–70.

17. [Rives, ed.], *Letters*, vol. 2, pp. 200–201; Hunt, ed., *Madison Writings*, vol. 7, pp. 204–375; vol. 8, pp. 77, 144; J. Q. Adams, *Madison*, p. 87; Henry Adams, *Jefferson*, vol. 2, book 3, p. 140; Perkins, *Prologue to War*, p. 43; Brant, *Madison*, vol. 4, pp. 106, 312, 442, 448, 461; Noble E. Cunningham, Jr., *The Jeffersonian Republicans in Power, Party Operations, 1801–1809* (Chapel Hill, 1963), pp. 98, 262–63; *Annals of Congress*, 10th Cong., 1st sess., pp. 2351–2712.

18. Cunningham, *Republicans, 1801–1809*, pp. 58–59, 215, 232.

19. *Ibid.*, pp. 111, 121; Adams, *Diary*, vol. 1, pp. 506, 512, 533; Adams, *Jefferson*, vol. 1, book 3, pp. 166–67.

20. Adams, *Diary*, vol. 1, p. 512; *National Portrait Gallery*, p. 10.

CHAPTER XI

1. Richardson, *Messages*, vol. 1, p. 466.

2. Reprinted from the *Alexandria Gazette* of June 24, 1812, in *Annals of Congress*, 12th Cong., 1st sess., p. 1653; the speech is entered as of June 4, 1812.

3. Hunt, ed., *Madison Writings*, vol. 8, pp. 99, 102, 174–75; Henry Wheaton, *Some Account of the Life, Writings, and Speeches of William Pinkney* (New York, 1862), p. 428; quotation of July 22, 1810, in [Rives, ed.], *Letters*, vol. 2, p. 448.

4. [Rives, ed.], *Letters*, vol. 2, p. 474; Hunt, ed., *Madison Writings*, vol. 8, pp. 96, 98–100, 102; Wheaton, *Pinkney*, p. 428. Robert Smith (*An Address to the*

People of the United States, dated Baltimore, June 7, 1811, p. 4), who was Secretary of State in 1810, charged that Macon's Bill No. 2 was "in fact the special contrivance of Mr. Madison himself." If Madison quietly sought passage of this bill, as Smith asserted, it was probably done in order to maintain at least a threat of economic coercion; that is, he preferred the act of May 1, 1810, to nothing. —See Hunt, *Madison Writings*, vol. 8, p. 141.

5. In a letter to David Humphreys, March 23, 1813, Madison said that he had repeatedly disavowed a policy of alliances. —Hunt, ed., *Madison Writings*, vol. 8, p. 239.

6. For repudiation of Erskine agreement, see Bradford Perkins, "George Canning, Great Britain and the United States, 1807–1809," *American Historical Review*, vol. 63, no. 1, October, 1957, pp. 18–20. In a letter to George Joy, January 17, 1810, Madison gave reasons why the British should have accepted the Erskine agreement without "a pledge that our own non-intercourse would be continued agst France & her dominions."—Hunt, ed., *Madison Writings*, vol. 8, p. 87.

7. *American State Papers, Foreign Relations*, vol. 3, p. 387; Hunt, ed., *Madison Writings*, vol. 8, pp. 115, 120.

8. Hunt, ed., *Madison Writings*, vol. 8, pp. 134–35, 157, 187, 190; [Rives, ed.], *Letters*, vol. 2, p. 519; Hamilton, ed., *Monroe Writings*, vol. 5, p. 365; Lawrence S. Kaplan, "France and Madison's Decision for War, 1812," *Mississippi Valley Historical Review*, vol. 50, no. 4, March, 1964, pp. 657–58.

9. Hunt, ed., *Madison Writings*, vol. 8, p. 209.

10. Hunt, ed., *Madison Writings*, vol. 8, p. 120; [Rives, ed.], *Letters*, vol. 2, p. 491. An Order in Council of April 26, 1809, made changes in the Order of November 11, 1807, that were favorable to U. S. trade with ports of northern Europe, but it was not viewed by Madison as a justification for optimism about the future in view of the way the British government repudiated the Erskine Agreement.

11. Madison's letter of November 15, 1811, in [Rives, ed.], *Letters*, vol. 2, pp. 516–17; Dolly Madison's letter in [Lucia Beverly Cutts, ed.], *Memoirs and Letters of Dolly Madison, Wife of James Madison, President of the United States* (Boston and New York, 1887), p. 74.

12. Hamilton, ed., *Monroe Writings*, vol. 5, pp. 206–9.

13. Hunt, ed., *Madison Writings*, vol. 8, pp. 242, 263; vol. 9, p. 274; [Rives, ed.], *Letters*, vol. 2, pp. 252, 562.

14. Monroe's confidential statement of March 30, 1812, to the House Committee on Foreign Relations as divulged by John Randolph, April 1, 1812, in *Annals of Congress*, 12th Cong., 1st sess., p. 1594; Reginald Horsman, *The Causes of the War of 1812* (Philadelphia, 1962), p. 242; Theodore Clark Smith, "War Guilt in 1812," *Massachusetts Historical Society Proceedings*, October 1930–June 1932, vol. 64, pp. 323–28. No better exposition of Madison's course can be found than that presented by Edward Coles in a letter to William C. Rives, January 21, 1856, in *William and Mary Quarterly*, second series, vol. 7, no. 3, July, 1927, pp. 163–64.

15. Richardson, ed., *Messages*, vol. 1, p. 499; *Annals of Congress*, 12th Cong., 2nd sess., p. 1296; 13th Cong., 3rd sess., pp. 1753–54; Henry Adams, *History of the United States of America during the Administration of James Madison* (2 vols., New York, 1930), vol. 1, book 6, pp. 289–98.

16. Hunt, ed., *Madison Writings*, vol. 8, p. 190; vol. 9, p. 195; [Rives, ed.], *Letters*, vol. 4, p. 360; Perkins, *Prologue to War*, pp. 400–401.

17. Hunt, ed., *Madison Writings*, vol. 9, p. 273.

18. Edward Coles to William C. Rives, January 21, 1856, in *William and Mary Quarterly*, second series, July, 1927, p. 163.

CHAPTER XII

1. Hunt, ed., *Madison Writings*, vol. 8, pp. 55, 89, 120; Walter Lowrie and Matthew St. Clair Clarke, eds., *American State Papers, Legislative and Executive, of the Congress of the United States . . . commencing March 3, 1789, and ending March 3, 1815. Foreign Relations* (Washington, D. C., 1832), vol. 3, pp. 349, 370, 222, 454, 459, 464; *Annals of Congress*, 12th Cong., 1st sess., p. 794; 2nd sess., p. 591; James Fulton Zimmerman, *Impressment of American Seamen* [*Columbia University Studies in History, Economics, and Public Law*, vol. 262, no. 1] (New York, 1925), pp. 156–59, 256; House report of November 29, 1811, in Meriwether, ed., *Calhoun Papers*, vol. 1, pp. 63–69; Horsman, *Causes*, p. 259; Perkins, *Prologue to War*, p. 429.

2. Richardson, ed., *Messages*, vol. 1, p. 493. Madison was aware of a belief in Indiana Territory that the British encouraged the Indians to resist Americans.— Logan Esarey, ed., *Messages and Letters of William Henry Harrison* (2 vols., Indianapolis, Ind., 1922), vol. 1, pp. 488, 539; *American State Papers, Foreign Relations*, vol. 3, pp. 464–68.

3. When he was Secretary of State, Madison's attempts to obtain from the Spanish government recognition of the Perdido River as the eastern boundary of the Louisiana Purchase or to buy all of its land east of the Mississippi were complicated by simultaneous attempts to settle maritime disputes with the belligerent powers. Between 1809 and 1813 serious negotiations with Spain were pointless; even if obtainable, any agreement would have been of doubtful value, since Spain was ruled by a puppet of Napoleon while the legitimate ruler was allied to Britain. As President, his policy toward Spanish Florida was definite and clear in its main outlines, but his methods were devious and clandestine. His West Florida policy was to assert that the Louisiana Purchase Treaty gave the U. S. title to territory as far east as the Perdido and to permit American occupation of any territory claimed by the U. S. where there was no danger of an armed clash between American and Spanish troops. His policy toward East Florida, to which no claims were asserted, was to use military force if necessary to prevent its transfer to another power and to occupy temporarily any areas where local Spanish officials were willing to cooperate with U. S. authorities. In 1810 and 1811 U. S. control was established in the region between the Mississippi and the Perdido, with the exception of the city of Mobile, which was not taken until April, 1813. In East Florida an agent representing Madison was disavowed in April, 1812, when a band of armed men under his direction attempted to take Fernandina and St. Augustine without the approval of local Spanish officials; nevertheless, U. S. troops and Georgia militia were not withdrawn until May, 1813. General Jackson took Pensacola in November, 1814, but left no occupying force when he moved on to New Orleans. In January, 1816, Monroe, as Secretary of State, resumed negotiations with the restored Spanish government but no agreement about Florida was reached until the second year of his presidency. A full examination of the relationship of Spanish Florida to the War of 1812 is to be found in Julius W. Pratt, *Expansionists of 1812* (New York, 1925).

4. Hunt, ed., *Madison Writings*, vol. 8, p. 191.

5. E. A. Cruikshank, ed., *Documents Relating to the Invasion of Canada and the Surrender of Detroit 1812* (Ottawa, 1912), p. 35; Alec R. Gilpin, *The War of 1812 in the Old Northwest* (East Lansing, Michigan, 1958), pp. 52–53.

6. Cruikshank, ed., *Invasion*, p. 44; H. A. S. Dearborn, *Defence of Gen. Dearborn against the Attack of General Hull* (Boston, 1824), p. 10; Richardson, ed., *Messages*, vol. 1, p. 515.

7. Hunt, ed., *Madison Writings*, vol. 8, pp. 206–7, 210–11, 216–17, 243, 263; [Rives, ed.], *Letters*, vol. 2, pp. 538, 540, 542, 560–63; vol. 3, p. 560; [Alexander J. Dallas], "An Exposition of the Causes and Character of the War," in *Annals of Congress*, 13th Cong., 3rd sess., p. 1453; *American State Papers, Foreign Relations*, vol. 3, pp. 464–68; Ingersoll, *Historical Sketch*, vol. 1, pp. 76–78.

8. Hunt, ed., *Madison Writings*, vol. 9, pp. 275–76. In his *War of 1812 in the Old Northwest*, Gilpin concluded that Hull had "some justification for surrender" (p. 122).

9. [Rives, ed.], *Letters*, vol. 4, p. 498; Hunt, ed., *Madison Writings*, vol. 8, p. 191.

10. Hamilton, ed., *Monroe Writings*, vol. 5, p. 212.

11. Hunt, ed., *Madison Writings*, vol. 8, p. 262.

12. *Ibid.*, pp. 215, 231, 319.

13. Hunt, ed., *Madison Writings*, vol. 8, pp. 264, 286, 300–302, 312–13; [Rives, ed.], *Letters*, vol. 2, pp. 256–57, 558; vol. 3, pp. 383–84, 561–63, 424; James F. Hopkins, ed., *The Papers of Henry Clay* [*The Rising Statesman* (Lexington, Kentucky, 1959)], vol. 1, pp. 713, 719–20; John Armstrong, *Notices of the War of 1812* (2 vols., New York, 1840), vol. 2, p. 140; John S. Williams, *History of the Invasion and Capture of Washington* (New York, 1857), p. 119; Ingersoll, *Historical Sketch*, vol. 2, pp. 164, 288; H. Adams, *Madison*, vol. 2, book 8, pp. 312–13; Freeman Cleaves, *Old Tippecanoe, William Henry Harrison and his Time* (New York, 1939), pp. 113–14, 120; Bradford Perkins, *Castlereagh and Adams, England and the United States, 1812–1823* (Berkeley and Los Angeles, 1964), pp. 44–46; Frank Arthur Updyke, *The Diplomacy of the War of 1812* (Gloucester, Massachusetts, 1965), pp. 169–75.

14. Hamilton, ed., *Monroe Writings*, vol. 5, p. 212; H. Adams, ed., *Gallatin Writings*, vol. 1, pp. 518–20.

15. *Annals of Congress*, 12th Cong., 1st sess., pp. 1541–43.

16. Hunt, ed., *Madison Writings*, vol. 8, pp. 208, 212; [Rives, ed.], *Letters*, vol. 2, p. 543; *American State Papers, Foreign Relations*, vol. 3, pp. 586–88; Alfred Thayer Mahan, *Sea Power in its Relations to the War of 1812* (2 vols., 1905), vol. 1, p. 275; Irving Brant, *James Madison, Commander in Chief, 1812–1836* (Indianapolis, Ind., 1961), pp. 61–62, 70.

17. Hunt, ed., *Madison Writings*, vol. 8, p. 186; Mahan, *War of 1812*, vol. 1, pp. 263–65; Perkins, *Castlereagh and Adams*, pp. 8–9.

18. H. Adams, *Madison*, vol. 2, book 7, pp. 5–11, 367–70.

19. Richardson, ed., *Messages*, vol. 1, p. 542.

20. *American State Papers, Foreign Relations*, vol. 3, p. 587.

21. *Ibid.*, pp. 585–88, 591–92, 595–96; [Dallas], "Causes" in *Annals of Congress*, 13th Cong., 3rd sess., p. 1458; Perkins, *Castlereagh and Adams*, p. 4; message of November 4, 1812, in Richardson, ed., *Messages*, vol. 1, p. 517.

22. Hunt, ed., *Madison Writings*, vol. 8, p. 213; *American State Papers, Foreign Relations*, vol. 3, pp. 585–88, 596.

23. *Annals of Congress*, 12th Cong., 2nd sess., pp. 1339–42; 13th Cong., 3rd sess., pp. 1285–99; *American State Papers, Foreign Relations*, vol. 3, pp. 585–86, 695–700; Elizabeth Donnan, ed., "Papers of James A. Bayard," in *American Historical Association, Annual Report for the Year 1913* (2 vols., Washington, D.C., 1915), vol. 2, pp. 204–6.

CHAPTER XIII

1. [Rives, ed.], *Letters*, vol. 2, pp. 57, 559, 582–84; vol. 3, pp. 399, 401; *American State Papers, Foreign Relations*, vol. 3, p. 703; *Annals of Congress*, 13th Cong., 3rd sess., pp. 1306, 1568–69, 1572.

2. *American State Papers, Foreign Relations*, vol. 3, pp. 703–4; *Military Affairs*, vol. 1, pp. 524, 541, 596; *Annals of Congress*, 13th Cong., 3rd sess., pp. 1307–11; Hunt, ed., *Madison Writings*, vol. 8, pp. 280–81; [Rives, ed.], *Letters*, vol. 3, p. 408; H. Adams, ed., *Gallatin Writings*, vol. 1, pp. 611–13; quoted words from Gallatin.

3. [Rives, ed.], *Letters*, vol. 3, pp. 403–4, 560–61; Hunt, ed., *Madison Writings*, vol. 8, pp. 279–80; vol. 9, pp. 277–80; Ingersoll, *Historical Sketch*, vol. 2, pp. 85–86; H. Adams, *Madison*, vol. 2, book 8, p. 33.

4. [Rives, ed.], *Letters*, vol. 3, pp. 383–84, 401, 404, 412–22; Ingersoll, *Historical Sketch*, vol. 2, p. 164; Irving Brant, *James Madison, Commander in Chief, 1812–1836* (Indianapolis, Ind.), pp. 260–61, 264–66, 277–78, 280–82.

5. Hunt, ed., *Madison Writings*, vol. 8, pp. 286–91.

6. *Ibid.*, p. 303; *American State Papers, Military Affairs*, vol. 1, pp. 524, 540–41, 596, 598; [Rives, ed.], *Letters*, vol. 3, p. 399; Williams, *Invasion*, pp. 60, 129; quoted words from Rush, in *Annals of Congress*, 13th Cong., 3rd sess., p. 1572.

7. *American State Papers, Military Affairs*, vol. 1, pp. 540–41, 596; *Annals of Congress*, 13th Cong., 3rd sess., pp. 1568, 1571–72; [Rives, ed.], *Letters*, vol. 3, p. 399; Williams, *Invasion*, p. 122.

8. *American State Papers, Military Affairs*, vol. 1, pp. 524, 536, 538, 540–41; *Annals of Congress*, 13th Cong., 3rd sess., p. 1570; [Rives, ed.], *Letters*, vol. 3, p. 409; Armstrong, *Notices*, vol. 2, p. 127.

9. *Annals of Congress*, 13th Cong., 3rd sess., pp. 1519–20.

10. B. Perkins, *Castlereagh and Adams*, pp. 63, 73; H. Adams, *Madison*, vol. 2, book 9, pp. 2–6.

11. Richardson, ed., *Messages*, vol. 1, p. 544.

12. *Ibid.*, p. 547.

13. *American State Papers, Military Affairs*, vol.1, p. 596; Hunt, ed., *Madison Writings*, vol. 8, pp. 294–95, 318; [Rives, ed.], *Letters*, vol. 3, pp. 422–23; Williams, *Invasion*, pp. 189–93, argued that "suggestions and advice had been freely given" by Armstrong.

14. Hunt, ed., *Madison Writings*, vol. 8, p. 296.

15. *Ibid.*, p. 297.

16. *Ibid.*, pp. 293–96; *American State Papers, Military Affairs*, vol. 1, pp. 527–29, 536, 539, 542, 555, 557.

17. Hunt, ed., *Madison Writings*, vol. 8, p. 293.

18. *Ibid.*, p. 292.

19. *Annals of Congress*, 13th Cong., 3rd sess., pp. 1610, 1648, 1651–52, 1674, 1682–83; Ingersoll, *Historical Sketch*, vol. 2, p. 123.

20. *Annals of Congress*, 13th Cong., 3rd sess., pp. 1530, 1544, 1674–75; H. Adams, *Madison*, vol. 2, book 8, pp. 144–48.

21. Hunt, ed., *Madison Writings*, vol. 8, pp. 297–300.

22. *Ibid.*; Hamilton, ed., *Monroe Writings*, vol. 5, pp. 373–74; Daniel C. Gilman, *James Monroe* (Boston, 1898), p. 123; Williams, *Invasion*, p. 277; Brant, *Madison Commander*, pp. 304, 306–10.

23. Brant, *Madison Commander*, pp. 303, 306–8; Hunt, ed., *Madison Writings*, vol. 8, p. 300.

24. Hunt, ed., *Madison Writings*, vol. 8, p. 301; Williams, *Invasion*, p. 106.

25. Richardson, ed., *Messages*, vol. 1, p. 547.

26. *Annals of Congress*, 13th Cong., 3rd sess., pp. 308–10, 689–91, 1122, 1518–50; Ingersoll, *Historical Sketch*, vol. 2, p. 170.

27. Richardson, ed., *Messages*, vol. 1, p. 550.

28. *Annals of Congress*, 13th Cong., 3rd sess., pp. 1310–24; Hunt, ed., *Madison Writings*, vol. 8, pp. 315–16.

29. *Annals of Congress*, 13th Cong., 3rd sess., pp. 381–83, 393, 397, 1285–1304; quoted words from speech by Alexander Hanson, October 10, 1814.

30. *Ibid.*, pp. 381–82; Perkins, *Castlereagh and Adams*, p. 112.

31. *Annals of Congress*, 13th Cong., 3rd sess., p. 1376; Ingersoll, *Historical Sketch*, vol. 2, p. 306.

32. *American State Papers, Foreign Relations*, vol. 3, pp. 709–10, 732; [Rives, ed.], *Letters*, vol. 2, p. 589.

33. Perkins, *Castlereagh and Adams*, pp. 101, 111, 132, 152; Updyke, *Diplomacy of War*, pp. 302, 312–13; George M. Dallas, *Life and Writings of Alexander James Dallas* (Philadelphia, 1871), pp. 392–93.

34. Hunt, ed., *Madison Writings*, vol. 8, p. 319.

35. Hunt, ed., *Madison Writings*, vol. 8, pp. 211, 215, 238, 241–42.

36. Ingersoll, *Historical Sketch*, vol. 2, pp. 235–38; H. Adams, *Madison*, vol. 2, book 8, p. 298.

37. Ingersoll, *Historical Sketch*, vol. 4, p. 66; Perkins, *Castlereagh and Adams*, p. 144.

38. Ingersoll, writing in 1848, said that "peace crowned his administration with revived and enduring favor."—*Historical Sketch*, vol. 2, p. 170. Estimates of his presidential leadership by men who knew him personally were quoted in the first chapter.

39. Richardson, ed., *Messages*, vol. 1, pp. 552–80.

C H A P T E R   XIV

1. [Rives, ed.], *Letters*, vol. 3, pp. 174, 301, 341, 578, 602, 613, 624.

2. *Ibid.*, vol. 3, pp. 49, 63–95, 265, 284, 291, 332, 368, 484, 500; vol. 4, pp. 35, 37, 57–60, 82, 274, 308.

3. *Ibid.*, vol. 3, p. 38.

4. Lester J. Cappon, ed., *The Adams-Jefferson Letters, The Complete Correspondence Between Thomas Jefferson and Abigail and John Adams* (2 vols., Chapel Hill, N.C., 1959), vol. 2, p. 508; Bergh, ed., *Jefferson Writings*, vol. 15, p. 110; Jefferson to Madison, April 17, 1817, letter in Library of Congress.

5. [Rives, ed.], *Letters*, vol. 3, pp. 603–4.

6. Quoted words in *William and Mary Quarterly*, April, 1945, p. 207.

7. Quoted words in [Rives, ed.], *Letters*, vol. 3, p. 575.

8. *Ibid.*, p. 527.

9. *Ibid.*, p. 238.

10. *Ibid.*, pp. 575–78; Hunt, ed., *Madison Writings*, vol. 9, pp. 224–31, 265, 310–11.

11. [Rives, ed.], *Letters*, vol. 3, p. 577.

12. Hunt, ed., *Madison Writings*, vol. 9, p. 469.

13. *Ibid.*, vol. 8, p. 426; Martineau, *Western Travel*, vol. 1, p. 192.

14. Hunt, ed., *Madison Writings*, vol. 9, p. 224.

15. *Ibid.*, vol. 8, pp. 439–47; vol. 9, pp. 265–66, 498–500; [Rives, ed.], *Letters*, vol. 3, pp. 170, 239–40; vol. 4, pp. 215, 274–77; Martineau, *Western Travel*, vol.

1, p. 192.

16. Martineau, *Western Travel*, vol. 1, p. 192.

17. *Congressional Globe*, 27th Cong., 1st sess. appendix, p. 73; William M. Meigs, *The Life of Charles Jared Ingersoll* (Philadelphia, 1897), p. 244.

18. [Rives, ed.], *Letters*, vol. 3, p. 518.

19. *Ibid.*, vol. 4, p. 114.

20. *Ibid.*, vol. 3, p. 483; also to Van Buren, September 20, 1826, in Hunt, ed., *Madison Writings*, vol. 9, p. 254.

21. [Rives, ed.], *Letters*, vol. 3, p. 573.

22. *Ibid.*, vol. 3, pp. 571–72, 592, 600, 636–60; vol. 4, pp. 6, 14–15, 232–60; Hunt, ed., *Madison Writings*, vol. 9, pp. 316–40.

23. Hunt, ed. *Madison Writings*, vol. 9, pp. 1–10, 22–25. He may have changed his opinion about the power of Congress to regulate the interstate slave trade. Harriet Martineau (*Western Travel*, vol. 1, p. 193) reported him as having said in 1835: "He believes that Congress has power to prohibit the internal slave trade."

24. Hunt, ed., *Madison Writings*, vol. 8, pp. 447–53; vol. 9, pp. 55–62, 65–68, 140–43, 177, 188, 235, 347–49, 527–28.

25. *Ibid.*, vol. 9, pp. 57–59, 76, 240, 527–28; [Rives, ed.], *Letters*, vol. 3, p. 483.

26. *Ibid.*, pp. 62–65, 73–76, 80, 84–87, 119, 204–11, 224–25, 228–32, 269–73, 293–95, 310–23, 334–36, 390–425; Hunt, ed., *Madison Writings*, vol. 9, pp. 342–44, 346–57, 383–403, 410–11, 511–14.

27. Hunt, ed., *Madison Writings*, vol. 9, p. 480.

28. *Ibid.*, pp. 431–32, 500–502.

29. *Ibid.*, pp. 302, 432–33, 501–2; [Rives, ed.], *Letters*, vol. 3, p. 629; vol. 4, pp. 261–66, 278, 333.

30. Hunt, ed., *Madison Writings*, vol. 9, p. 244.

31. Clark, *Dolly Madison*, pp. 458, 484; Martineau, *Western Travel*, pp. 191–92; Brant, *Madison Commander*, pp. 446–48, 501–2, 510–11.

32. [Rives, ed.], *Letters*, vol. 3, pp. 241, 341, 441, 505, 626; vol. 4, p. 12; Hunt, ed., *Madison Writings*, vol. 9, pp. 192, 245.

33. [Rives, ed.], *Letters*, vol. 3, pp. 500, 520.

34. *Ibid.*, vol. 4, pp. 66, 164, 299, 355.

35. *Ibid.*, p. 182.

36. *Ibid.*, vol. 4, p. 179; Hunt, ed., *Madison Writings*, vol. 9, p. 488.

37. [Charles J. Ingersoll], letter of August 6, 1836, in Washington [D. C.] *Globe*, August 12, 1836; Martineau, *Western Travel*, vol. 1, p. 190.

38. [Margaret Bayard Smith], "Mrs. Madison," in *National Portrait Gallery*.

39. *Globe*, August 12, 1836; Martineau, *Western Travel*, vol. 1, p. 195; Hunt, ed., *Washington Society*, p. 234.

40. [Rives, ed.], *Letters*, vol. 3, p. 322.

41. Ingersoll, "Madison," in *National Portrait Gallery*; *Niles Register*, July 16, 1836, p. 343; November 12, 1836, p. 175.

42. *Niles Register*, November 12, 1836, p. 175.

43. Hunt, ed., *Madison Writings*, vol. 9, pp. 245–46.

Selected Bibliography

The primary sources for the life of Madison are his own writings. "James Madison's Autobiography," edited by Douglass Adair, in the *William and Mary Quarterly*, April, 1945, pp. 191–209, summarizes his career and makes suggestions to a prospective biographer about the use of his papers. His recollections can be found in letters written during his retirement; in his "Detached Memoranda," edited by Elizabeth Fleet, in the *William and Mary Quarterly*, Oct., 1946, pp. 534–68; and in Herbert B. Adams, *The Life and Writings of Jared Sparks* (2 vols., Boston, 1893). A large collection of Madison manuscripts is in the Library of Congress. His extant writings are being edited by William T. Hutchinson and William M.E. Rachal and published as *The Papers of James Madison*, six volumes of which have appeared (Chicago, 1962–69). At present, for his published writings after 1783, one must rely upon [William C. Rives, Philip R. Fendall, and James C. McGuire, eds.], *Letters and Other Writings of James Madison, Fourth President of the United States, Published by Order of Congress* (4 vols., Philadelphia, 1865); Gaillard Hunt, ed., *The Writings of James Madison* (9 vols., New York, 1900–10); and Edmund C. Burnett, ed., *Letters of Members of the Continental Congress* (8 vols., Washington, D. C., 1921–36).

Among the published letters of his contemporaries, the following are the most useful: Julian P. Boyd, ed., *The Papers of Thomas Jefferson* (17 vols., Princeton, N. J., 1950–65), which will eventually supersede Paul Leicester Ford, ed., *The Writings of Thomas Jefferson* (10 vols., New York, 1892–99) and Albert Ellery Bergh, ed., *The Writings of Thomas Jefferson* (20 vols., Washington, D. C., 1905–7); Stanislaus Murray Hamilton, ed., *The Writings of James Monroe* (7 vols., New York, 1898–1903; John C. Fitzpatrick, ed., *The Writings of George Washington* (39 vols., Washington, D. C., 1931–44); Henry Adams, ed., *The Writings of Albert Gallatin* (3 vols., Philadelphia, 1879); Harold C. Syrett and Jacob E. Cooke, eds., *The Papers of*

Alexander Hamilton (13 vols., New York, 1961–67), which will eventually supersede John C. Hamilton, ed., *The Works of Alexander Hamilton* (7 vols., New York, 1850–51) and Henry Cabot Lodge, ed., *The Works of Alexander Hamilton* (12 vols., New York, 1904); Lucia Beverly Cutts, ed., *Memoirs and Letters of Dolly Madison, Wife of James Madison, President of the United States* (Boston, 1887); and the correspondence of Joseph Jones in *Proceedings of the Massachusetts Historical Society*, second series, vol. 15 (Boston, 1901), pp. 116–61 and of Edmund Pendleton in *ibid.*, vol. 19 (Boston, 1905), pp. 107–67.

Of the biographies of Madison, one is based upon an exhaustive investigation of original manuscripts: Irving Brant, *James Madison* (6 vols., Indianapolis, 1941–61). The subtitles for the volumes in Brant's biography are: *The Virginia Revolutionist*; *The Nationalist, 1780–1787*; *Father of the Constitution, 1787–1800*; *Secretary of State, 1800–1809*; *The President, 1809–1812*; *Commander in Chief, 1812–1836*. William C. Rives, *History of the Life and Times of James Madison* [to 1797] (3 vols., Boston, 1859–68) was written by an experienced Virginia politician who was personally acquainted with his subject and thoroughly immersed in his papers. Abbot Emerson Smith, *James Madison: Builder* (New York, 1937) is more readable and has more interesting insights than Gaillard Hunt's *The Life of James Madison* (New York, 1902). Sydney Howard Gay's *James Madison* (Boston, 1899) is unsympathetic and superficial in its adverse judgments. Of the short sketches, Charles Jared Ingersoll's [in vol. 3 of *The National Portrait Gallery of Distinguished Americans*, edited by James B. Longacre and James Herring (4 vols., Philadelphia, 1834–39)] is the most perceptive appreciation.

Brief introductions to Madison's political thought are: Edward McNall Burns, *James Madison, Philosopher of the Constitution* (New Brunswick, N. J., 1938); *The Complete Madison, His Basic Writings* (New York, 1953), an anthology of excerpts edited by Saul K. Padover; Adrienne Koch, *Madison's "Advice to My Country"* (Princeton, N. J., 1966); Adrienne Koch, *Power, Morals, and the Founding Fathers* . . . (Ithaca, N. Y., 1961); Neal Riemer, "The Republicanism of James Madison," *Political Science Quarterly*, March, 1954, pp. 45–64. Commentaries on the ideas in *The Federalist* are in the introduction to *The Federalist* (Cambridge, Mass., 1961), edited by Benjamin F. Wright and in Gottfried Dietze, *The Federalist, A Classic on Federalism and Free Government* (Baltimore, 1960). Articles on special characteristics of his political thought are: Ralph L. Ketcham,

"James Madison and the Nature of Man," *Journal of the History of Ideas*, Jan., 1958, pp. 62–76; Irving Brant, "Madison: On the Separation of Church and State," *William and Mary Quarterly*, Jan., 1951, pp. 3–24; Irving Brant, "Madison and the Empire of Free Men," *Journal of the Illinois State Historical Society*, Winter, 1955, pp. 402–26; Douglass Adair, "The Tenth Federalist Revisited," *William and Mary Quarterly*, Jan., 1951, pp. 48–67; Douglass Adair, "That Politics May Be Reduced to a Science: David Hume, James Madison, and the Tenth Federalist," *Huntington Library Quarterly*, August, 1957, pp. 343–60.

Other articles of biographical interest are: Louis C. Schaedler, "James Madison, Literary Craftsman," *William and Mary Quarterly*, Oct., 1946, pp. 515–33; Theodore Bolton, "The Life Portraits of James Madison," in *ibid.*, Jan., 1951, pp. 24–39; and Patricia P. Clark, ed., "Madison Family Bible [genealogical] Records," *Virginia Magazine of History and Biography*, Jan., 1958, pp. 80–83.

Biographies of contemporaries with whom Madison was associated over a long period of time are: Katharine Anthony, *Dolly Madison: Her Life and Times* (New York, 1950); Allen C. Clark, *Life and Letters of Dolly Madison* (Washington, D.C., 1914); Dumas Malone, *Jefferson and His Time* [to 1801] (3 vols., Boston, 1948–62); Nathan Schachner, *Thomas Jefferson, a Biography* (2 vols., New York, 1951); Henry S. Randall, *The Life of Thomas Jefferson* (3 vols., New York, 1858); Adrienne Koch, *Jefferson and Madison: The Great Collaboration* (New York, 1950); William P. Cresson, *James Monroe* (Chapel Hill, N. C., 1946); Dice Robins Anderson, *William Branch Giles: A Study of the Politics of Virginia and the Nation from 1790 to 1830* (Menasha, Wis., 1914); Robert Ernst, *Rufus King, American Federalist* (Chapel Hill, N. C., 1968).

For Madison's early life, the first volume of the biographies by Brant and Rives are the fullest. Irving Brant, *James Madison and American Nationalism* (Princeton, N. J., 1968) is a brief interpretation of the 1780's. For the Philadelphia Convention of 1787, the main sources are: Max Farrand, ed., *The Records of the Federal Convention of 1787* (4 vols., New Haven, Conn., 1937) or Charles C. Tansill, ed., *Documents Illustrative of the Formation of the Union of the American States* (Washington, D. C., 1927). Jacob E. Cooke, in his introduction to *The Federalist* (Middletown, Conn., 1961), summarizes the dispute about which of the *Federalists* Madison wrote and presents an exact chronology of their publication in the newspapers. His role in the ratification struggle can be traced in David McCarrell, "The Formation of the Republican Party in Virginia" (doctoral dissertation, Duke University, 1937), and Harry Ammon, "The Republican Party in Virginia, 1789–1824" (doctoral dissertation, University of Virginia, 1948), both of which made extensive use of the Madison papers in the Library of Congress. Also, for the period 1787–89: Hugh Blair Grigsby, *The History of the Virginia Federal Convention of 1788* (2 vols., Richmond, Va., 1890–91); vol. 3 of Jonathan Elliot, ed., *The Debates in the Several State Conventions, on the Adoption of the Federal Convention at Philadelphia in 1787* ... (5 vols., Philadelphia, 1881); Robert Allen Rutland, *The Ordeal of the Constitution* ... (Norman, Okla., 1965); Jackson Turner Main, *The Antifederalists, Critics of the Constitution, 1781–1788* (Chapel Hill, N. C., 1961); Forrest McDonald, *We the People, the Economic Origins of the Constitution* (Chicago, 1963); Edward Dumbauld, *The Bill of Rights and What It Means Today* (Norman, Okla., 1957); Robert A. Rutland, *The Birth of the Bill of Rights, 1776–1791* (Chapel Hill, N. C., 1955); and biographies of Patrick Henry, George Mason, James Monroe, Edmund Randolph, Edmund Pendleton, and John Marshall.

The main source for Madison's speeches in the first four Congresses is the report of proceedings generally called *The Annals of Congress* (Washington, D. C., 1849). A brief account of "The Formation of the Republican Party in Virginia, 1785–1796," by Harry Ammon, is in the *Journal of Southern History*, Aug., 1953, pp. 283–310; for lengthy accounts of the same subject, see the dissertations by McCarrell and Ammon previously listed. Noble E. Cunningham, *The Jeffersonian Republicans, the Formation of Party Organization, 1789–1801* (Chapel Hill, N. C., 1957) assigns an important place to Madison.

"James Madison," by Charles E. Hill, is in the third volume of Samuel Flagg Bemis, ed., *American Secretaries of State and their Diplomacy* (10 vols., New York, 1927–29). The more subdued role of Madison in party politics after he became Secretary of State can be seen in Noble E. Cunningham, *The Jeffersonian Republicans in Power; Party Operations, 1801–1809* (Chapel Hill, N. C., 1963).

Madison's presidential messages, inaugural addresses, and proclamations are in vol. 1 of James D. Richardson, ed., *A Compilation of the Messages and Papers of the Presidents, 1789–1797* (10 vols., Washington, D. C., 1896–99). Diplomatic correspondence for the period 1801–17 is in his letters and in

American State Papers, Foreign Relations, vols. 3 and 4. Diplomatic histories containing much about Madison during the period 1801–12 are: Bradford Perkins, *The First Rapprochement, England and the United States, 1795–1805* (Philadelphia, 1955); Bradford Perkins, *Prologue to War: England and the United States, 1805–1812* (Berkeley, Cal., 1963); Paul A. Varg, *Foreign Policies of the Founding Fathers* (East Lansing, Mich., 1963). "An Exposition of the Causes and Character of the War," written by Alexander J. Dallas [printed in *Annals of Congress,* 13th Cong., 34th sess., pp. 1416–79 and in George M. Dallas, *Life and Writings of Alexander James Dallas* (New York, 1871)] accurately recapitulates the intricate arguments that Madison had made in his diplomatic disputes with Great Britain. Irving Brant, "Joel Barlow, Madison's Stubborn Minister," *William and Mary Quarterly,* Oct., 1958, pp. 438–51, and Lawrence S. Kaplan, "France and Madison's Decision for War, 1812," *Journal of American History,* March, 1964, pp. 652–71, are on Madison's policy toward Napoleon before 1812. Two anthologies that reprint writings representing varying points of view are: Bradford Perkins, ed., *The Causes of the War of 1812, National Honor or National Interest?* (New York, 1962), and George Rogers Taylor, ed., *The War of 1812, Past Justifications and Present Interpretations* (Boston, 1963). Theodore Clarke Smith, "War Guilt in 1812," *Proceedings of the Massachusetts Historical Society,* June, 1931, pp. 319–45, demonstrates the relationship of Madison to the so-called War Hawks in the spring of 1812. Abbot Smith, "Mr. Madison's War: An Unsuccessful Experiment in the Conduct of National Policy," *Political Science Quarterly,* June, 1942, pp. 229–46, convincingly argues that President Madison was influenced by his earlier views on the diplomatic and war-making powers of the executive, and, evaluating his methods by standards prevalent in the mid-twentieth century, concludes that his leadership was a failure. A condensed version of Irving Brant's apologia for Madison's presidential leadership is: "Timid President? Futile War?" in *American Heritage,* Oct., 1954, pp. 46–47, 85–89. Marcus Cunliffe briefly interprets his war leadership in Ernest R. May, ed., *The Ultimate Decision* (New York, 1960). Roy J. Honeywell, "President Jefferson and His Successor," *American Historical Review,* Oct., 1940, pp. 64–75, shows that President Madison was not dominated by Jefferson. Recent histories of the War of 1812 have less on Madison than Charles Jared Ingersoll, *Historical Sketch of the Second War between the United States of*

America and Great Britain ... (4 vols., Philadelphia, 1845–52). Leonard White, *The Jeffersonians: A Study of Administrative History, 1801–1829* (New York, 1951) has less on Madison's presidency than on Jefferson's. James Sterling Young, *The Washington Community, 1800–1828* (New York, 1966), is a study of personal and social relationships among politicians and administrators in the capital that stresses the lack of unified direction of national party politics. The relationship of the President to three members of his cabinet can be studied in biographies of Gallatin, Dallas, and Rush; to the Secretary of War in the memoirs of John Armstrong; and to army commanders in the biographies, memoirs, or correspondence of William Henry Harrison, William Hull, Henry Dearborn, James Wilkinson, and Andrew Jackson. Excellent biographies of the peace commissioners have been written by Henry Adams (Gallatin), Raymond Walters (Gallatin), Samuel Flagg Bemis (John Quincy Adams), Bernard Mayo (Henry Clay), Glyndon G. Van Deusen (Clay and Morton Borden (James Bayard). Two scholarly studies of wartime diplomacy are: Frank Arthur Updyke, *The Diplomacy of the War of 1812* (Gloucester, Mass., 1965) and Bradford Perkins, *Castlereagh and Adams, England and the United States, 1812–1823* (Berkeley, Cal., 1964). Henry Adams, *History of the United States of America during the Administration of Thomas Jefferson* (2 vols., New York, 1930) and *History of the United States of America during the Administration of James Madison* (2 vols., New York, 1930), written in the 1880's, are still of immense value for the period 1801–17.

Not mentioned in the preceding paragraphs are many letters, memoirs, biographies, books by historians, and articles in journals which contributed to the author's knowledge of the events with which Madison was associated. A small proportion of the unmentioned histories and biographies and most of the letters and memoirs, published and unpublished, appear at some place in the footnotes. Regretfully, the others are too numerous and the space too limited to permit more than a few of these to be noted here; these are selected because of the scope of their contents and/or the value of their annotated bibliographies: Merrill Jensen, *The New Nation: A History of the United States during the Confederation, 1781–1789* (New York, 1950); Russell Blaine Nye, *The Cultural Life of the New Nation, 1776–1830* (New York, 1960); John Chester Miller, *The Federalist Era, 1789–1801* (New York, 1960); Marshall Smelser, *The Democratic Republic, 1801–1815* (New York, 1968); George

Dangerfield, *The Awakening of American Nationalism, 1815–1828* (New York, 1965); Curtis Nettles, *The Emergence of a National Economy, 1775–1815* (New York, 1962); Francis S. Philbrick, *The Rise of the New West, 1754–1830* (New York, 1965); John R. Alden, *The South in the Revolution, 1763–1789* (Baton Rouge, La., 1957); Thomas P. Abernethy, *The South in the New Nation, 1789–1819* (Baton Rouge, La., 1961); Richard Beale Davis, *Intellectual Life of Jefferson's Virginia, 1790–1830* (Chapel Hill, N. C., 1964).

Index